BORIS GODUNOV

TSAR OF RUSSIA

BORIS GODUNOV

S. F. PLATONOV

BORIS ▨ GODUNOV

TSAR OF RUSSIA

TRANSLATED FROM THE RUSSIAN BY

L. Rex Pyles

WITH AN INTRODUCTORY ESSAY

S. F. PLATONOV: EMINENCE AND OBSCURITY

BY

John T. Alexander

ACADEMIC INTERNATIONAL PRESS

1973

THE RUSSIAN SERIES / Volume 10

Sergei F. Platonov **BORIS GODUNOV**

Translation of *Boris Godunov* (Leningrad, 1921)

Library of Congress Catalog Card Number: 73-176467
ISBN: 0-87569-024-6
A Catalog Card follows the Index

Printed in the United States of America

ACADEMIC INTERNATIONAL PRESS
Box 555 Gulf Breeze, Florida 32561

To
MARY RINEHART HOGE
Historian, Professor, Poet, and Friend

CONTENTS

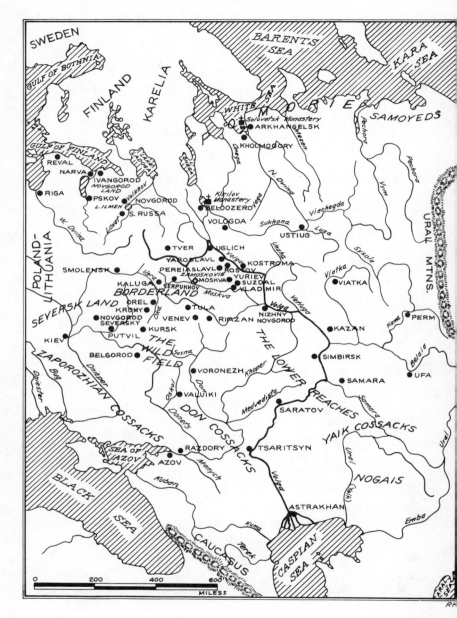

MUSCOVY AT THE TURN OF THE SEVENTEENTH CENTURY

INTRODUCTION

S. F. PLATONOV: EMINENCE AND OBSCURITY

Author or editor of more than 100 published works, exemplar of a major school of Russian historiography, member of the Academy of Sciences and director of its library and research institute for Russian literature, occupant of the chair of Russian history at a leading university for twenty-six years, participant in a score of scholarly organizations, director of a women's pedagogical institute for thirteen years, lecturer in numerous higher and secondary schools, tutor to children of the Imperial family — do such accomplishments usually delineate the career of an obscure person? For a variety of reasons, however, obscurity is the present lot of a once famous historian: Sergei Fedorovich Platonov (1860-1933).

To be sure, Platonov has not been forgotten entirely. Historians of Russia inside and outside the Soviet Union still value his works. If Soviet presses have so far reprinted only one of Platonov's many publications, second-hand copies are in brisk demand, while publishers in the Netherlands have lately reissued his major writings. Even so, Platonov's fame outside his native land is largely confined to academic historians who read Russian. Only five of his works have been translated, four into English. And because Platonov died after having been arrested, imprisoned, and then exiled to the provinces, his reputation in his own country has suffered. His photograph still hangs in the office of the History Faculty of Leningrad State University, and a few of his students are still alive in the Soviet Union and beyond its borders. Otherwise- he is scarcely remembered. Neither his work nor his career has attracted any detailed study. His published memoirs consist of four articles, which present only a fragmentary account of his long and active life.[1] His voluminous personal papers remain unpublished and scarcely consulted. Finally, Platonov had the historical misfortune — though he himself doubtless thought otherwise — to be born a generation after the most celebrated of modern Russian historians, Vasily Osipovich Kliuchevsky (1841-1911). Kliuchevsky's genius created a vision of Russian history so brilliantly conceived and superbly written that it seemed to exhaust, for a time at least, all possibilities of creative historical synthesis. In the penumbra of Kliuchevsky's supreme popularity in Russia and abroad, the works of scholars like Platonov often appeared derivative, pedantic, and esoteric. Besides, Kliuchevsky had the good fortune to pass from the scene before the worldwide cyclone unleashed in 1917. Platonov's generation was less fortunate.

There is ample reason to study Platonov and his works. By any standard, he was a significant scholar — as writer, researcher, educator, administrator, editor, and reviewer. His work exemplified the effulgent flowering of Russian historiography during the late Imperial period. He was also a talented teacher who personally trained a whole generation of historians and archivists, whose lectures inspired thousands of students, and whose sophisticated popularizations of Russian history reached a far broader audience than did the works of, say, Kliuchevsky. Platonov contributed importantly to the development of Russian educational institutions — especially in the field of higher education for women. Moreover, his career may offer some insight into the social and intellectual trends of late Imperial and early Soviet Russia. While Russian educational institutions of the post-reform era, with their emphasis on classical languages and rigid discipline, were avowedly conservative, they contributed to the modernization of the country by facilitating social mobility; thus they produced in the persons of Platonov and his generation a splendid intellectual elite. Many of the achievements of this elite were transmitted to its Soviet successors. Platonov's success demonstrates the possibilities of social advancement under the last three Tsars — he attained the title of privy councilor, the third highest position in the Table of Ranks — just as his fate illustrates the perilous status of intellectuals under a totalitarian regime.

I

We know little about Platonov's family or his early life. He was born on June 16, 1860, in the Ukrainian town of Chernigov where his father was a printing press technician in state service. His parents were both Great Russians, with perhaps some Moldavian blood on his mother's side, and they were descendants of peasants in the Moscow region. Since the term peasant might apply to a broad legal category, Platonov's social origins cannot be precisely determined from published information. One of his grandfathers may have been a serf or, perhaps, a state peasant; in any case, Platonov's father was a free urban dweller. Sergei Fedorovich was apparently an only child. His father was literate and held a good job, and in 1869 the family moved to St. Petersburg where Platonov attended a classical gymnasium (1870-1878). These facts indicate that Platonov was in no sense a country boy of deprived

background. His parents lived comfortably, and they valued
education and culture. At age nine their son began reading
Pushkin and Karamzin; study at a gymnasium opened the
door to higher learning.[2]

In the spring of 1877 young Sergei contracted typhus. He
later remembered this illness as having marked the boundary
between childhood and young manhood. "Before it I was a
carefree youngster; recovering from the illness, however, I felt
as if I were beginning a new life . . ."[3] His search for this new
life lasted about three years. Instrumental in guiding him were
new friends and associations. Platonov spent the summer of
1877 with relatives in Moscow regaining his health. There he
experienced an intellectual awakening through contact with
the household of Evgeniia Antonovna Selivanovskaia,
especially through friendship with her granddaughter Evgeniia
Nikolaevna Kalaidovich. Six years older than Platonov, this
young woman introduced him to the spiritual delights of
literature and history. She inspired him with the high idealism
then current among student circles of Moscow University. "Up
to that time I had had no need to look forward and to delineate
subsequent paths in life. Now before me, like a guiding beacon,
stood the university — the depository of the humanistic
knowledge which molds character, which gives meaning to
life."[4] He returned for his final year of secondary school in St.
Petersburg resolved to pursue higher education.

Learning became fun. Outside school Platonov wrote
poetry, read Taine, Lewes, [5] and Mill — even Büchner's then
popular *Kraft und Stoff,* though its materialism repelled him.
His new teacher of Russian literature, Vladislav Feofanovich
Kenevich, a commentator on Krylov's fables, cultivated the
young man's belletristic talents. At Kenevich's urging Platonov,
though skeptical of his supposed gift for poetry, decided to
enter the historico-philological faculty of St. Petersburg

University where he matriculated in September, 1878. He intended "to specialize in the study of the history of literature in the broad sense of that term." [6]

Like many college freshmen, the eighteen-year-old Platonov found the university a great disappointment. The classical curriculum bored him. The philologists seemed dull or incompetent. More stimulating were the lectures of the prominent historian K.N. Bestuzhev-Riumin and of the jurists V.I. Sergeevich and A.D. Gradovsky. A man of cosmopolitan culture and immense reading, Bestuzhev-Riumin artfully conveyed to his audience a lively enthusiasm for, and encyclopedic knowledge of, Russian history as a dimension of national self-knowledge. "Work in the scholarly field of our own history appeared before us in an aureole of spiritual zealousness and promised the highest spiritual satisfaction." [7] Luckily for Platonov and his fellow students, they first met Bestuzhev-Riumin (1829-1897) at the apogee of his intellectual powers. Thereafter he became absorbed in other matters; his Slavophil proclivities became manifest, his health declined, and his scholarly influence waned.

In V.I. Sergeevich (1835-1911), an historian of Russian law, Platonov encountered the speculative boldness and oratorical brilliance of an accomplished lecturer. A.D. Gradovsky (1841-1889), a liberal historian of state law, shared Sergeevich's popularity with the student body. "Both professor-jurists observed several oratorical devices unknown to the philologists," recalled Platonov: "their speech was refined and cultivated; the students were named 'kind sirs;' the lecturer 'requested their leave' to dwell on this or that question and so on. All this worked upon the mood, imparted a solemn-serious tone to the discourse." [8] Although Platonov later concluded that Sergeevich's scholarship was superficial, he treasured the jurist's pedagogical virtuosity.

In contrast, Platonov respected Gradovsky both for his pedagogy and for his scholarship. A liberal Westernist in orientation, Gradovsky captivated the students with his biting, carefully camouflaged, political comments. Under his influence, as Platonov recollected,

> took shape my conceptions about the state and society, about the purposes of the state, about the relationship of the state to the individual, and about the blessing of personal liberty and independence. To the 'liberal' Gradovsky I am obligated, by the way, for the stubbornness with which I have always opposed any spirit of party or clique, jealously guarding the right of each individual to the use of his powers in whatever direction inner motivation may attract them. [9]

Both Gradovsky and Bestuzhev-Riumin, though poles apart in their political convictions, impressed the young Platonov by their passionate commitment to the moral value of history. Both men "penetrated the heart and the conscience, stirred the soul, compelled one to seek the ideal and moral principles. In their presentation history gave material for the evaluation of the present and compelled a youth to think over his relationship to the people [narodnost] and the state." [10] This moral element acted powerfully in resolving Platonov's personal search for a calling. The study of history attracted him by its intellectual charms, its relevance to present concerns, and its psychological nourishment.

Unlike many students of that time, Platonov did not plunge into politics. He shied away from debating circles. He spent much of his free time reading at home, corresponding with his Moscow friends, or attending the capital's flourishing theaters. He was not exactly a loner, but rather a thoughtful youth searching intensively for moral values during a period of

great social ferment. Perhaps impelled by his early reading of
liberal and positivist philosophy, Platonov drank deeply of the
intellectual currents of the 1870s emphasizing the dignity and
worth   of   independent,   individual   activity.   While
fundamentally apolitical throughout his career, he exemplified
classical liberalism with its stress on the value of individual
liberty as the mainspring of social and moral progress. He did
not   admire   those   of   his   fellow   students   who   staged
conspiratorial meetings and demonstrations. Most of such
would-be revolutionaries struck him as "limited dullards" or
"notoriously shallow and worthless lads." Their political
gatherings *(skhodki)* seemed "disorderly assemblages that
depended upon cultivation of the crude mass." [11] Much later in
life Platonov mused that, had he been temperamentally suited
for   political   activity,   he   might   at   best   have   become   a
behind-the-scenes operative. Demonstrations appalled him. He
did not feel personally oppressed and wished only to pursue his
education without interruption.

Platonov's first year at the university left him restless and
dissatisfied. His second year proved even less satisfactory. His
father fell seriously ill, requiring constant attention from Sergei
and his mother. Only two months into the academic year,
Platonov's studies ground to a halt. His sporadic attendance at
lectures — except those of Bestuzhev-Riumin — was aggravated
by irksome police surveillance which, he later learned, had
begun in the summer of 1878 "upon the most improbable
pretext, unconnected with the university." [12] Kenevich, whose
influence had guided the young *gimnazist* into the study of
literature, had died in the fall of 1879. Even before his death,
Platonov's ardor for literary studies had begun to cool under
the faucet of an ineptly taught, stultifying classical curriculum.
By contrast, history and the history of law seemed to him more
scientific in method, more congenial to national pride, and

more intellectually pleasing in their understanding of the past.
Faced with the necessity of selecting a major subject, Platonov
in the spring of 1880 chose history. His intellectual and
spiritual wandering came to an end.

In later life Platonov remembered his third year at St.
Petersburg University with unalloyed enthusiasm. His father
seemed to be recovering his health, which allowed Sergei to
return to his studies full-time. The whole structure of study
changed. Gone were the endless hours of boring lectures and
required language instruction. Bestuzhev-Riumin took charge
of the future historians and tailored their assignments so as to
evoke independent, diligent, and mature study. Bestuzhev
himself gave special courses which did not require the usual
end-of-the-year exams. In 1880-81 he lectured on his favorite
subject — Russian historiography. Each student was to select a
topic for a research paper which he would "defend" at a
colloquium during the fourth and final year of study. Final
grades were assessed for the paper and its presentation. In a
word, the system was what is nowadays termed an "honors"
course. [13.]

Beyond his continuing admiration for Bestuzhev-Riumin,
Platonov gravitated intellectually toward two new professors:
I.V. Jagic, a specialist in Slavic linguistics, and — especially —
Vasily Grigorevich Vasilevsky (1838-1899), the founder of
Byzantine studies in Russia. Vasilevsky taught a general course
on medieval history and, for history majors, an advanced
course on Russo-Byzantine relations. Here Platonov was
introduced to the critical analysis of historical texts. Vasilevsky
would bring documents to class in order to demonstrate how an
historian extracted living history from dead sources. "We
entered into the very process of scholarly research and
creativity," recollected Platonov, "and began to understand
the alluring fascination of successful scientific labor." [14]

Like Bestuzhev-Riumin, Vasilevsky was something of a
pedagogical innovator. Besides lecturing, he had the students in
his general course read the works of several major scholars —
Guizot, Granovsky, Thierry, and others. He proposed to the
students in his special course that they write brief analyses
(referaty) of selected historical problems. He prevailed on
young Platonov, who sat in the first row, to investigate "the
place of residence of the Tetraxsite Goths." [15]Platonov's
report displayed attributes to which he clung the rest of his
scholarly career: a fervent aspiration to originality and a horror
of slavish repetition of others' conclusions. Thus he took issue
with Vasilevsky's own views on the problem, marshaled the
Greek texts in favor of a different location, and accompanied
the paper with his own map of the region in question. The
exercise also manifested Platonov's life-long fascination with
historical geography.

Pleased with his pupil's efforts, Vasilevsky devoted an
entire class period to discussing his work. "This was my first
acquaintance with Vasilevsky, which served as the beginning
of my long and close relationship with an unforgettable
teacher." [16]Indeed, Vasilevsky acted as Platonov's intellectual
mentor and took a fatherly interest in his progress. Although
Platonov did not become a Byzantinist, he imbibed
Vasilevsky's methods and consciously modeled himself after
him. His warm remembrance of Vasilevsky bespeaks those
qualities he himself strove to cultivate:

> Many-sided scholarship, breadth of intellectual
> horizon, most acute power of observation, [and]
> extraordinary critical sensitivity distinguished Vasil-
> evsky as a scholar who in talent had no equals among
> the Russian historians contemporary to him.
> Originality and elegance of construction, proportion
> and power of argumentation, the peculiar beauty of

a style which knew how and loved to transpose into
the present the merits of archaic rhetoric and even its
mannerism, [and] finally, the unrivalled humor in
which Vasilevsky's mind was so rich — such are his
virtues as a writer. As a man he was exceptionally
kind and benevolent, distinguished by unwavering
tolerance and magnanimity. He did not know how to
be hostile or to quarrel, and affected everyone by
means of his unwavering moral virtue and kindliness.
No wonder his pupils and comrades on the faculty
responded to him with profound devotion, often
even with adoration. [17]

For his research paper in Russian history Platonov
decided to study the Muscovite *Zemsky Sobor* (assembly of the
land). He chose this theme partly under the influence of
contemporary events — "the dictatorship of the heart"
established under Count Loris-Melikov in February, 1880, to
combat revolutionary terrorism by reconciling state and
society. Loris-Melikov's policies inspired hopes that
reconciliation might take the form of a representative
assembly. More broadly, the Era of Great Reforms had
stimulated widespread interest in representative institutions,
and both Westernist and Slavophil historians plumbed the
Russian past to discover precedents. Hence there was
considerable scholarly and journalistic discussion of the
Zemsky Sobor. In view of Platonov's ties to Moscow and the
interest in legal and institutional history that Gradovsky and
Sergeevich had already implanted in him, the subject held
obvious attraction. Bestuzhev approved Platonov's choice and
mentioned a few bibliographical leads, but refused to give any
further guidance. Bestuzhev's colleague E.E. Zamyslovsky
assisted Platonov, however, with the initial phase of his
research. [18] .Platonov's theme led him to examine the so-called

Time of Troubles at the turn of the sixteenth and seventeenth centuries; for it was during that epoch of dynastic disarray, civil war, and foreign intervention that the Zemsky Sobor had assumed paramount significance. This historical period became his lifelong specialty.

Sure of his field of study, Platonov began to gather a library of books on Russian history. He discovered the Archaeographic Commission, where he first examined old manuscripts and state documents. He gradually purchased its publications of sources and became an intimate of the institution which sponsored much of his subsequent research. Later he would long be among its most active members (1894-1929). [19]

If the academic year 1880-81 was intellectually satisfying for the budding historian, it was politically and emotionally unsettling. The student body was in constant ferment. During a solemn ceremony at the university in February, 1881, somebody slapped the Minister of Public Education, A.A. Saburov, in the face. Demonstrators in the balconies raised a commotion and rained down proclamations. Though order was quickly restored, the agitation continued at the customary benefit ball. Only with great difficulty were the malcontents prevented from disrupting the event, but they distributed plenty of leaflets "and created such a hot atmosphere," recalled Platonov, "that I personally with pleasure quit the ball." [20] Three weeks later terrorists killed Tsar Alexander II.

The assassination stunned Platonov and many of his fellow students. Unlike some, however, he did not thereafter become a convinced conservative or reactionary. He remained a mild Westernist in intellectual outlook and shunned politics even more than before. While he maintained his respect for Bestuzhev-Riumin, whose conservative Slavophil sympathies became more pronounced in these years, he felt uncomfortable among the chauvinistic patriots who had come to dominate Bestuzhev's St. Petersburg salon. [21]

More congenial to Platonov was the company of fellow students who placed scholarship above politics. Hence in the months following the assassination he eagerly participated in founding a student organization dedicated to the pursuit of knowledge and mutual assistance. Chartered by the government as the "Student Scientific-Literary Society," this organization partially reconciled conservative and radical student opinion by providing a legitimate forum for scholarly discussion. Prominent in its establishment and varied activities were the Oldenburg brothers, Fedor and Sergei, while its faculty advisor was a popular professor of Russian literature and liberal Slavophil, O.F. Miller (1833-1889). The society attained a membership of more than 300, collected a library of some 5,000 volumes, and sponsored numerous activities until disbanded by government order in 1887. Platonov's standing in the society is indicated by its sponsorship of his first scholarly publication: "Remarks on the History of the Muscovite Zemsky Sobors" (1883). [22]

Membership in this organization facilitated Platonov's new friendships, many of which lasted the rest of his life. At the same time he became a member of an intimate circle *(kruzhok)* consisting of I.A. Shliapkin, K.A. Ivanov, and V.G. Druzhinin. They all loved Russian history and literature; all became teachers. Their discussions gradually became a regular affair, the number of participants grew, and beginning in 1884 Platonov stood at the center of a "circle of Russian historians" which included such scholars as M.A. Diakonov, A.S. Lappo-Danilevsky, N.D. Chechulin, S.M. Seredonin, E.F. Shmurlo, and others. [23] These vital, gifted young historians proved enormously creative. They constituted the sophisticated, critical yet sympathetic milieu in which liberal, independent scholarship flourished. Informal gatherings of this sort cushioned Russian university scholarship from the debilitating loss of autonomy imposed by the new, restrictive university statute of 1884.

Having passed his third-year exams in the spring of 1881, Platonov spent the summer working on his Zemsky Sobor project. He soon exhausted the materials previous researchers of the institution had used, discovered some sources they had overlooked, revised some of their views, and formulated several novel observations and conclusions. "Independent work immeasurably diverted and comforted me in the difficult circumstances of my family situation at that time." His father's health had collapsed, never to return. Forced to retire, he had to subsist on the family's modest savings. The younger Platonov had never known need, had never had to request scholarship assistance or seek employment. Now he had to rush to complete his studies in order to become the family's breadwinner. He finished his composition, prior to his father's death in November, 1881, with the hope that it might serve as his candidate's thesis as well as fulfilling the requirements of Bestuzhev's colloquium. In January, 1882, Platonov submitted his essay to Bestuzhev-Riumin. That same month he commenced giving private lessons in a St. Petersburg *pension*. His long teaching career began even before he had a degree. [24]

Bestuzhev-Riumin approved Platonov's work on the Zemsky Sobor as his candidate's thesis, but still requested his student, who was then submerged in teaching and preparing for final exams, to offer another work to the colloquium. Platonov was "astonished, grieved and even insulted" at this unrealistic suggestion. He finally told Bestuzhev that he could not do it. Despite this misunderstanding, Bestuzhev-Riumin later proposed that his pupil upon graduation "remain at the university in preparation for the professorial calling." Platonov eagerly accepted. Soon thereafter, however, Bestuzhev-Riumin fell ill and left for Italy to convalesce, ending his intellectual sponsorship of Platonov. [25]

In inviting Platonov to study further, Bestuzhev deprecated his own impact on the young scholar, in whom he saw a pupil of Sergeevich. But Platonov's appreciation of Bestuzhev's erudition had never been uncritical. Vasilevsky had facilitated his intellectual independence, and in his final year of undergraduate study another powerful stimulus emerged: the radiant mind of Kliuchevsky. From friends in Moscow Platonov heard rapturous praise of the brilliant young successor to S.M. Soloviev. In 1880 he obtained a lithographed copy of Kliuchevsky's lectures on the reign of Catherine II. For a *referat* on the Boyar Duma he read the first chapters of Kliuchevsky's noted work about that institution, serialized in 1880-81 in the journal *Russian Thought*. Bestuzhev-Riumin's sour appraisal of the Moscow scholar did not disillusion Platonov, who was impressed by the breadth and multiple dimensions of historical understanding that Kliuchevsky's intellect laid bare. Platonov never concealed his debt to Kliuchevsky, whose works he "read and re-read" and whose influence he experienced "powerfully and profoundly." He subsequently came to know Kliuchevsky well, though not with blind adoration.[26] Only Vasilevsky had a greater effect on Platonov. If Platonov is usually depicted as a disciple of the St. Petersburg school of Russian historiography, the early and continuous influence upon him of Kliuchevsky's Moscow school should not be underestimated. Platonov believed that the academic year 1881-82, when he began to appreciate Kliuchevsky's achievement, lent final direction to his scholarly pursuits.

II

Invitation to post-graduate study did not permit the young *kandidat* to give up teaching. On the contrary, over the next seven years he taught Russian language and Russian history twenty or more hours per week in several secondary schools. Because of low salaries, it was common practice to hold multiple teaching positions simultaneously. In 1884-1889 Platonov lectured at a school sponsored by the Society of St. Petersburg Merchants. Having become a qualified docent by passing preliminary exams for the *magister* degree in 1886, he began lecturing at the fashionable Imperial Lyceum *(Aleksandrovskii litsei)* at Tsarskoe Selo, where he taught college level courses in Russian history until 1891. It was probably this position that brought Platonov to the attention of the Imperial family. He later served as tutor in Russian history to the children of Grand Duke Mikhail Aleksandrovich and Grand Duchess Olga Aleksandrovna, the brother and sister of Nicholas II, in the years 1895-1902.[27] When Bestuzhev-Riumin's failing health forced his virtual retirement after 1882, his chair at St. Petersburg University passed to E.E. Zamyslovsky. Platonov was among those graduate students who replaced Bestuzhev in his other principal position — teaching and administering the so-called St. Petersburg Higher Women's Courses. This institution was an outgrowth of the movement for women's education; at the time Russian universities were exclusively male.

   The prototype of higher women's courses had opened in St. Petersburg in 1870, with an enrollment of about 900 students. The institution languished until 1878, when Bestuzhev-Riumin obtained a modest government subsidy and reorganized the courses. They were henceforth known unofficially as the Bestuzhev Courses. The two faculties — historico-philological and physico-mathematical — offered a four-year program staffed by teachers and professors from other institutions including a few Academicians. By 1881 there were 938 students regularly enrolled and 42 auditors. Similar institutions appeared in Moscow, Kazan, Kiev, and Odessa, with total enrollment reaching 2,000 in 1881.

Higher women's courses in other cities were closed in 1886, primarily for political reasons — to combat revolutionary activities among the young women. The Bestuzhev Courses alone managed to survive, although their enrollment shrank to only 144 in 1889 before rebounding slightly to 557 in 1894. Financial woes plagued the institution; in 1892-93 Platonov and other professors taught there after hours without payment. Nevertheless, growth resumed during the reign of Nicholas II, especially after 1905. By 1906, when the Bestuzhev Courses added a juridical faculty, their enrollment totaled 2,396; by 1912, nearly 6,000. [28]

Platonov played a major part in the success of the Bestuzhev Courses. He taught Russian history there for thirty-three years (1883-1916). From 1885 to 1889 he served as dean of the historico-philological faculty. He accompanied the girls on excursions to old Russian towns, organizing in 1910 a trip to the Solovetskii Monastery on the White Sea. His lectures enjoyed exceptional popularity. He lectured in the largest auditorium of the institution, as students from other faculties flocked to hear him. "Professor S.F. Platonov literally resurrected the past in front of his listeners," remarked a former student. "He had no need of outlines or textbooks, but reproduced old charters, documents from memory. Those in his course said that he lectured about each epoch in the language of that time, interspersing his discourse with quotations and references to chronicles, diplomatic correspondence, the statements of the very heroes of the story." [29]

Platonov devoted much attention to teaching techniques. His own undergraduate study had impressed on him the necessity of presenting history so as to attract and inspire his listeners. Hence he concentrated upon a seemingly simple, straightforward delivery of the facts, yet laced his lectures with pungent character sketches, piquant details, colorful quotations, and sly humor. The drama of historical events fired his imagination, and he employed rhetorical devices to capture the attention of his audience. One former student singled out his "celebrated pauses."

> When he was finishing any presentation, before drawing a conclusion, making a summary — he would fall silent and for a long time look into the audience with a sort of searching gaze, as if reading the necessary answer in our strained silence.
>
> And then — a dry, laconic, as if closing gesture of the right hand — and we would hear: "Aleksei Mikhailovich poised one foot over the threshold dividing Old Russia from Europe, and thus with an uplifted foot remained there till the end of his reign." [30]

Platonov was neither a facile showman content to dazzle his audiences nor a fact-pusher intent upon cramming their heads with information. The same woman who remarked on his pauses also attested to his intellectual inspiration. "We learned to understand that it's not enough to know an event — one has to comprehend the causes that gave birth to it; it's too little to know what a person is, one has to grasp why he became what he is. These lectures greatly enriched us." [31]

Even after having achieved scholarly eminence, Platonov maintained his interest in pedagogy and women's education. In 1903 he joined hands with several fellow teachers to revitalize the Imperial Women's Pedagogical Institute in St. Petersburg.

As its director until his retirement in 1916, he was instrumental
in building the institute into a first-class teachers'
college. [32] Commented one contemporary who taught there:
"One must give high credit to Platonov's ability and tact for the
high reputation of this women's institution of learning, which
had contributed much to the practical and theoretical training
of teachers." [33]

Platonov committed his scholarly as well as his
organizational talents to improving the teaching of history in
secondary schools. He wrote what immediately became the
standard textbook of Russian history, the first part of which
appeared in 1909, the second a year later. By 1911 it had
already gone into its fourth edition. Counting abridgements,
fourteen Russian editions have appeared to date, the latest in
Buenos Aires in 1945. Translations into English, French, and
German have extended its influence outside Russia. The work
is a solid piece of scholarship; its presentation is clearly
arranged and lucidly set forth. As P.B. Struve remarked, one
cannot imagine Kliuchevsky, for example, expending his
intellectual energies on a simple textbook. [34] Significantly,
Platonov's text appeared after the revolution of 1905 had
inaugurated a semi-constitutional regime in Russia, with
substantially broadened civil liberties. His book marked a great
advance, intellectually and politically, over the notoriously
chauvinist and obscurantist textbook of D.I. Ilovaisky
previously used. [35]

III

The pedagogical and administrative contribution of Platonov
to Russian secondary education appears truly remarkable in
view of his multiple involvements in higher education and his
dedication to research. His scholarly promise was manifested

early and was brilliantly realized. Bestuzhev-Riumin wrote of him in December, 1883: "Platonov is really very gifted, and probably, will go far. Not that I made him a scholar, of course, but partly himself, partly Zamyslovsky. My own influence I do not see."[36] The young *kandidat* completed course work for his magisteral exam in 1885 and began to publish serially his *magisterskaia dissertatsiia* late in 1887. In February, 1888, with the rank of privatdocent, he commenced lecturing at St. Petersburg University. There he publicly defended his magisteral dissertation, entitled *Old Russian Legends and Tales about the Time of Troubles of the 17th Century, as an Historical Source,* in September, 1888. That same year it appeared in book form and won its author an Uvarov Prize of the Imperial Academy of Sciences in 1890. [37]

Under ordinary circumstances the holder of a magister's degree in history could not expect to obtain a chair at a major university until he achieved the doctorate. But at the end of 1889 E.E. Zamyslovsky fell mortally ill. The faculty did not desire an outsider, so in the spring of 1890 they named Platonov to the chair with the rank of acting professor of history. His selection was probably due to the influence of Vasilevsky, who had written of him on January 6, 1890: "the younger of the two, [the other candidate was E.F. Shmurlo] Platonov, is much more even-tempered, more precise and harmonious. He has an amazingly well structured head, his thinking, just as his research, is always distinguished by clarity and precision, [and] is expressed with complete exactitude." [38]

Vasilevsky counseled Platonov to hurry with his doctoral dissertation, as the doctorate would be required to hold the chair. After consultation with Bestuzhev-Riumin, Platonov elected to pursue the subject of Boris Godunov, hoping to complete within two years a study of his career. As it happened, this project burgeoned into the much more ambitious study which insured Platonov's fame: *Outlines of the History of the Troubles in the Muscovite State in the 16th and 17th Centuries* (St. Petersburg, 1899). He kept his chair, however, until retirement from teaching in 1916, while in 1900-1905 he functioned as dean of the Historical Faculty.

A principal cause for the delay in Platonov's doctorate stemmed from his editorial labors. He served in 1890-1895 as chief assistant to Vasilevsky, editor of the monthly *Journal of the Ministry of Public Education*. From 1888 to 1910, moreover, he edited ten different sources and collections of sources. Indeed, he first collected and edited the sources on which both his magisteral and his doctoral dissertation were based. Entitled *Monuments of Old Russian Writing Relating to the Times of Troubles* (St. Petersburg, 1891) [*Russian Historical Library,* vol. XIII], the collection proved so valuable to literary and historical scholars that it was reissued, in expanded form, in 1909 and again in 1925. This dimension of Platonov's scholarship manifested his profound faith in the discipline of history as a progressively developing, valuable cultural and intellectual enterprise. Here his labors contrast sharply with those of Kliuchevsky, who took little interest in such molelike endeavors though he gladly utilized their fruits. [39]

Platonov also gave a series of lectures on the critical analysis of sources, which the students of the Petersburg Archaeological Institute had lithographed in 1905. He transmitted the methodology of source criticism which Vasilevsky and others had learned in German universities, brought back to Russia and widely diffused. The German *Quellenkunde,* translated into Russian *istochnikovedenie,* became the hallmark of the St. Petersburg School of Russian historiography which Platonov personified for his generation.

To the present day this methodological orientation retains
great influence among Leningrad historians.[40]

During Platonov's twenty-six years as a professor at St.
Petersburg University, he supervised the recruitment and the
training of an entire generation of historians. Among his most
distinguished students were A.E. Presniakov, N.P.
Pavlov-Silvansky, S.V. Rozhdestvensky, B.A. Romanov, A.I.
Zaozersky, I.I. Lappo, M.A. Polievktov, A.A. Vvedensky, A.I.
Andreev, P.G. Liubomirov, and G.V. (George) Vernadsky. All
these scholars wrote important works; several supplied crucial
training to subsequent generations of historians both in the
Soviet Union and abroad. Professor Vernadsky still remembers
his post-graduate study under Platonov in the years 1911-1917.
He mentions, for instance, that Platonov had doubts about his
choosing to write his magisteral dissertation on Russian
freemasonry in the eighteenth century; "but when I explained
to him at length my reasons he agreed to approve it. This was an
example of the breadth of his mind and his attentive attitude
toward the interests of young scholars."[41]

Platonov enjoyed a close relationship with his advanced
students. On Wednesday evenings he held a regular open-house.
Professor Vernadsky recollects of these informal gatherings:
"As the soiree advanced, someone would ask Platonov to say a
few words about a historical problem he was working on, or
about a new book, or to relate some episode of his recent
travels, for example about his search for old manuscripts in
various Russian monasteries. His talks were exceedingly vivid
and interesting."[42]

In addition to editorial work and teaching, which
included periodic lectures at two local military colleges — the
Military Juridical Academy and the Academy of the General
Staff — Platonov was active in a host of scholarly organizations.
A 1916 recording of his titles found him a member or honorary

member of twenty-four different societies, commissions, and institutes. He traveled widely, too, crisscrossing the western part of the Russian Empire from the White Sea to the Crimea, the Caucasus, and the southern Urals. He visited Constantinople, Greece, and Western Europe, his last European journey being to Berlin and Paris in 1928. [43]

Platonov became widely known to the Russian public through his writings and lectures. In 1899 students began lithographing his university course of lectures on Russian history, which by 1917 was in its tenth edition. His collected articles were issued twice, in 1903 and, in expanded form, in 1912; his magisteral dissertation also required a second printing, in 1913. His doctoral dissertation — the crowning achievement of his career — was reissued twice, in 1901 and 1910; a projected fourth edition was interrupted by revolution and civil war. Furthermore, students and colleagues dedicated *Festschriften* to him in 1911 and 1922. When Platonov retired from teaching and administration in 1916, his books provided a handsome income, and he anticipated a period of unhampered scholarly productivity. [44] This was not to be.

IV

Not a member of any political party though a liberal conservative in outlook, Platonov had to return to work if only to survive in post-revolutionary Russia. From April, 1918 to May, 1923 he was delegated by Petrograd University to work in the newly established Chief Archives Administration. He supervised one of its seven subdivisions and headed its Petrograd committee. He also assisted in training cadres of archivists to staff the new institutions; his prominence and organizational ability facilitated the establishment, in the summer of 1918, of the so-called Petrograd Archival Courses.

In May, 1920, he addressed the opening and closing sessions of the first conference of Petrograd archival workers. [45]

Platonov spent the civil war years in Petrograd. He took up lecturing again and appeared before various audiences, from scholarly gatherings such as the Petrograd House of Scholars (*Dom uchenykh*) to Red Army groups and workers' clubs. As before, he regularly attended the monthly sessions of the Archaeographic Commission, whose members unanimously elected him chairman in December, 1918. A corresponding member of the Academy of Sciences since 1908, Platonov was elevated to full membership in 1920. That same year he became chairman of the Academy's Standing Historical Commission (*Postoiannaia istoricheskaia komissiia* [PIK]), which since 1903 had been publishing historical sources. Platonov's dual chairmanship of PIK and the Archaeographic Commission, which from 1922 came under the jurisdiction of the Academy, presaged their amalgamation in 1926 as the Standing Historico-Archaeographic Commission (PIAK). He remained chairman until 1929. [46]

Despite myriad difficulties, Platonov strove to reactivate the publication activities of both commissions. Only his personal intercession in 1921 with M.N. Pokrovsky (1868-1932), the Bolshevik historian and head of the Chief Archives Administration in Moscow, enabled the Archaeographic Commission to obtain access to manuscripts in Moscow archives. Also in 1921 Platonov was chosen as one of the eight Petrograd members of the newly established Central Bureau of Scientific Societies and Institutions. [47]

Because of the economic disruption and its attendant paper shortage, he was able to publish only a few brief articles. But in 1921 *Boris Godunov,* the first of a series of popular studies, appeared in print — to the acclaim of "bourgeois" historians, but to the chagrin of militant Bolsheviks like Pokrovsky. Indeed, Pokrovsky denied its value and ended his review on a bitter note: "The little book is printed with extraordinary splendor for the present time. The bourgeoisie knows how to print its own. But when will we learn?" And yet Ia. L. Barskov, a friend of Platonov's, lauded his book as Marxist in the best sense of the term![48]

The tragic figure of Boris Godunov had long stirred Platonov's sympathies. The elderly historian evidently perceived in the cataclysm suffered by Russia in 1917–1921 an analogue to Boris's fatal dilemma: a capable ruler overwhelmed by an unfathomable social crisis. He interpreted Boris's personal tragedy as a product of the larger tragedy inherent in the violent dissolution of traditional Muscovite society. Accordingly, *Boris Godunov* is more than a biography or apologia. It provides a subtle study of a society in turmoil, and of one man's valiant efforts to stave off a revolution that proved stronger than he.

Although Platonov did not become a convert to Marxism, his long-standing interest in social and economic history proved adaptable to some of the new historiographical currents. Thus he took an active part in a scholarly commission established in 1921 by the Petrograd Soviet of Professional Unions to investigate the history of labor in Russia. He contributed to its journal, *Archive of the History of Labor in Russia,* of which ten issues came out between 1921 and 1923.[49] He published in several other of the numerous short-lived periodicals of that era, such as *Affairs and Days* (1920-1922) and *The Russian Historical Journal* (1917-1922), serving as chief editor of the latter and also of *The Russian Past* (5 issues, 1923).

Soviet authorities respected and trusted Platonov sufficiently to invite his participation as an historical expert in the negotiations for the Treaty of Riga between the Soviet Republic and Poland in 1920.[50] This commission casts some doubt on the standard charge of Soviet authors that Platonov reacted negatively to the October Revolution. That same year he accompanied a research expedition to the Murmansk region. This journey was part of a broad inquiry into the resources and colonization of the Russian North — an effort initiated by a special "Committee on the North" of the Russian Geographical Society under the auspices of the Academy of Sciences. Platonov headed the historical section of the enterprise and wrote several articles on the subject, which were later collected and published as *The Past of the Russian North* (1923).[51]

Platonov was fortunate to survive the civil war; many Russian historians of his generation did not. He recalled in 1927 how eight years earlier, when communications had been severed between northern and southern Russia, newspapers in the South and abroad had carried reports of his death. "With great curiosity I read my obituaries, and in several of them found information about my life and activities that was very curious, but to me personally completely unknown up to that time."[52] His wife and six grown children (five daughters and a son) also survived, one of the daughters emigrating to western Europe.

"In his political views Platonov was a monarchist," states the entry in a recent Soviet historical encyclopedia. "After 1917 his political views changed little. He was arrested, banished to Samara (present-day Kuibyshev), where he died" (on January 10, 1933).[53] No charges, no details, no reasons given — such reticence is typical of Soviet commentaries on the events of 1928-1931 that engulfed Platonov and many other intellectuals. Evidently, Platonov himself left no account of his personal time of troubles; so the only available sources are official pronouncements, on the one hand, and hearsay evidence from former Soviet prisoners, on the other. Lack of sources therefore precludes full explication of the intricacies of the tragedy.

What seems clear, in retrospect, is that Platonov fell victim to repression not because of anything he did, but because of his position in the Academy and the scholarly world in general. When the Academy was purged of its "bourgeois" elements, i.e., most of its members and staff, Platonov was singled out as a target. Some writers have blamed this persecution on Pokrovsky's alleged personal antipathy for Platonov.[54] This charge may be overly specific, however, as Pokrovsky's political influence had never been great and was already on the wane by 1929.[55] Yet Pokrovsky's "political" approach to history and disdain for "bourgeois historians" proved convenient weapons in the national crisis of 1929-1932. In any event, as Loren Graham has shown, the Sovietization of the Academy of Sciences was an organic outgrowth of the social reorganization and institutional remolding that constituted the first five-year plan. "The replacement or reform of the Academy was almost certainly only a matter of time," he writes; "this institution without a single Party cell and with an uncensored press, even for works in history and the social sciences, was an anomaly in Soviet society."[56] Platonov apparently led the defense of the Academy's autonomy and thus suffered special persecution.

The few facts available are generally clear; the personal story behind them is not. When the Party authorities encountered opposition to their proposed reorganization of the Academy, they moved to purge the institution. Platonov, who since 1925 had also served as director of the Academy's Library and of its research institute for Russian Literature *(Pushkinskii dom)*, was relieved of many of his duties in the fall of 1929. He and others were publicly accused of concealing historical documents, including Nicholas II's act of abdication. This "archives affair" was designed, it seems, to arouse public outrage against the Academy. Platonov was finally arrested in November, 1930, and three months later was charged with complicity in a "Monarchist plot." But the "Academic case," in which Platonov was only one of the accused, never came to trial.[57] For reasons still unknown, it was quietly liquidated in 1931. That summer Platonov and three other Academicians were exiled internally. Accompanied by one of his daughters, whose sentence to convict labor was commuted to exile, Platonov was sent to live in a wretched house on the outskirts of Samara on the Volga.[58] Disfranchised, unemployed, far from books, he died eighteen months later from heart disease and malnutrition. The fate of his children is not known.[59]

In the post-Stalin years, particularly after 1956, many former "unpersons" have been rehabilitated in the Soviet Union. Recent Soviet treatments of the late 1920s and early 1930s have admitted that excesses occurred in that era.[60] Still, in most cases these posthumous rehabilitations have not extended to non-Marxists, and Soviet authors continue to portray the triumph of Marxist historiography as an essentially intellectual victory achieved over the remnants of "gentry-bourgeois-kulak" idealogy. The particular circumstances of Platonov's fate — like that of many others — are simply ignored.

The tragic irony is that, had Platonov lived longer, he might have regained his position when Soviet historiography after the downfall of Pokrovsky's "school" swung back, around 1934, to a more orthodox and nationalistic approach to Russian history. Several prominent non-Marxist historians — B.D. Grekov (1882-1953) and E.V. Tarle (1875-1955), to mention two Leningrad scholars whose cases were very similar to Platonov's — survived the Pokrovsky period and became respected figures of the Soviet historical profession. Had Platonov been younger, he might have followed a similar path. His historical views appear quite similar to those of National Bolshevism, which with its statist assumptions dominated

Soviet historiography from the mid 1930s until the post-Stalin era.[61] Indeed, the single work of Platonov's to be reissued under the Soviet regime — his *Outlines of the History of the Troubles* — came out in 1937 in a substantial printing of 10,000 copies. In 1964, however, when a prominent Soviet historian during his visit to the United States was asked whether Platonov's works would be republished in the Soviet Union, like the then recent multi-volume editions of Soloviev, Kliuchevsky, and Pokrovsky, he only shook his head and said "not soon." An unfortunate byproduct of Pokrovsky's recent partial restoration to grace may be continued oblivion and opprobrium for his contemporary rivals like Platonov.[62]

V

What of Platonov's works? Do they place him in the forefront of Russian historians? They do indeed. If quantity is used as an index, his total literary output approximates that of Kliuchevsky. A listing of his works (including sources and studies edited) in 1922 totaled 98, but this figure does not encompass such notable later studies as *The Time of Troubles* (1923), *Ivan the Terrible* (1923), *The Past of the Russian North* (1923), *Muscovy and the West* (1925), *Peter the Great* ((1926), and *From the Social History of the Petrine Epoch* (1926). Most of these appeared in article as well as book form, while six of the books he published in the 1920s in the Soviet Union were also issued by emigre presses in Western Europe. To this total should be added numerous editorial credits, articles, reports, reviews, obituaries, and the various translations of his books. A rough estimate of his publications in the period after 1922 would swell his bibliography by at least thirty items.

The 1920s constituted a sparkling epilogue to Platonov's already distinguished career. While his works of that period drew heavily on earlier research, they incorporated sophisticated analysis and masterful presentation. As S.N. Valk has noted, "each of them gave something new and fresh."[63] These products of Platonov's last decade attest to his continuing concern for the diffusion and popularization of accurate historical knowledge. His works enjoyed scholarly as well as popular success; they raised issues — the origins of serfdom, for example — that dominated scholarly discussion during the nest decades.[64]

Tremendous public recognition accrued to Platonov during his lifetime. The multiple editions of his main works have been mentioned. His writings achieved an enormous popularity that has continued abroad and, to a lesser extent, in the Soviet Union long after his death. Central to their success, in my opinion, is Platonov's felicitous combination of intimate knowledge of the sources, painstaking care, critical perceptiveness, and literary style. Thus Kliuchevsky applauded Platonov's "ability to pick out, in mosaic fashion, petty facts scattered in various sources, and to form them into a whole sketch. . . ."[65] Platonov's erudition is made gracefully accessible, too. His boyhood attraction to literature, his love for the classics, both Russian and foreign, his admiration for the artistry of Kliuchevsky all impelled him to see in history a special mode of creative literature. In comparison with Kliuchevsky, however, Platonov exercised considerably greater restraint in communicating his scholarship. His passion for factual exactitude and for clarity of presentation found expression in simple, laconic language. Platonov eschewed, just as Kliuchevsky pursued, the use of aphorism and paradox. Yet Platonov's prose is not pale and lifeless; on the contrary, it breathes vitality from an ingenious blending of rhythmic phrasing, rich vocabulary, and poetic devices. His mastery of the sources combined with an acute sense of phrasing to enrich the texture of his language with colorful quotations. He had an eye for the *bon mot* in the work of others, as when he quoted Soloviev to describe the Russian peasantry before enserfment as embodying a "fluid consistency." [66]

Some critics have branded Platonov an imitator of Kliuchevsky's style and borrower of his conceptual framework.[67] This is true only to the extent that every sensitive Russian historian after Kliuchevsky had to contend with his genius. Platonov learned much from Kliuchevsky; he did not conceal or deny his debt. Indeed, he was supremely conscious of the traditions of Russian historiography and visualized himself as a link in a long chain of progressively evolving historical scholarship.

If Platonov largely adopted the framework of Russian history that Kliuchevsky had wrought, he made an original contribution in his distinguished studies of the Time of Troubles. Here he gave an acutely perceptive analysis of Muscovite society on the eve of the Troubles, displaying in the process a staggering knowledge of local and regional history. He reinterpreted the *oprichnina* of Ivan the Terrible, demonstrating its broad significance to the intra-elite antagonisms and socioeconomic cleavages of the time.[68] Boris Godunov emerges in a strikingly different, much more positive, light thanks to Platonov's subtle argumentation. Finally, in tracing the course of the Troubles proper (1598-1613), Platonov employed a disarmingly simple threefold scheme, as he examined first the "dynastic struggle," then the "social struggle," and finally the "struggle for nationhood." Far from being an oversimplification of the convoluted sequence of events, Platonov's scheme was based upon detailed analysis which showed how the three different phases interpenetrated to produce a gigantic social upheaval in which individual patriotism and heroism were strangely interwoven with the self-interested rivalries of the various social and regional groupings of the population. The result is a magnificent interpretation of a crucial epoch, for Platonov conceived the Time of Troubles as an historical divide separating the patrimonial regime of medieval Muscovy from the bureaucratic autocracy of modern Russia. So imposing has Platonov's authority loomed over this epoch, that few scholars have ventured to contest his conclusions and, as a result, the period has suffered relative neglect during the past four decades. [69]

Platonov's scholarship exemplifies the creative response of his own St. Petersburg school, with its devotion to the careful and subtle use of sources, to the intellectual stimulus of Kliuchevsky's Moscow school, with its socioeconomic and geopolitical emphases. His historical works, whether large or small, exude a marvelous sense of discovery, tempered by a sober appreciation of the interaction between past and present. Platonov, like Kliuchevsky, never became a Marxist; he could not bear to see individuals dwarfed by impersonal forces. An optimist and devotee of classical liberalism, he was also acutely aware of the way in which historical tradition circumscribes the actions of individuals.

Without access to Platonov's personal papers, it is impossible to detail the evolution of his philosophical and political views. It seems likely, however, that he became more pessimistic and more conservative in the latter decades of his life. P.B. Struve recalled meeting Platonov on a tram several months before the outbreak of World War I. He was astounded at the historian's fatalistic attitude toward Russia's future. "Platonov scented — such was the sense of his sharply candid discourses and references — a bloody palace revolution in the style of the 18th century, but in the atmosphere of the 20th century. . . ." [70] All the same, he evidently welcomed the February Revolution and, despite Soviet claims to the

contrary, accepted the October Revolution. In contrast to
many other "bourgeois" intellectuals, Platonov was not
expelled from the country nor did he choose to emigrate. And
this was not because he had no opportunities to leave: he was
sent abroad on official business in 1923.[71] Whatever his
personal attitude toward Bolshevism, Platonov worked loyally
for and occupied a prominent position under the new Soviet
regime, whose trust and respect he seems to have retained right
up to the moment of his arrest.

If Platonov's writings of the 1920s took on a Marxist
terminological overlay, that fact should not be used to infer a
similar change in his philosophical outlook. On this point
Soviet commentators are probably right: his views did not
change substantially. Still, their classification of Platonov
as a representative of the "official-preservative attitude of
bourgeois-gentry historiography" smacks of dogmatism.[72]
Platonov was not a radical in politics, nor a materialistist
in philosophy, but that does not mean that he was a reactionary dreamer. Rather, he appears to have been an essentially
apolitical liberal conservative, a Russian patriot, a man of
exemplary integrity, an educator dedicated to the enlightenment of his nation, and a scholar committed to the value
of independent investigation of the past. His career illuminates
the achievements and tribulations of late Imperial Russia, just
as it highlights the triumph and the tragedy of the Soviet Union.

John T. Alexander

University of Kansas

TRANSLATOR'S PREFACE

Boris Godunov is a powerful statement of the riddle of Boris himself, and of his time and place. The work sets before the reader Platonov's penetrating resolution of the enigmas of Russian history with which it deals. The character of this puzzle — and the challenges with which the author must deal — are artfully posed in the incredible list of allegations against Godunov cited by Platonov in Chapter One, Part I. In confronting what is part of the very marrow of the Russian historical experience as pared to its core by one of the most distinguished and skilled Russian historians, the translator encounters both a supremely gifted analyst and a writer of no mean artistic accomplishment. Choosing not to confine himself to a direct expository prose, Platonov embellished his structurally simple style with a stimulating overlay of rich imagery, poetic turn of language and extensive use of sixteenth and seventeenth-century speech. In what is essentially a straightforward translation, I have attempted to retain Platonov's power and art. At the same time, to the best of my ability, I have tried to render the text as precisely and accurately as possible. The reader must determine the degree to which the alchemy of translation has yielded the precious metal of Platonov's scholarship, unique style and force.

For this translation I have used the edition published in 1921 in Petrograd. Russian names and terms have been transliterated by a modified Library of Congress system. No hard or soft signs have been indicated nor have ligatures been employed. *Ya* and *yu* are used initially instead of *ia* and *iu*. The soft sign before *e* in neuter nouns has been replaced by *i*. Plurals of all family names have been anglicized as the differences in spelling between the singular and plural forms of various adjectival surnames tend to change the shape of the word for the English-speaking reader. Thus the plural of Nagoi is rendered Nagois, instead of Nagie. Common nouns, on the other hand, retain the Russian plural, i. e., muzhiki instead of muzhiks. Platonov makes much use of quotations, the marks for which have been retained in most cases. All quotation marks used to indicate passages from other texts appear in this translation. The spelling of names and terms sanctioned by time and usage have been omitted from the system of transliteration: for example, Alexander and Cossack instead of Aleksandr and Kazak.

Stressed *e* is spelled simply as *e,* thus Fedor and not Fedor. Foreign names have been retained in their national spelling, although Platonov used Russian spelling throughout the original. Parentheses are Platonov's; words and phrases in brackets are mine. The footnotes have been placed at the end of the book. Platonov used very few and they are so indicated after each of his citations. To make the text easier to follow, I have employed shorter sentences and paragraphs than those used by the author. A list of sources used in preparing the translation follows the notes, as do Platonov's own references.

Many persons deserve special credit for their aid and support in this work. In particular, thanks are due Professor John T. Alexander of the University of Kansas, whose many and extremely helpful suggestions were of material assistance. I would also like to express my gratitude to Professors Edward Keenan of Harvard University, and John Bross of New York University, for their guidance in translating especially intricate passages extracted by Platonov from old Russian texts. I thank my colleagues, Professors James Hayes and David Tatem of the University of Maine, for their aid in rendering passages from German and Latin. Mr. Richard D. Kelly deserves special acknowledgement for his excellent map and for the reproduction of the sketch in Chapter Three. Mr. John R. McConnell, the Rev. Edward R. Greene, Mrs. Nancy L. Clark, and my mother, Mrs. Rex E. Pyles, by their many suggestions concerning style and readability for the non-specialist, contributed measurably to my work. I must express my gratitude to Mr. Stefan D. Gurin and residents of the Russian community in Richmond, Maine for their special assistance in interpreting certain obscure idiomatic expressions and passages. Peter von Wahlde, who made this book possible, also offered much support and helpful criticism. Finally, special thanks and sincere appreciation go to my wife, Florence, who not only read portions of the early draft and typed much of it, but who unfailingly gave her continual support and encouragement throughout the whole endeavor. Without this, most certainly, the present translation would never have been completed. Of course, any deficiencies or inadequacies must remain my own responsibility.

L. Rex Pyles

University of Maine at Orono

S. F. PLATONOV

BORIS GODUNOV

TSAR OF RUSSIA

CHAPTER ONE

THE CAREER OF BORIS

I   BORIS IN SCHOLARLY LITERATURE

The personality of Boris Godunov has long captured the fancy of historians and writers of fiction. For in the great historical drama which took place in Moscow at the turn of the sixteenth and seventeenth centuries Godunov was destined to play the role of both victor and victim. The personal characteristics and private affairs of this political figure evoked from his contempories both praise which became eulogistic, and censure which turned into vicious slander. It has behooved calmer investigators of events and persons to dispense with both extremes in order to glimpse the true face of Boris and to render a just appraisal.

This work was first undertaken by a young contemporary of Godunov, a seventeenth-century state secretary [diak] and the author of The Annals [Vremennik], Ivan Timofeev, "a reader and writer of annalistic books." He ultimately confessed, however, after having made a most curious and interesting personality study of Boris, that he could not comprehend the "slave-tsar" and could not understand whether good or evil predominated in Boris. "At the very hour of his death no one knew which side prevailed in his affairs — good or evil," wrote Timofeev.

During the early years of the nineteenth century Boris appeared as a similar riddle to the illustrious Karamzin. Over the crypt of the Godunovs in the Trinity Monastery,[1] Karamzin rhetorically exclaimed: "The cold ashes of the dead have no advocate other than our conscience. All is silent round the ancient grave. . .what if we besmirch these ashes? What if, unjustly, we torment the memory of the man by believing false notions which have been established in the chronicles through stupidity and enmity?"

The same question has been posed to the historian of our time. Until now historical material concerning the personal life of Boris has been so unclear and the political role of Boris so complex, that it has not been possible either to state with any assurance the motives and principles of his activities, or to give an unerring appraisal of his moral qualities. This fact explains the continued existence of literary discrepencies with respect to Boris. If in drama and historical fiction Boris has usually appeared with the characteristics of a schemer and a scoundrel, this role has been not so much an expression of the author's historical convictions as a device of dramatic conception, of creative thought.

In scholarly literature also, even as late as the last few decades, Boris has appeared to many writers as a somber villain, who came to the throne through intrigue, deceit, violence and crime (N. I. Kostomarov, I. D. Beliaev, Kazimir Waliszewski). The hagiographic tradition of the Lives of the Saints continued to influence these writers. In the seventeenth and eighteenth centuries this tradition enjoyed the force of an officially established doctrine, and only in the nineteenth century did it begin to yield to the efforts of free and scholarly criticism.

Professor A. Ya. Shpakov, one of the most recent researchers dedicated to the "historiography" of Boris, has noted this tradition. His sarcastic and doleful words have shown that this tradition aroused profound indignation. Professor Shpakov, in touching upon the epoch of Boris, was amazed at the abundance of charges against Boris and at their flippancy.

The history of Boris Godunov, described in chronicles and various other literary monuments, and passing from these into the writings of many historians, is extremely simple. After the death of Ivan the Terrible [1584], Boris Godunov exiled Tsarevich Dmitri[2] and the Nagoi family to the town of Uglich. He incited Bogdan Belsky to make an attempt on the life of Tsar Fedor Ivanovich and then had Belsky banished to Nizhni Novgorod. He threw Ivan Fedorovich Mstislavsky into prison where he had him strangled. He summoned Maria Vladimirovna (the wife of Magnus, 'King of the Livonians,' daughter of Prince Vladimir Andreevich of Staritsa) in order to force her to take the veil, and killed her daughter Evdokia. Furthermore, he ordered the boyars slaughtered and all the princes Shuisky strangled, sparing for some reason Vasili Ivanovich and Dmitri Ivanovich. Then he established the patriarchate in order that his benefactor Job might sit on the patriarchal throne. He killed Dmitri, falsified the official notice of the murder, and tampered with the investigation and the decision of a church assembly concerning this deed. He set fire to

Moscow, then summoned the Crimean khan in order
to divert the attention of the people from the
murder of Dmitri and the Moscow Fire.
Furthermore, he murdered his niece Feodosia, and
disgraced Andrei Shchelkalov after having
treacherously and evilly repaid him for his fatherly
assistance. He poisoned Fedor Ivanovich and seated
himself on the throne. He tampered with the
Zemsky Sobor, [3] and had the people beaten into
crying out that they wanted only him to be tsar. He
blinded Simeon Bekbulatovich. He concocted an
affair about a conspiracy of 'Nikitiches' [that is,
Romanovs], Cherkasskys and others in order to
exterminate the tsarist 'root.' All of them he
slaughtered and imprisoned. Finally, he murdered
his own sister, Tsaritsa Irina, because she would not
recognize him as tsar. He was hated by 'all persons of
high rank in the land' and by the boyars in general,
for he plundered, ruined, and murdered them. He
was hated by the people, for he introduced serfdom.
He was hated by the clergy, for he abolished their
privileges and connived with aliens, fawning upon
them, inviting them to live and work in Russia, and
permitting them to practice their own religion
freely. He was hated by the Muscovite merchants
and the rabble, for he had offended their beloved
Shuiskys and Romanovs, and so forth. Subsequently
he poisoned his daughter's fiance, could not
withstand [the onslaught of] the Pretender,[4] and
poisoned himself. That is all. [5]

This list of charges against Godunov, supported by
specific references, was neither contrived nor even exaggerated.
It was simply a collection of everything that historians had

believed and had disbelieved — that which they set forth as fact and that which they dropped as absurd and incredible. Boris's misfortune lay in the fact that those who wrote about him in olden times did not venture out of the area of legend and slander inscribed in chronicles and memoirs.

Matters began to change when, with a shift in scholarly interests, the attention of historians was directed away from the personality of Boris and toward the study of his epoch as a whole. Serious and free investigation of Boris's times led to the discovery of his administrative talents, and Boris came to be portrayed in a new and more favorable light. It is true that the new material has not won all historians to Boris. But as soon as it became possible to switch from "annalistic narratives" to "documented data," Boris's defenders and admirers began to multiply. This is not to mention the "historiographer" [Georg Friedrich] Müller, who in the eighteenth century still did not dare be candid in his opinions concerning Boris for fear of reprimand and punishment by the authorities. M. F. Pogodin, in the time of Nicholas I [1825-1855], was a freer and more daring historian. He must be acknowledged as the first open apologist for Godunov. According to the opinion of one of his university students: "His voice took on a lively, sincere expression when he spoke of Boris Godunov, and with enthusiasm he proved to us that Boris Godunov was not and could not have been the murderer of Tsarevich Dmitri." And Pogodin's affection for Boris passed from the classroom into print.

Pogodin was followed in 1830 by N. S. Artsybashev, who acquitted Boris of the murder of the tsarevich. In 1836 A. A. Kraevsky wrote a general panegyric of Boris. And in 1850 P. V. Pavlov defended Boris in a favorable statement on the significance of all the activities of Godunov as ruler and politician. Later several other writers, including K. S. Aksakov

(1858), E. A. Belov (1873) and A. Ya. Shpakov (1912) spoke
out in various ways in favor of Boris.

Yet one cannot conceal that such authorities as S. M.
Soloviev [1820-1879] and V. O. Kliuchevsky [1841-1911]
remained at least very cold, if not openly hostile towards Boris.
Their historical insight, however, permitted them to discern in
Boris not just the traits of a dramatic villain, but also the
qualities of a true statesman. Precisely from the time of
Soloviev's *History,* Boris became the object not so much of
accusation as of serious study. Perhaps the further successes of
historical research will create an even better background for
Boris and give his "long-suffering shade" the opportunity for
historical justification.

II   THE FAMILY OF THE GODUNOVS.
       BORIS'S SERVICE CAREER.
       THE APPEARANCE OF BORIS
       GODUNOV IN THE GOVERNMENT.

It is not difficult to collect data for the "service record" of
Boris Fedorovich Godunov. Quite a bit has been preserved. He
came from a long line of Muscovite "free servants" who prided
themselves on the fact that "from time immemorial they had
never served anyone except their own sovereigns." According
to a genealogical tradition (which no one has ever disputed), an
ancestor of the Godunovs was Chet, a member of the Tatar
gentry *[murza],* who around the year 1330 came from the
Horde to serve Grand Prince Ivan Kalita and who was baptized
Zakhari. Besides the Godunovs, from the line of Chet also came
such "families of honor" as the Saburovs and the Veliaminovs.

If these families were not at the very summit of Muscovite

aristocracy, they were at least at a level very close to the summit, whose members received *Duma* ranks[6] and served at court. Alexander Pushkin was hardly correct from the historical point of view when in the play *Boris Godunov* he put in the mouth of Prince Shuisky scornful words about Boris: "Yesterday's slave, a Tatar, son-in-law of Maliuta, son-in-law of a hangman, and in his heart himself a hangman."[7] The Shuiskys could, of course, look down their noses at the unprincely Godunov clan, which was not princely nor even of boyar rank prior to Ivan the Terrible's favor. But no one in the sixteenth century could call Godunov "yesterday's slave" and a "Tatar." For two and a half centuries the family had been Orthodox. From the 1570's members of the family such as Dmitri Ivanovich, Ivan Vasilievich and Boris Fedorovich Godunov had entered the Duma.[8]

The personal career of Boris Godunov began early. About age twenty, around 1570, he married the daughter of the tsar's favorite, Grigori (Maliuta) Lukianovich Belsky-Skuratov,[9] and became a personage at court. His intimacy with the terrible tsar may be seen from the fact that he occupied a post and fulfilled duties "close" to the sovereign himself. He was in the tsar's "bodyguard" [immediate retinue] and was a "young friend" at the tsar's weddings.[10] Around thirty years of age Boris obtained the rank of boyar, being "proclaimed" boyar in 7089 (1580-1581)[11] from among the *"kravchie"* or *"kraichie"* (an important post: the *kraichii* attended the sovereign's table, set courses before him upon receiving them from the *stolniki* [gentlemen of the table], and tasted each dish). All such data concerning Boris and the tsar indicate that he was Ivan's personal favorite, and that he owed his early successes not so much to his "pedigree" as to the tsar's affection for his family, if not for Boris himself.

The marriage (probably in 1580) of Tsarevich Fedor

Ivanovich to Boris's sister, Irina Fedorovna Godunova, is also
proof of the tsar's favor for the Godunov family. By choosing a
Godunov to be his son's wife, Ivan brought the Godunovs to
court — into his own family. As the tsar's relative Boris, in
November, 1581, could plausibly intervene in a family quarrel.
According to a credible account in a chronicle, Boris received a
severe beating from the tsar because "he had dared to enter into
the tsar's private chambers" and to intercede for Tsarevich Ivan
Ivanovich whom, it is well known, Ivan the Terrible beat to
death.[12] The tsar also wounded Boris, "causing him much
torture and opening terrible wounds." Because of such "insult"
Boris fell ill and was a long time recovering. Upon visiting him
at home, Ivan restored him to favor, and until Ivan's death
Boris "remained close to him, to the sovereign." At the hour of
Tsar Ivan's death in 1584, Boris found himself numbered among
the first dignitaries of state and took part in the formation of
the government under Ivan's successor, Tsar Fedor Ivanovich,
who was completely incompetent.

    In the second year of Tsar Fedor's reign Boris achieved a
position of governmental ascendancy. Around 1588 he became
the formally recognized regent of the state, "brother-in-law of
His Tsarist Majesty" and "a goodly ruler" who "governed the
land at the hand of the great sovereign." For ten whole years
(1588-1597) Boris ruled in Muscovy, until the death of the
childless Fedor opened his road to the throne. Finally, in 1598
the "Lord Protector of Russia" (as the English called Boris) was
elected tsar by the Zemsky Sobor and became "the Great
Sovereign Tsar and Grand Prince of All Russia, Boris
Fedorovich." Such was Boris's worldly pathway — brilliant,
extraordinarily successful and, as we shall see, full of thorns.

    Boris entered the sphere of government and began his
political activity at a very difficult time for the Muscovite state.
The country was experiencing a complex crisis. The

consequences of the unsuccessful wars of Ivan the Terrible, an internal governmental terror called the *oprichnina,* and confused movements of the masses from the center of the state to the outlying districts had shattered the social order by the end of the sixteenth century. This state of affairs brought ruin and destruction to economic life and created such widespread turmoil that everyone was tortured by an expectation of coming woes. The government itself admitted to the "great emaciation" and "exhaustion" of the landowners. It repealed every kind of tax privilege and exception "for the time being until the land returns to order."

Struggle against the crisis was becoming an urgent problem in the eyes of the government, but at the same time complications within the ruling class itself were coming to a head. A power struggle was in the offing. Internal unity and strength were essential to the government. But dissension was growing and collapse threatened. It fell to Boris to take on the grave responsibility of establishing authority and pacifying the country. In the resolution of these tasks he displayed his own unquestionable political talent, and yet ultimately the crisis caused his own eternal condemnation and the downfall of his family.

III   THE PROBLEM OF SOVEREIGN POWER IN
      MUSCOVY. THE OLD MUSCOVITE BOYARS.
      THE *KNIAZHATA* OF THE SIXTEENTH
      CENTURY. THE ORDER OF SUPREMACY.
      PATRIMONIAL ESTATES. THE OPRICHNINA
      OF IVAN THE TERRIBLE – DIRECT AND
      INDIRECT CONSEQUENCES

We shall begin the story of Boris's activities with the problem of the establishment of power and the struggle to retain that power. This problem was one of the most burning and complex

issues of Muscovite life at that time. The passion and brutality
of Ivan the Terrible lent to the matter a special sharpness,
brought this problem out of the area of theory and books into
real life, and stained with wasted blood the innocent victims of
the tsar's mistrust and lust for power.

The unification of the Great Russian regions under
Muscovite authority and the concentration of power in the sole
person of the Muscovite grand prince were accomplished very
shortly before the time of Ivan the Terrible through the
energies of his grandfather and, partly, of his father. In 1574
Ivan assumed the title *Tsar* [13] and adorned his "autocracy"
with magnificent fictions of kinship (real and imagined) with
the ecumenical dynasties of the "old" and "new" Rome.[14] He
was ruling in a young, newly-arisen state. There was no firm
order in this state, nor was there any conception of "antiquity"
or of "duty" which might have been inviolable and
indisputable for all. Everything was still subject to
consolidation and definition. To be sure, the authority of the
"great sovereign" had achieved extraordinary scope and was
expressed in forms that astonished foreign observers. The
words of the Austrian Baron Herberstein are
well-known.[15] The grand prince of Muscovy "surpasses in
power all the monarchs in the world. He wields his power over
the clergy as well as the laity, disposing of the lives and
property of all, unhindered and at his own will." This fact was
obvious and indisputable. But in the eyes of the Russian people
of the sixteenth century the authority of the grand prince still
required legal and moral justification.

Muscovite political writings of the sixteenth century
eagerly discussed questions of the limits of princely and tsarist
authority, and of the possibility and necessity of opposing a
prince who trespassed the divinely established limits of his
authority. Impious and cunning rulers were examined. "Such a

tsar is not God's servant, but the devil's, and not a tsar but a torturer." Finally, it was stated that the tsar's authority was limited by the law of God and had jurisdiction only over the body, but not over the souls of the people subject to him. At the basis of such considerations lay the dogma of Christian morality and religious obligation. These arguments did not strive to place external limitations on princely and tsarist arbitrary rule. On the contrary, all ecclesiastical writing was imbued with the notion of the divine establishment of the power of the pious Muscovite monarch, and with the necessity of obeying the "true tsar" who is "God's servant," whom God has set in "his place" and whose judgment is incontestable. While imposing upon the "autocrat" the responsibility to be "true, right, and pious," the ecclesiastical writers also imposed upon the subjects of such a tsar the obligation to serve him faithfully and meekly.

The idea of the necessity of placing a "limit" upon the personal authority of the great sovereign, even if he were lawful and pious, appeared in a different group — namely among the boyars. These aristocrats were guided not so much by pious as by practical considerations. It has long been admitted by historians that Muscovy owed its first political successes to the Muscovite boyars. Beginning in the fourteenth century there had formed in Muscovy a defined circle of boyar families who had bound their destinies with those of the princely clan, and who had successfully labored for the good of Muscovy and its princes even when those princes themselves proved — because of youth and other reasons — incapable.

The dynasty admitted the services of its boyars; the populace was aware of them, too. The biographer of Dmitri Donskoi [1359-1389] put into his mouth special praise for the boyars. "I was born before you and grew up with you — and ruled with you. . .together we watched over my patrimony. . .I

gave you honor and love. . .under your rule I held towns and
great districts. . .I rejoiced with you, I grieved with you. You
were not called boyars, but princes of my land." Thus spoke
Dmitri to the boyars. And to his children he said on his
deathbed: "Love your boyars; without their will you can do
nothing." The alliance of the dynasty and the boyars appeared
strong until the middle of the fifteenth century when fortune
sent to both parties a peculiar trial in the form of a crowd of
service princes appearing in Moscow — the kniazhata, as Ivan
the Terrible called them.[16]

The gathering of Great Russian lands under the authority
of Moscow was accompanied by the appearance in Moscow of
the princes who had once ruled these lands. If they did not, of
their own free will, flee from the Great Russian sovereigns to
Lithuania, and if they were not expelled by them, then there
was nowhere else for them to go but to Moscow. Arriving there
they would humbly beg the great sovereign to be allowed into
his service. They placed themselves and their lands at his
disposal. The grand prince would be gracious to them and
receive them into his service. After having obtained from them
their districts as political possessions, he would return their
districts to them "in patrimony," that is, in hereditary private
ownership. Thus was accomplished the reduction of a "sovereign prince" into a servitor, a "slave" of the great sovereign
of Muscovy.

After the Muscovite authorities had installed their own
order in a prince's district and had extracted from it all that the
grand sovereign needed, the district was handed over to the
disposal of the hereditary owners on a new basis. It was
converted into a simple privileged possession, where the
holders held a charter of immunity and styled themselves as of
old — "sovereigns" [gosudari] — having ceased to be so in fact.
A chronicler of Yaroslavl — a local patriot — recounts with

bitter sarcasm the conversion of Yaroslavl into a Muscovite district. Under the year 1463 he relates the discovery of the relics of the grand prince of Yaroslavl, Fedor Rostislavich, and his two sons, and says: "These seemed to all the princes of Yaroslavl not to be wonderworkers for good. They bade farewell to all their patrimonies forever, and gave them to Grand Prince Ivan Vasilievich.[17] The grand prince, in return for their patrimonies, presented them with districts and villages. Now for a long time Aleksei Poleuktovich, state secretary to the grand prince, had petitioned the old Grand Prince Vasili the Blind [1425-1462] concerning them, that the land might not come to be theirs. But afterwards in that same city of Yaroslavl there appeared a new wonderworker, Ioann Agafonovich, from that most fruitful land of Yaroslavl. Whoever possessed good land, he took it away. And whoever possessed a good village, he took that away too and delivered it to the grand prince. And he who was a good and worthy man, be he boyar or *syn boyarskii*,[18] this man took note of him. The multitude of his wonders cannot be described, for as you know, the devil appears in the flesh."

This sorrowful tale points out that the princes of Yaroslavl did not receive back from Moscow even their former lands, but in their place, "in return for their patrimonies," they received new districts and villages. In the sixteenth century these princes had sunk to the level of a large nest of petty and poor landowners attached to the Muscovite court. This came about after the destruction of their principalities by the "wonderworkers" from Moscow such as Aleksei Poleuktovich and Ioann Agafonovich. One can understand the feelings of these princes for the Muscovite "wonderworkers" and for those who had inspired them, the Muscovite sovereigns.

Prince Andrei Mikhailovich Kurbsky, in the words of Ivan the Terrible "a treacherous Yaroslavl ruler," came from the ranks of these very princes of Yaroslavl. Having escaped Ivan's clutches and flown across the Lithuanian border, the prince did not spare Ivan and his forebears. "It has long been the custom of the princes of Muscovy," wrote Kurbsky, "to desire the blood of their brothers, to destroy them for the sake of their damned patrimonies and for the sake of their own insatiability." In the words of Kurbsky, his ancestors and kin — the Yaroslavl princes — were not addicted to this custom. "This chain (that is, branch) of service princes was never in the habit of eating the bodies and drinking the blood of their brothers, as some have long been accustomed to doing," Kurbsky taunted Ivan, meaning by "some" the lengthy bloodthirsty line of the Muscovite "chain" of princes. An emigrant, who had escaped the clutches of the tyrant in Moscow, could be so outspoken. But the service princes were forced to remain silent. Bondage had driven them to Moscow and had put them into the hands of Muscovite authority. They had to perform their services humbly, side by side with the common untitled boyars and servants of the great sovereign.

But the same hatred of the enslaver and the same memories of former independence that so filled Prince Kurbsky also boiled and flourished in the hearts of the service princes. Under the heel of the Muscovite dynasty the service princes did not forget that they too were a dynasty — "that all the traditional powers of the Russian land" (V. O. Kliuchevsky says of them) "were the same powers by which they had formerly ruled the land in appanages."[19] But the service princes had previously ruled the land in parcels and independently; now, gathered together in Moscow, they "were ruling all the lands together."

Such an understanding of the matter was not peculiar to the service princes alone. Everyone recognized them as "sovereigns" and, in contrast to them, called the Muscovite tsar "great sovereign," considering (in the words of Joseph Volotsky)[20] the great sovereign to be "the sovereign over the sovereigns of all the Russian lands."

At first the service princes in Moscow did not mix with the common boyars but formed their own class. "The princes and the boyars" was the usual formula for official Muscovite listings. Only in the course of time did there arise the custom of granting place among the boyars to the most eminent of the service princes. For those who were "a little poorer" in rank, there was place among the okolnichie. [21] In such fashion the service princes gradually entered in among the boyars, the old "eternal" Muscovite servitors.

But this was only an official, outward equalization of princes with plain boyars. Each group understood its own distinction. Guided by the "Genealogy of Sovereign Rulers" (the official listing of princely and boyar families in service), the princes demanded for themselves a superior position at court and in the service. They considered the ordinary boyars beneath them in "pedigree" for, according to an expression of the time, they came "not from the great and not from the appanage princes."

Occasionally the service princes were prepared to call "honored" or "great" boyars "slaves" with respect to themselves, the "sovereigns." Several "half-wits" among the princes of Rostov went so far as to express (in 1554) displeasure at the marriage of Ivan the Terrible to Anastasia Romanova because, in their opinion, it was an unworthy marriage. Ivan "took his woman" and thereby "forced out" the service princes who had apparently anticipated his marriage to a tsarevna or a princess, according to the example set by Ivan III and Vasili III.

But the old Muscovite boyars displayed their own haughtiness in response to this princely arrogance. They recalled a time when their ancestors worked in Moscow against the appanages, and created a unified opposition in the state to the separatism of the appanage princes. Their boyar clans had been in Moscow at a time when the predecessors of the service princes were still in their appanages or were serving not in Muscovy, but in other grand principalities (Tver, Riazan, and others). The old boyars also expressed the idea that they were native to Moscow, that they had "from time immemorial belonged to the sovereign, and had served no one except their own sovereigns, the Muscovite princes."

The memory of former merits and the principle of indigenousness aided select personages from the untitled boyars to be retained among the first ranks of the Muscovite dignitaries of princely origin. V. O. Kliuchevsky writes that "the native clan of old Muscovite boyars, which came into being in the fourteenth century, remained together and survived the influx of aristocratic princes into Moscow. Pressed down by these princes from above and excluded from the highest rank of service, these boyars held sway over the second rank of service in the sixteenth century. In their turn, they attempted to bring pressure to bear upon both the boyar newcomers from appanages and the second layer of former appanage princes in order 'to force their way upward to their old relatives.'"

Many princely family branches fared badly because of this rivalry of the "old nest." While plain servitors like the Morozovs, the Saltykovs, the Sheins, the Zakharins, the Sheremetevs, the Buturlins, the Saburovs, the Godunovs, and the Pleshcheevs were retained at the summit of the service and court aristocracy, many princes sank to the bottom of the service and "became impoverished." There were, for example, many fallen family branches among the princes of Yaroslavl and Rostov. "There are great and small among the princes of

Yaroslavl and Rostov, and they are not of equal rank," it was said officially in the seventeenth century. Of the princes Prozorovsky, Ivan the Terrible wrote scornfully that such Muscovite sovereigns as they numbered "more than a single hundred." The Englishman [Giles] Fletcher expressed this fact even more pointedly. According to his report there were so many princes in Moscow that they had been reduced in rank. "Of this sort there are so many that the plentie maketh them cheap: so that you shall see dukes glad to serve a meane man for five or six rubbels or marks a yeare, and yet they will stand highly upon their *bestchest [bescheste]* or reputation of their honours."

If the appearance in Moscow of the service princes turned out to be a heavy trial for the native Muscovite boyars, the service princes were also distasteful and disloyal servants for the Muscovite rulers. We have just seen how Prince Kurbsky quarrelled with Ivan the Terrible. It can be assumed that these same feelings of enmity toward the sovereign were also expressed by other spokesmen of the princes. Ivan in his missives to Kurbsky intimated many times that such hostile ideas and speeches of the princes were well-known to him. He said directly to Kurbsky: "Many times you have attacked me, insulted me, vexed me, and reproached me!" Some of these "vexations" and "reproaches," of course, were not politically threatening. The central authorities were upset, in the first place, by the constant claims of precedence made by the service princes, and in the second place by the princely patrimonies which remained in the hands of the service princes.

Order of precedence *[mestnichestvo]* was a very well-known custom in old Russia. This was the tradition that at every gathering nobles were seated according to "pedigree" and "family," that is, according to degree of aristocracy. This

custom was recognized and accepted by absolutely everyone —
boyars, the sovereign, and all others alike. They knew that "the
sovereign grants *pomestie* estates [22] and monies for service, but
not family" status. This is why persons of high birth were
allowed to take first place by family status, to quarrel over
these posts and not seek the will or favor of the great sovereign
in order to occupy them. Sovereigns could remove individuals
objectionable to them; they could even destroy such persons
through disfavor. They could "elevate" their personal favorites
to top rank. But they could not remove the whole group of
princely aristocrats from their superior positions in
government, nor could they govern the state without this
group. It therefore became necessary to devise some sort of
general measure against the princely aristocracy in order to free
the monarch and his government from the collaboration of
such a suspect and unreliable helpmate. The need of such a
measure for the success of the Muscovite autocracy seems
completely clear.

    Less clear is the problem of the so-called princely
patrimonies. Those patrimonial estates which Moscow had left
in possession of their former owners still worried the Muscovite
sovereigns and aroused their suspicious attention. From the
time of Ivan III until the close of the sixteenth century,
restrictive decrees were made concerning these patrimonies.
The service princes were forbidden to sell their lands to anyone
whomsoever without knowledge of the grand prince.
Sometimes the circle of persons who could inherit and acquire
such lands was limited and defined. Sometimes the government
resorted to confiscation of these lands. In short, Moscow never
took its eyes off princely landholding. In return the service
princes, when their influence on affairs increased during the
minority of Ivan the Terrible, above all else concerned
themselves with their own princely patrimonies. Ivan

complained that under him the service princes reclaimed the "towns and villages" that had been taken from them by his grandfather, and permitted the free turnover of princely patrimonies, the sale and alienation of which had been forbidden by the Muscovite sovereigns before Ivan.

Precisely what evoked such jealous attention from the central authorities to this princely landownership cannot be ascertained from the documents. The decrees were issued without clear motives. One can only surmise that important patrimonies lay at the foundation of the economic power of the princes, and that the government may have feared this power of the princely landowners. Moreover, the service princes, the age-old owners of appanage patrimonies, preserved a strong hereditary bond with their population. The service princes had long been the legitimate and rightful "sovereigns" of their lands and their populations. As privileged landowners they had administrative and judicial jurisdiction over the population. They bestowed "in substance and in perpetuity" small hamlets to the clergy and to their own "service" people. In short, these princes had ruled their lands almost singlehandedly. In the event of need they could have thrown their subjects into a political struggle against Moscow, especially in those instances when they enjoyed the affection of the populace. This very fact evidently alarmed the Muscovite sovereigns. By vigilant surveillance and attentive calculation the Muscovite sovereigns thought to render princely patrimonies harmless, and to take away from their owners the possibility of employing their material resources to harm Moscow.

We may presume that the persistent policy of distrust and suspicion adopted by Moscow *vis-à-vis* the princes slackened somewhat during the first years of the reign of Ivan the Terrible. This impressionable tsar, because of his youth and his

lively nature, fell under the influence of a small circle of
friends. This small circle proved to be "cunning" and
"treacherous." Evidently it conducted a policy favorable to the
princes. At least Ivan, having freed himself from these
"friendly" influences, accused members of the circle of just
that: they had attempted to "take power" from the
unsuspecting and trustful sovereign. He also claimed that they
had led boyars "into opposition" to him. He declared that they
had willfully and illegally distributed ranks and patrimonies,
leaving to the tsar only "the honor of first place" (that is,
leaving for the tsar nothing more than a presiding chair in their
midst). In short, they restricted, insofar as was possible, the
personal authority of the tsar, while they tried to remove from
the princes the restrictions which had been imposed by a stern
Moscow. That is how Ivan the Terrible viewed the matter.

During his illness (in 1553) there was an attempt on the
part of the boyar-princes to hand over the reins of government
not to Ivan's son but to his cousin Vladimir, a younger
kinsman of the royal family ("from a fourth-rate appanage!"
exclaimed Ivan). When this attempt was revealed, Ivan
completely abandoned his sympathetic feelings for his former
friends and gradually began to feel differently about them.
There grew in Ivan a fear of the treacherous boyars, an
awareness of the necessity of taking general measures against
them, and a feeling of animosity toward the servitors "who
desired their traitorous custom of being rulers" in their former
appanages. For a whole decade (1554-1564) Ivan's awareness
of vague, obscure enmity and his mood of irritation continued.
There was a constant search for measures that could be taken
for the defense of tsarist power and authority against the claims
of the unreliable group of the high princely aristocracy.
Finally, at the end of 1564 and the beginning of 1565, Ivan
devised his celebrated oprichnina.

Not all of Ivan's contemporaries clearly understood just what this oprichnina was. Russians thought that he was simply "playing with God's people" when he divided his kingdom into the oprichnina and the *zemshchina,* and gave to the oprichnina "a portion of the people to despoil and to put to death." They did not see the meaning in this "game" of the despot to "create a great division throughout the land and to look with suspicion upon all that occurs," as wrote Ivan Timofeev. The intricacy of the execution of these measures conceived by Ivan the Terrible concealed their aim and purpose from the uninitiated simple observer. But Ivan undoubtedly had an idea and a purpose in mind. Giles Fletcher, who visited Muscovy about five years after the death of Ivan the Terrible and who possessed political information from the entire English colony in Russia, explained in detail what the oprichnina did there. According to his account, the oprichnina was directed against the aristocracy. It dispossessed the "appanage princes" of their hereditary lands and evicted them from their old traditional patrimonies.

A comparison of Fletcher's comments with extant Russian documents from the sixteenth century gradually discloses the complete picture of Ivan's actions in the oprichnina. In essence, the tsar decided to apply to the regions in which were located patrimonies of the service boyar-princes the so-called "removal." Such "removals" were usually employed by Moscow in conquered lands. The grand princes of Muscovy, upon subjugating some region, would remove from it the most prominent and, for them, dangerous persons into the interior regions of Muscovy. They would then establish in the conquered lands inhabitants from native Moscow areas. This was a tried and tested method of state assimilation which destroyed local separatism at the root.

It was this decisive procedure, usually directed against

outside enemies, that Ivan turned against internal "treason."
He decided to remove the princes from their appanage nests
and to send them to new areas. Fletcher claimed that the tsar,
having established the oprichnina, seized the patrimonies of the
princes for himself, with the exception of an extremely
unimportant portion. He then gave other lands to the princes in
the form of "pomestie estates" (an allotment of state land) for
service, which they ruled at the tsar's pleasure. These estates
were in regions so remote that the princes had neither the love
of the people nor influence, for they had not been born there
and were not known there. According to Fletcher, this measure
achieved its end: "The chiefe nobilitie (called *udelney knazey
[udelnye kniazia]* are equalled with the rest: save that in the
opinion and favour of the people they are of more account, and
keepe stil the prerogative of their place in al their publike
meetings." The removal of the princes and the confiscation of
their patrimonies was not executed directly and simply by
Ivan. He surrounded the affair with such actions and began it
with such an approach that he evidently aroused the general
bewilderment of his subjects.

Ivan began by completely abandoning Moscow and the
state. He agreed to return upon the request of the Muscovites
only on the condition that no one thwart him in his struggle
with treason "to disgrace some, to execute others and to take
their lives and property, and to establish for himself in his realm
an oprichnina — a special court for all his needs." The special
royal court comprised boyars and gentry ("thousands of
heads" — oprichniki), court servants, Moscow streets and
settlements assigned "to the oprichnina," and various towns
and districts which the sovereign "took into the oprichnina."

Having established himself in the new court, Ivan began to
include in the oprichnina an increasingly great amount of
land, namely that land which constituted old appanage Russia

and in which were concentrated the patrimonies of the princes. From the lands taken into the oprichnina the tsar "sorted out his servants," that is, the landowners. Some he "received" into the new service. Others he "sent away;" in other words, he drove them from their holdings, giving them new land (and instead of their patrimonies, pomestie estates) in the borderlands. Clan after clan, family after family, the princes fell under a strange scrutiny. In the great majority of cases they lost their old way of life and were ejected from their hereditary nests.

In the course of the last twenty years of Ivan's reign [1565-1584] the oprichnina enveloped half of Muscovy and ravaged all the appanage nests therein, smashing princely landholdings and tearing asunder the bond between the appanage "rulers" and their appanage territories that had so frightened Ivan the Terrible. But the achievement of the oprichnina was accompanied by consequences which were hardly necessary or desirable. In place of the destroyed "princely patrimonies," which had represented large landed economies, there grew up petty pomestie estates. Along with their formation a complex economic culture, created by many generations of princely landowners, was destroyed. Peasant self-government, which had flourished on the large patrimonial estates, perished. Boyar slaves were freed, and exchanged the well-fed life of the boyar's household for hungry homelessness.

The very nature of Ivan's reform — conversion of large scale and privileged forms of land ownership into small pomestie estates encumbered by service and fiscal obligations — was bound to evoke the dissatisfaction of the populace. And the methods of implementing this reform evoked even greater dissatisfaction. Reform was accompanied by terror. Disgrace, exile, and the execution of persons suspected of treason, scandalous acts of violence committed by oprichniki against the "traitors," the bloodthirstiness and dissoluteness of Ivan himself — torturing and destroying his subjects during orgies which have become legendary — all this frightened and embittered the people. They saw in the oprichnina only unfathomable terror and did not divine its basic political aim, which the government evidently did not explain directly to the people.

Such was the notorious oprichnina. Directed against the aristocracy, it terrorized society as a whole. Having as its aim the consolidation of state unity and supreme authority, it disrupted the social order and sowed general discontent. The aristocracy was broken and dispersed. But those of the aristocracy who remained did not fare any better in their relations with the Muscovite dynasty. The remaining aristocrats held onto their spirit of opposition and remembered their sovereign traditions and claims. The entire population trembled before the "terrible" tsar, unable to explain why "the sovereign killed so many in his disfavor and dislodged people both in the zemshchina and the oprichnina."

Ivan had not yet closed his eyes in death [1584] when Moscow seethed in open dissent over the question of the future of the oprichnina. The service princes, who had been held under the tyrant's iron heel, were raising their heads and considering plans for their return to power. Observing Muscovite society in the years following Ivan's death, Giles Fletcher found that "this wicked pollicy and tyrannous practise" of Ivan the Terrible "hath so troubled that countrey, and filled it so full of grudge and mortall hatred ever since, that it wil not be quenched (as it seemeth now) till it burne againe into a civill flame." He proved to be a prophet. The oprichnina itself, to a significant degree, caused the great troubles that almost destroyed the Muscovite state.

These were the circumstances in which the boyar, Boris

Fedorovich Godunov, appeared at the helm of power in Moscow.

IV   THE BOYARS AT THE END OF THE
     SIXTEENTH CENTURY. THE ANCESTRAL
     NOBILITY AND THE ROYAL FAMILY.
     RELATIONS BETWEEN THEM

At the beginning of the reign of Tsar Fedor Ivanovich [1584—98] relations among the Muscovite boyars were not as they had been prior to the oprichnina. Formerly the service princes had comprised a large circle of aristocrats who held their heads high and looked down upon the untitled boyars. The oprichnina had exterminated this circle. The decrease in the ranks of the old titled or "princely" boyars was so great by the beginning of the seventeenth century that, according to V. O. Kliuchevsky, of the great boyar families of earlier times there survived only the Mstislavskys, Shuiskys, Odoevskys, Vorotynskys, Trubetskois, Golitsyns, Kurakins, Pronskys, several of the Obolenskys including the last of their generation, Kurliatev — "and that is about all." The remaining high aristocracy had fled, been put to death, died out, or was brought to ruin — in short, had disappeared from the summit of Muscovite society. With such decrease, one can even say with such utter destruction, the only aristocrats who survived were those who bowed obediently before the tsar and joined the oprichnina. They laid aside all their old claims and recognized the power of the new order. "Both great and small live by the sovereign's grace."

The fate of the princes Shuisky is quite indicative in this respect. They considered themselves by ancestry to be the most high-born of the princes. As a native Great Russian clan, the

Shuiskys placed themselves not only higher than all the other
sons of Riurik *[Riurikovichi]*,[23] but also higher than the
venerable sons of Gedimin *[Gediminovichi]*.[24] And the Poles
considered the Shuiskys *jure successionis haereditariae* [within
the law of hereditary succession], the natural successors to the
Muscovite tsardom after the end of the dynasty. The Shuiskys
themselves, of course, knew of their genealogical precedence.
They said that their ancestors were a "great fraternity" among
the princes and "were accustomed to sitting in high places."
But under Ivan the Terrible this venerable and great fraternity
humbly went to serve in the oprichnina and preserved its
existence only by absolute obedience to the despot. It may be
said even that the Shuiskys were the only ones among the most
eminent Riurikovich clans all of whose branches not only
survived but also prospered during the period of the
oprichnina. It would seem that under the new conditions of life
and service that prevailed, the old proprietary memories and
claims of the Shuiskys should have withered. But in fact they
flourished, and as soon as Ivan died, the hope of restoring the
earlier order of Muscovy began to glimmer.

Other very aristocratic princes who survived the
oprichnina began to feel as did the Shuiskys. Having once lain low
under the terror of the oprichnina, at its end they raised their
heads and were alert, together with the Shuiskys, to regain their
lost primacy at the court of Ivan the Terrible's heir, Tsar Fedor.
But, as shall be seen later, the princes were not successful. The
remnants of the princely aristocracy did not comprise a solid,
homogeneous and united group. Marriage alliances, contracted
to please Ivan, had brought untitled elements into their
families. The accidents of career often made them dependent
upon people who were, by comparison, "low-born." The
princes were broken up into small parties and families of
motley composition, far from being always in agreement

among themselves. The old ideals still held sway over the minds of the leaders of this group and united them in common aspirations — in intrigues and in attempts to seize power and influence. But these intrigues and attempts did not have much strength, went no further than court circles and usually acquired the cast of pretty everyday stratagems. The princes entered the broad arena of state intrigue only through the affair of the pretender, some twenty years after the death of Ivan the Terrible.

Thus in the oprichnina the service princes lost their former power. Moreover, during the time of the oprichnina, at the Muscovite court a new group hostile to princely traditions had taken shape — a purely court aristocracy. The marriages of Ivan the Terrible himself and of his sons had brought among the tsar's kinsmen non-princely families of Muscovite boyars. Successively the Zakharin-Yurievs, the Godunovs, and the Nagois had come to court. As a rather crude joke said of them, "God was in a headdress;" that is, their fortune lay in women's headdresses. [25] The presence at court of a tsaritsa's female relatives strengthened the position of their male relatives. The sovereign, after persecuting the princes, in their place "raised on high" his wife's kinsmen and gave them the leading posts vacated by the princes. Thanks to the tsar's largesse, the families related to the tsar became firmly established in the Muscovite government and administration, and they brought with them their numerous kinfolk and in-laws.

The tsar's brothers-in-law, the Zakharin-Yurievs and the Godunovs in particular, took good advantage of their positions at court. By the end of the sixteenth century both these clans had become large nests of relatives, each of which was united behind a family close to the relatives of the tsar. Among the Zakharins this leadership rested in the family of the tsar's brother-in-law, Nikita Romanovich Yuriev. Among the

Godunovs it rested in the family of Boris Fedorovich Godunov, who was also the tsar's brother-in-law. Around the Yurievs were grouped their "brethren and good friends," the princes Repnin, the Sheremetevs, their "sons-in-law" the princes Cherkassky, the Sitskys, Prince Troekurov, Prince Lykov-Obolensky, Prince Katyrev-Rostovsky, the Karpov family, the Shestunovs and many other less noted families (the Mikhalkovs, Shestovs, Zheliabuzskys). Like the Romanov-Yurievs, the Godunovs themselves were numerous and also had their own circle (Skuratov-Belskys, Kleshnins and others).

This aristocracy was a far cry from the princes who remembered their appanage antiquity and dreamed of a return to the pre-oprichnina order. This court aristocracy had received its court and service ascendency at the "special court" of Ivan the Terrible during the time of the oprichnina and, perhaps, because of it. Whether or not they were oprichniki did not matter. They could not object strongly to Ivan's policies as could the true service princes. Whether titled or not, they had been drawn into a new circle of interests, maintained favor at court, and ceased being "princes" in spirit and class ideals. For them a return to the former order would have meant the loss of their prestigious positions so newly acquired at court.

And so by the end of the sixteenth century the interrelationships among the boyar groups had changed considerably in comparison with the beginning of that century. Instead of the long-time servitors and newly arrived "princes," we have before us two groups of mixed composition. Both had served "of old" in Moscow and both had become quite intermixed through marriages and other everyday intimacies. Both were, therefore, variegated in composition and had been made equal in the oprichnina both in terms of service and in precedence. But in one of these groups the old spirit still lived.

In it the appanage tradition was preserved, and there burned a hatred for the oprichnina for it had been directed against just this group.

The other party was devoted to Moscow as the ancient place of service and was strongly attached to the dynasty to which these people had become related and to which they had bound their family interests. The group devoted to Moscow, in contrast to the circle of the old spirit, aspired to preserve the oprichnina, or more precisely, the service and court order which had been created at court as a result of the oprichnina and which had brought about the fall of the princely nobility. The oprichnina (or "court" as it came to be called in 1572) was the most critical issue over which the boyar groups quarrelled, divided, and were prepared to fight among themselves. The outcome of this struggle would decide the second and equally critical question — which of the boyar groups would occupy the position of supremacy at court and in the government?

That is how matters stood in Muscovy at the moment of Ivan the Terrible's death and in the first days of the reign of his successor, Tsar Fedor Ivanovich.

V   THE TSAR'S FAMILY AFTER THE DEATH
        OF IVAN THE TERRIBLE. THE RIOT OF
        1584. NIKITA ROMANOVICH YURIEV,
        BORIS, AND THE SHCHELKALOVS. BORIS'S
        STRUGGLE WITH PRINCE MSTISLAVSKY
        AND THE SHUISKYS. BORIS'S TRIUMPH

Ivan the Terrible died, unexpectedly for those around him, on March 18, 1584. Two sons remained: the elder, Fedor, by Ivan's first marriage, and Dmitri, by his seventh marriage. It was rumored that Fedor, who was already twenty-seven, was

mentally retarded. "It is said that he has little intelligence,"
wrote the Polish-Lithuanian ambassador, Leo Sapieha, in April
of 1584. [26] "The tsar is slightly mad," said King Johann III of
Sweden in an official speech in 1587. "The Russians in their
own language call him *'durak'*" [silly fool]. The younger
"Tsarevich" Dmitri had been born in 1582 to the seventh wife
of Ivan the Terrible, Maria Fedorovna Nagaia. Although the
tsar had celebrated his "wedding" properly, the union was not
a canonical marriage. The legitimacy of Ivan's last son was open
to some question. At any rate, of the two heirs only the elder
was undoubtedly a legal successor, and both required
guardianship — the one because he was underage, the other
because he was mentally retarded.

There was no doubt in Moscow that the throne belonged
to the elder. Young Dmitri and his family were hurriedly sent
to an "appanage" — to that same "appanage" town of Uglich
which Ivan himself had willed in 1572 to his youngest son (at
that time, Fedor). It is curious that the very alert diplomat, Leo
Sapieha, mentions nothing of Dmitri in his letters. Sapieha
arrived in Moscow at the time of Ivan's death and had the
opportunity to learn a great deal through his informers.
Obviously, Dmitri's name then played no part in the question
of succession. The banishment of Dmitri with his mother and
her relatives was not a notable event for the Muscovites. The
Nagois and their "tsarevich" were simply taken away out of
caution, as out of caution and suspicion Moscow generally took
the most diverse measures in order to forestall possible
complications in all important moments of its political life.

The physical and mental incompentence of Tsar Fedor
naturally posed the question of a regency. It was rumored that
Ivan himself had designated which of his boyars were to
surround Fedor and to "maintain the tsardom." Contemporaries gave the names of the most important boyars,

those worthy to rule the state. The historian Karamzin believed the reports of these contempories and created the notion that during the reign of Fedor a boyar "pentarchy" in fact functioned. It consisted of princes Ivan Fedorovich Mstislavsky and Ivan Petrovich Shuisky, the boyars Nikita Romanovich Yuriev and Boris Fedorovich Godunov, and Ivan's favorite, the master of arms, Bogdan Yakovlevich Belsky.

Other historians, following Karamzin, have spoken of this pentarchy. But a closer look at the documents of the period reveals no such "pentarchy." Only Fedor's closest relatives gathered round him during his reign: his maternal uncle, Nikita Romanovich Yuriev; his second cousin, Prince Ivan Fedorovich Mstislavsky and his son, Fedor Ivanovich; and the tsar's brother-in-law, Boris Fedorovich Godunov. Prince Ivan Petrovich Shuisky held an important position at court by virtue of kinship and marriage into these three families. Finally, Bogdan Yakovlevich Belsky strove to maintain his position as the tsar's favorite. He had enjoyed the great favor and trust of Ivan during the latter's last years, although he had not been made a boyar. These persons were not on equally friendly terms with one another. Evidently Belsky was quite willing to intrigue against the others, while Godunov bided his time, not appearing in the front ranks for the present.

On April 2 an intrigue came to light. After the reception of the Lithuanian ambassador, Leo Sapieha, when the boyars had departed from the Kremlin to their homes for dinner, Belsky, supported by the *streltsy*,[27] closed the Kremlin and attempted to persuade Tsar Fedor to retain the "court and oprichnina" as it had been during the reign of his deceased father. Evidently in this way Belsky intended to give himself the primary position as senior oprichnik and to remove from the tsar the "*zemsky* boyars,"[28] Prince Mstislavsky and Prince Yuriev.

The boyars immediately received word of what was
occurring at the Kremlin and rushed there. Belsky's streltsy,
however, refused them admittance into the Kremlin. Only
Mstislavsky "with two companions" and Yuriev "and one
other person" managed to penetrate the line and get through.
Then their people began to raise a clamor. They feared Belsky
would harm their masters. The streltsy turned on the people. A
crowd came running and gathered around the fracas. All of this
took place at the Kremlin walls on Red Square where there was
always a crowd at the trading stalls. It was rumored that Belsky
wished to slaughter — or had already slaughtered — the boyars.
The crowd burst into the Kremlin. The streltsy began firing
into the crowd and, according to the account of Leo Sapieha,
killed about twenty persons. A real civil riot began. The people
prepared to storm the Kremlin. "Military personnel" joined the
crowd, among them gentry from various towns. They procured
a large cannon (the "tsar-cannon" according to the chronicle)
and with it sought to "knock out" the Spasskie Gates. From
the Kremlin the assault was forestalled. The zemsky boyars
somehow managed to deal with Belsky in the palace and to free
Tsar Fedor from his power. The boyars then went out to the
people in the Square and asked them about the cause of their
insurrection. The crowd demanded Belsky because he "wanted
to exterminate the tsarist line and the boyar families."

Animosity against the intriguer was so great that it was
easy for the boyars to get rid of him. They did not hand him
over to the crowd, but decided to banish him to Nizhni
Novgorod. They immediately informed the crowd of this
action in the name of the tsar. Moscow was quieted, and Belsky
disappeared from the scene for a long time. It was rumored that
he had tried to retain the oprichnina in power not for himself,
but in order "from Tsar Fedor to gain for his confidant the
tsardom of Muscovy." Some saw in this confidant Boris

Godunov. However in 1584 it was still too early for Boris "to gain the tsardom."

The whole Belsky affair transpired without the participation of Boris, with the result that he neither won nor lost. The most senior boyars came out ahead in the affair. The oprichniki, together with Belsky, officially left the court and the state. Nikita Romanovich Yuriev remained in control. To him belonged, by general acknowledgment, the actual guardianship of his blood-nephew Tsar Fedor and with it governmental primacy.

Nikita Romanovich Yuriev was old. In August, 1584, he fell seriously ill — in all likelihood from a stroke — and left the political arena. It quickly became evident that his position as the tsar's regent and ruler of the state would be filled by the tsar's brother-in-law, Boris Godunov. But this fact did not appear so obvious at first glance. At the head of the list of boyars stood old Prince Ivan Fedorovich Mstislavsky, not Godunov. In addition to seniority of rank, he, like Boris, possessed for that time a precious advantage — kinship with the tsarist family. True, this kinship was not close (Ivan Fedorovich Mstislavsky was the son of a cousin of Ivan the Terrible, or the grandson of a sister of Grand Prince Vasili III), but the kinship was of long standing and therefore comparatively valuable. Godunov, however, had outmaneuvered Mstislavsky, for the illness of Nikita Romanovich revealed the closeness of the Yurievs to Godunov and also attested to some kind of agreement between these boyars, an alliance or connection of their families.

The basis for such an accord is clear. Both families belonged to the newest circle of the Muscovite court aristocracy; both held the favor of Ivan and kinship with Fedor; and both had the same rivals and enemies. Their alliance was natural. But it did not simply exist, it was conscious and

formulated. Contemporaries knew that Nikita Romanovich
Yuriev "entrusted to Boris the care of his offspring." These
"offspring" were still young. They needed care, support, and
guidance in the difficult life at court, and the sick old man
entrusted them to the same boyar to whom he had given the
guardianship over the tsar. In turn Boris "swore a mighty oath
— that the brethren and the tsardom might have an attendant."
That is, Boris swore to consider them as brothers and helpers in
the business of government.

Thus there arose a "sworn alliance of friendship" between
the two most prominent families at court, who did not wish to
let favor and power out of their hands. These families were able
to defend their court influence by themselves. In the
consolidation of power in government they were aided by two
of the most prominent and clever dealers of the time, the state
secretaries and brothers, Andrei and Vasili Shchelkalov. The
elder, Andrei Yakovlevich, was very close to Nikita
Romanovich. The two of them had served Ivan for many years.
Andrei Yakovlevich had later become close friends with Boris,
too. It was reported that he was Boris's "mentor and tutor" in
matters of everyday life. It was "as if he (Andrei) were trying to
move from a lower to a higher position, from the ranks of the
petty to the ranks of the great in order to become a nobleman,"
in the words of Ivan Timofeev. Between Boris and the
Shchelkalovs there supposedly existed a "Christian oath" that
the three of them together would seek a predominant position
in the government — "an attachment to the tsardom" as a
contemporary expressed it. Thus by the time of the illness of
Nikita Romanovich a firm alliance of political men had formed
in Moscow, an alliance which directed its strength against the
hereditary aristocracy in favor of selected families of the tsar's
kin.

The transfer of power from Nikita Romanovich Yuriev to

Boris evidently was badly received by the boyars of greatest ancestry and led to "boyar dissension and disunity." In the words of a chronicler, the boyars were "split in two." The Godunovs constituted one side — Boris and "his uncles and brothers." The other consisted of Prince Ivan Fedorovich Mstislavsky. To the Godunov side "came also other boyars and state secretaries and persons of Duma rank and many people in service." With Prince Mstislavsky were the princes Shuisky and Vorotynsky, the Golovins, the Kolychevs, "and other service people, and the Muscovite rabble." A struggle ensued for influence and position at court, and Boris, in the words of the chronicle, "prevailed."

Under Ivan the Terrible the matter would not have been settled without bloodshed. Now the struggle was solved more gently. At first the princes Golovin suffered. At the end of 1584 they were removed from their posts (as treasurers). One of the Golovins fled to Lithuania. Thereupon the elder Mstislavsky, Ivan Fedorovich, who had served at court since 1541, was banished to the Monastery of St. Cyril and there shriven as a monk. 29 According to the vague report of a chronicler, other opponents of Boris were sent off to remote towns and a few put in prison. But this "persecution" was obviously not far-reaching. The chronicler does not name Boris's banished and imprisoned victims, except those mentioned above. From the documents it may be seen that while the aged Mstislavsky became a monk, his son, Prince Fedor Ivanovich, inherited his primacy in the list of boyars. Thus even the family of Boris's chief opponent did not suffer.

The removal of the aged Mstislavsky coincided with the death of Nikita Romanovich Yuriev (in the spring of 1585). Boris Godunov and the princes Shuisky, who had come to the fore after the removal of Mstislavsky, now stood at the top of the boyar class in opposition to each other. The Shuiskys

wanted to continue the struggle against the favorite and
conducted it so cautiously and so shrewdly, and in such
complex fashion, that it is very difficult to fathom their
designs. For some reason or other they drew the low social
elements into their intrigue. "They began to do treason (a
government report said of them), to plot every kind of evil with
trading *muzhiki*." [30] The word "trading" must in this case
mean "people of the marketplace" *[ploshchadnye]*. [31]

The Shuiskys incited the Moscow street rabble against
Boris. During the first half of 1587 there was a street
disturbance in Moscow directed against the rule of Godunovs.
"In the city of the Kremlin they sat in siege and set a strong
guard." When the siege had been broken and the crowd dealt
with, an "inquiry" was begun — an investigation in which the
princes Andrei Ivanovich and Ivan Petrovich Shuisky were
proclaimed to be the chief culprits. The sovereign's disgrace
overtook them: they were banished, their property
confiscated. Rumor had it that the Shuiskys' personal guards
took care to hasten their end while in exile. Friends of the
Shuiskys — the Kolychevs, Tatevs, and others — were also
exiled. Their "people" (slaves) and the "trading muzhiki" were
tortured. Six or seven of them were even executed, "their heads
chopped off." Muscovite justice always banished a boyar and
executed a "muzhik brigand" for one and the same offense.

Contemporary accounts do not state directly the nature
of the guilt of those tortured and exiled. We may only surmise
that "the square" had attempted to present a "communal
petition" concerning matters suggested by boyars hostile to
Boris and by the metropolitan of Moscow, Dionisi. Dionisi and
certain of the boyars dared to request no less than that the tsar
remarry because his present marriage was childless. They
petitioned "from all the land" that "the tsar remarry and grant
the tsaritsa of his first marriage, Irina Fedorovna, release to

take the veil, so that the tsar might have offspring by this new marriage."

The point was that the tsar had no children. That the tsar had a brother, Dmitri, apparently never entered anyone's mind. The boyars, along with the metropolitan, feared the end of the dynasty and tried to avoid this disaster by having the barren tsaritsa removed. Concern for the well-being of the dynasty was, of course, reasonable and loyal. But this concern had been inspired by the Shuiskys and their supporters, not solely out of love for the dynasty and the state, but also in the hope that with the tsaritsa's removal her brother, whom the petitioners hated, would also fall.

The calculation was subtle and clever, but it turned out to be in vain. The petitioners were quite mistaken. Had Irina actually been barren, their petition would have made sense, but the tsaritsa had had several miscarriages before her daughter Feodosia was born (1592). Therefore talk of divorce was premature and very tactless. The interference of the common people in such an intimate affair could be seen as impudent and criminal. Preserving the decency and dignity of authority, Boris could say that the Shuiskys "committed treason before the sovereign, told lies, contrived all kinds of evil with trading muzhiki. But the trading muzhiki, hoping for the sovereign's mercy, started plundering, stuck their noses into someone else's business, and united with idlers." Metropolitan Dionisi, who had supported the "idle" petition, found himself compromised. He had to give up the metropolitanate and enter a monastery because he too "had joined the idlers."

Thus Boris, appearing in a defensive rather than an aggressive posture, triumphed completely in his clashes with the most prominent representatives of the aristocracy. He had not intrigued. In the words of a chronicle, he had merely "overpowered" the enemies who had threatened him. He had won wardship of the tsar and "maintained" power under him. However, "his enemies opposed him and did not surrender to him in anything." The persecution of the boyars appeared as punishment for resistance to lawful authority and for encroachment upon the tsar's family life. The persecution did not resemble the cruelties of Ivan the Terrible. Boyars were not killed (openly, at least); persons were banished or executed after investigation and trial. Boris could be maligned and slandered, but he could not be compared with Ivan and called a tryant and a despot. The style of authority had changed. In consequence the government now could charge that the muzhiki, "hoping for the sovereign's mercy," had plundered.

VI   BORIS, RULER OF THE STATE. HIS TITLE,
       RIGHTS, AND THE CONDITIONS OF HIS
       RULE

By the summer of 1587 there was no one left in Moscow who could compete with Boris. Nikita Romanovich Yuriev was dead, Ivan Fedorovich Mstislavsky was in exile, and the Shuiskys were in disgrace. Yuriev's children, known in Moscow by the surname "Nikitich" and Romanov, were for the time being under the "supervision" of Boris, "behind his back" as the old expression says. The younger Mstislavsky had no personal influence, nor did the other boyars attempt to dispute Boris's supremacy. Boris celebrated his victory and took a series of steps to regulate and legalize his position of power under the incompetent tsar. These measures were very clever and interesting.

Officially, of course, Tsar Fedor Ivanovich was not considered that which the king of Sweden, having adopted an expression of Muscovite popular speech, had called him — a silly fool. Nothing was said about the incompetency and feeble-mindedness of Fedor. Rather, his extraordinary devotion and piety were emphasized: "very pious and gracious to all, gentle and not given to anger, clement, loving of the poor and hospitable to strangers." Evidently Fedor's religious devotion was known to all. This devotion had two consequences. First, Fedor pleased God by his piety and brought God's grace to the tsardom. Fedor was given a peaceful and prosperous reign, and the pacific tsar ruled more effectively through prayer than through reason. Second, as the benefactor of his people and a willing servant of God, Fedor did not consider it essential that he himself handle administrative affairs. He avoided "worldly annoyances." Withdrawing from the fuss and bustle of everyday business and turning to God, Fedor entrusted to Boris Godunov the authority to conduct the affairs of state. In Tsar Fedor "the religious life was protected by the diadem." In him "monasticism and tsardom were adorned and bound together inseparably."

The tsar, a monk without cassock and vows, "expending all the time of his life in spiritual exploits," could not function without an administrator. Under such a sovereign the "government" of Boris achieved extraordinary credibility. He was not merely the guardian of the weak-minded tsar. He was a confidential and trusted aide and, through kinship, executor of the "will of the shining tsar by the grace of God." In Moscow they liked to point to Boris's special intimacy with the tsar and to the unique confidence of the tsar in Boris — of course, by command of the ruler himself. As early as 1585 one of the Muscovite diplomats, speaking officially while abroad in Poland, said that "God has filled with reason and understanding this great man — our great boyar and equerry, brother-in-law of our sovereign and brother of our sovereign's lady, and he grieves and cares for this great land."

In 1586, long before Boris had attained the rights of regency in international affairs, the "great man" was presented

to the English as the tsar's "vital friend" and "ruler of the
state" (lieutenant of the empire). Reports from Moscow
indicated that foreign governments maintaining relations with
Muscovy had become accustomed to addressing Boris as
co-ruler and relative of the Muscovite sovereign. In this way
Boris strove to create for himself the general impression of a
person belonging to the dynasty and the natural co-ruler of the
most pious sovereign.

The exceptional governmental position of Boris required,
besides general everyday recognition, an official expression. In
the writings of several foreign contemporaries (Bussow [32] and
Petreus [33]) is found a notation to the effect that "Tsar Fedor,
finding government a burden, supposedly granted the boyars the
right to choose an aide and deputy for him." Boris was selected
as the tsar's aide. Then, with the customary ceremony in the
presence of the grandees, Fedor removed the golden chain of
office and placed it on Boris, saying "that with this chain he
removed from himself the burden of government and placed it
upon Boris, retaining for himself the right to decide only the
most important affairs." He supposedly wished to remain tsar
("Ich will Kayser seyn"), but Boris was to become the ruler of
the state *(Gubernator der Reussischen Monarchie)*. N. M.
Karamzin was among the first to doubt this story. He believed
that it did not really conform to Muscovite custom. Boris
hardly needed such a ceremony of election by the boyars and
investiture by the tsar: it would only have provoked his boyar
competitors. Boris achieved his end by other means.

In the first place Boris gained, through the tsar's favor, an
exceptionally magnificent and expressive title. Gradually this
title became: "Brother-in-law and Ruler to the Great Sovereign,
Servant and Boyar-Equerry, and Court *Voevoda*, [34] Protector
of the Great States and of the Tsardoms of Kazan and
Astrakhan." The ambassador to Persia, Prince Zvenigorodsky,

clarified the significance of this title in the following manner. "No one is like unto Boris Fedorovich. . .many tsars and tsareviches, [35] princes and children of princes serve our great sovereign, but every tsar and tsarevich and prince [must] beg love and concern from the tsar through Boris Fedorovich, and Boris brings their petitions to the tsar and intercedes for them all." The immoderate hyperbole of this comment was intended to explain properly Boris's "government" and his ascendency over all of the titled servants of the Muscovite sovereign.

In the second place, Boris prevailed upon the Boyar Duma to decree — in the tsar's own presence — that Boris officially have the right of conducting relations with foreign governments in his capacity as a high governmental personage. This right was granted on the basis that "the Equerry and Boyar Boris Fedorovich Godunov write letters now and in the future" to foreign courts "for the honor and increase of His Tsarist Majesty's name; [and] that His Majesty's Intimate Equerry and Boyar Boris Fedorovich Godunov start contacting great rulers." From that time on (1588-1589) it began to be general procedure in the ambassadorial office "to write letters from Boris Fedorovich in ambassadorial books as well as in other books, together with the sovereign's letters."

As ruler, Boris entered the international sphere and thereby stood at last outside the usual order of Muscovite service, having risen above it to be the supreme arbiter of Muscovite policy. The manner in which Boris's participation in diplomatic negotiations "was written in ambassadorial annals" clearly tended toward an exaggerated exaltation of the "ruler." For example, here is how — in the official Muscovite version — the ambassador of the Holy Roman Emperor [Rudolph II] appealed to Boris for aid against the Turks. "And the ambassador spoke and begged humbly of Boris Fedorovich: His Imperial Majesty entreats Your Grace, O Boris Fedorovich, brother-in-law of His Tsarist Majesty, the Great Sovereign Tsar and Grand Prince Fedor Ivanovich, Autocrat of All Russia, and is most hopeful that Your Majesty will not despise the petition of his brother, His Imperial Majesty, but will grant aid against the enemy of all Christians, the Turkish Tsar." Boris gave a simple and favorable reply to the Emperor's humble request. "Of those matters concerning which you spoke with me, I will inform His Majesty and you will have an answer at another time." Whether or not Boris answered the ambassador in this way does not matter. The official record made Boris a third "majesty" between two other "majesties" — the tsar and the emperor. Boris was the ruler of the state who "ruled the land at the hand of the great sovereign."

In the third place, Boris established for his own official appearances at the tsar's court, as well as at his own "court," a diligently contrived "rank" (etiquette), the subtleness of which was directed, like the official records, to making him not a mere servant of the tsar but a co-ruler "of His Majesty." At court during ambassadorial receptions, Boris was present in a special role. He stood by the throne itself, "higher than the tsar's bodyguard," while the boyars sat at some distance "on benches." In the last years of Fedor's reign, during such ceremonies Boris usually held "the golden apple of tsarist rank" that served as a manifest sign of his "authoritative government." When at official feasts "they drank the sovereigns' cup," along with toasts to the tsar and other sovereigns, there followed a toast to Boris. "They drank the cup of the servitor and boyar-equerry, Boris Fedorovich." Foreign ambassadors arriving in Moscow, after their presentation to the sovereign, were presented also to Boris, and with great ceremony.

Boris maintained his own court and staff of courtiers. The ceremony of "meeting" ambassadors at Boris's court, their presentation to the ruler, their release and refreshment (packages of foodstuffs) was an exact copy of the tsar's receptions. Officials of Boris's court "presented ambassadors" to him. A "steward" met them on the palace stairway, a "treasurer" led them into the throne room. Boris's noblemen, "the chosen few persons in golden robes and golden hats," sat in the throne room just as the boyars sat with the tsar. Other persons were stationed "from the gates about the whole court and on the porch, and in the passageways and in the entryway." The ambassadors brought Boris presents ("remembrances") and styled him "Most August Dignitary" and "Most High Majesty."

In every way the ambassadors were given to understand that Boris was the true bearer of authority in Moscow, that all affairs were executed "by command of the great sovereign but by order of the brother-in-law of His Tsarist Majesty." After one of his receptions Boris would honor the ambassadors in their quarters with his food and drink, just as did the tsar. And in abundance and luxury his table did not yield to the tsar's. For example, Boris sent his nobleman Mikhail Kosov to the quarters of the ambassador of the Holy Roman Emperor with food and drink, "and one hundred and thirteen dishes of food were sent and also drink in eight tankards and in eight vessels."

Add to the enumerated distinctions of Boris the fact that during his regency quite substantial personal wealth was concentrated in his hands, and there emerges the final feature characterizing his station. Englishmen in Moscow during Boris's time were frankly astonished at his wealth. Fletcher, a very sober and well-grounded observer, reports to us an exact sum for Boris's yearly income — "93,700 rubbels and more." Unfortunately this sum is not subject to documentary verification. In listing the various items in this figure, Fletcher exceeds his own total and, according to various categories, estimates Boris's income at 104,500 rubles. Fletcher's calculations include the following: incomes from patrimonies (in Viazma and Dorogobuzh) and from pomestie estates in many districts; incomes from the Vaga region, from Riazan and Seversk and from Tver and Torzhok; incomes from quit-rent properties in Moscow itself and surrounding areas along the Moscow River; a salary for his position as equerry; and finally, a pension from the sovereign.

Of all the Muscovite grandees only Boris's brother-in-law, Prince Glinsky, received an income somewhat approaching his. According to the reckoning of Fletcher, Glinsky received up to 40,000 rubles a year. The remaining aristocracy supposedly trailed far behind Boris and Glinsky in wealth. Jerome Horsey, another Englishman well acquainted with Russian affairs during Boris's time, exaggerates his calculation of Boris's wealth even more than does Fletcher. By Horsey's calculation, the incomes of Boris Godunov were equal to 185,000 pounds sterling (either marks or rubles). "Prince Boris Pheodorowich . . .and his house be of such authoritie and power, that in 40 dayes warning they are able to bring into the fielde 100 thousand souldiers well furnished." [36]

However exaggerated these opinions, they attest to the fact that Boris had concentrated in his hands all that was required for political hegemony: court favor and influence, governmental primacy and, for that time, immense wealth. Between about 1588-1589 "the authoritative government" of Boris was legitimatized and consolidated. It was impossible to struggle against him. There were no longer any lawful means for carrying on such a struggle, nor did anybody have the strength for it. "From this time on," says the historian K. N. Bestuzhev-Riumin, "Muscovite policy is Godunov's policy."

VII BORIS'S   ADMINISTRATIVE   ABILITIES.
CONTEMPORARY   OPINIONS OF BORIS.
HIS PERSONAL QUALITIES

Had the supremacy and power of Boris Godunov been based
solely upon intrigue, servility, and adroitness at court, his
position in government would not have been so firm and
enduring. But without any doubt Boris possessed an
outstanding mind and administrative talent. His qualities
surpassed those of all his rivals. Contemporary references to
Boris's personal characteristics agree in acknowledging the
exceptional quality of his gifts. Ivan Timofeev characterized
more vividly than others Boris's intellectual strength. He found
that although there were intelligent rulers in Moscow, their
minds were but a shadow or likeness of Boris's. And in this
connection he noted that Boris's superiority was generally
recognized, "understood by all." No less laudatory of Godunov
was another contemporary, the author of "brief writings about
the Muscovite tsars." He said that "Tsar Boris flourishes in
grandeur and his manner surpasses the multitude of
people...the man is very splendid in reason and very kind
spoken, well-assured and a lover of the poor, and very ordered
and thrifty."

Foreigners echoed the opinion of the Muscovites. Bussow,
for example, says that general opinion held that no one was
more able than Boris to govern intelligently and wisely. The
Dutchman Isaac Massa, generally hostile toward Boris,
nevertheless recognized his abilities. [37] In his words, Boris
possessed a fine memory, and although he ostensibly did not
know how to read or write, still knew more than those who did.
Massa felt that had matters gone as Boris wished, he would have
accomplished many great things. In short, contemporaries
considered Boris an outstanding man and believed that he came
to power by merit, and exercised it well. In the words of Prince

Ivan Khvorostinin, "he clothes himself in the wisdom of the life
of this world as a kind and good giant, and receives glory and
honor from tsars."

Despite the widespread opinion about Boris's illiteracy,
he must be considered an enlightened man for his time.
Those who considered Boris illiterate were simply mistaken.
Several signatures of his have been preserved on letters
"of bestowal." [38] Knowledgeable contemporaries evidently
pointed out not that Boris was illiterate, but that he was not in
the least bookishly learned. "Of scholarly studies he is not
informed and he is not versed in simple letters," said Ivan
Timofeev, "and wonder! the first despot in Russia to be
unlettered!" "And wonder! the first tsar not to be bookread!"
he repeats in another place. Avraami Palitsyn thought the
same. [39] He wrote that Boris, "though he understands the tsar's
government, is not practiced in divine writing." Thus Boris did
not belong to the number of erudite people. However, in "the
affairs of the tsar" and as a practical official, politican and
administrator, he was by no means unlearned and ignorant. On
the contrary, there is every reason to believe that Boris's
intellectual horizon was unusually broad for that time and that
he not only understood well the problems and interests of the
state in the spirit of old Muscovite tradition, but appeared as an
advocate of cultural innovation and borrowing from the West.

Boris startled his contemporaries in his display of
humanity and goodness, so unexpected and so unusual after
the tyrannical ways and savage brutality of Ivan the Terrible.
Through the mouths of his agents Boris himself boasted
officially that he had established order and justice everywhere,
and that "his regime is such as there has never been before.
Neither the great nor the powerful torment any man, not even
the poor orphan." Boris was "extremely competent" (in the
words of a contemporary), and not only did he wish to appear

"enlightened" and "loving of the poor," he was indeed so. He labored hard for the poor and the downtrodden. Boris's contemporaries, who were not his unconditional supporters, tell us of this. Timofeev sings Boris's praise most highly. Though Timofeev's language seems somewhat pretentious to us, nevertheless it may be rendered thus: Boris was "a generous giver" and he meekly attended to all the supplications of the people. He was "gracious to all in his answers," "a quick avenger of the helpless and widows," and "a diligent watcher over the government of the land." "His love of justice had no price." "He was an exterminator of all falsehood," and "his domestic life passed quietly and inoffensively for all." "His injunction to those who ravaged the weak was gentle unless the offenders did not heed him." "He was a strong guardian of the wronged against the hands of the powerful." "He ordered the eradication of the impious and ungodly sale of wine for drunkenness." "He mercilessly killed those given to all sorts of bribery, so loathsome was it to him." "Against every evil that contravened the good he was as implacable as he was an unflattering rewarder of good."

A certain difficulty of language and an inclination to tautology cannot, of course, detract from the power of this astonishing characterization. It recreates for the reader an idealized image of an unselfish, kind, just and attentive ruler. And such a ruler Boris was, according to Timofeev's picture, until he was "seized with the love of power." The praises of the author of the so-called "Chronograph of the Second Redaction" equal Timofeev's in force. Boris "was strong in his hatred of bribery;" "he attempted much to rid his tsardom of the unwelcome business of brigandage and thievery and every sort of illegal practice, but it was by no means possible." "He is enlightened by nature and charitable in disposition, even more so in speech, and is loving of the poor." "His generous giving reaches forth to all," "and so as flowers the date tree, so flowers he in virtue."

Palitsyn is less inclined toward the exaltation of Boris. But even in his writings the following eloquent words are found. "Tsar Boris was very concerned about piety and the needs of the tsardom." "He lived for the welfare of the poor and lowly and his charity to them was great." "Fiercely did he root out evil persons." "And for such popular actions he was loved by all."

Information about one curious habit of Boris's has been preserved. Generally affable and gentle in his relations with people, he was quick to promise aid and assistance. In such instances he would often grab the pearled collar of his shirt and say that he was ready to share even this with those in want. This habit was noticed by many of his contemporaries. Germans, who had personally observed Boris, made reference to this gesture. Konrad Bussow related that "he grabbed his pearl collar with his fingers and said: 'We would divide the same with you.'" And the Imperial Ambassador, Warkotsch, stated that "he, however, would be prepared at any time to help one with gold and treasure, even including his coat and his shirt all the way up to the throat."

Boris's gesture confused one Muscovite witness, however. Avraami Palitsyn, describing the coronation of Boris, said that while standing to be blessed under the uplifted arm of Patriarch Job, Boris "delivered a very high-sounding speech. 'O Father and great Patriarch Job, may God be witness. No one in my realm shall be poor or lowly!' And pulling up his long shirt he said, 'Even this last shall I share with all!'" To Palitsyn Boris's "speech" seemed "high," that is, overly assured and even "an abomination to God," and he censured those who were in sympathy with Boris. Yet all those present in the church were in sympathy with him, for Boris's "speech" was evidently liked and created an impression. Palitsyn noted that Boris's "words were gratifying to all who heard them."

Such was the "bold" ruler of Muscovy. Although descended from old Muscovite aristocracy, he fashioned his career not by "his high birth" but through court favor, and became a member of the sovereign's family by marriage. By reason of his position at court he was opposed to the boyar service princes. He therefore met active opposition among the princely families at the beginning of his political career and inevitably had to struggle for power with the Mstislavskys and the Shuiskys. This same struggle brought Boris close to the circle of Nikita Romanovich Yuriev and, after the latter's death, seemingly placed Godunov at the head of an entire faction of court aristocracy. Boris, who had become the guardian of the children of Nikita Romanovich, also found himself at the head of his own family, the Godunovs. In all essentials he acted as guardian to the whole tsarist family and represented the interests of all members of the court circle which had grown up around Ivan the Terrible in place of the old aristocracy, which Ivan had destroyed.

Boris's victory over the princes Shuisky, Mstislavsky, and others was a lasting one, for Boris proved to be a talented politician. He strengthened his position of authority not only through favors and intrigue, but also by intelligent statesmanship. "And for such popular actions he was loved by all." In other words, Godunov was able to gain popularity by showing good will and the administrative art of a ruler.

CHAPTER TWO

THE POLICY OF BORIS

I   THE INTERNATIONAL POSITION OF
MUSCOVY AFTER THE DEATH OF IVAN
THE TERRIBLE. BORIS'S EXECUTIVE
PROBLEMS

After the death of Ivan the Terrible Muscovy experienced
extreme exhaustion as a result of the extraordinary political
tension of his reign. The prolonged war with Lithuania and
Sweden for control of the Baltic coast had ended quite
unsuccessfully. Ivan ceded to his foes everything that he had
managed to conquer in the initial, happier period of the war,
together with some of his own lands. Admirers of King
Stefan Batory [1] have unjustly claimed that Ivan was defeated
by the king's superior abilities. Karamzin stated that "if the
life and genius of Batory had not failed before the death of
Godunov, then the glory of Russia might have been tarnished
for centuries during the very first decade of the new
century." Karamzin sincerely believed that "thus the fate of
states is dependent upon a person, upon an event, or upon
the will of Providence!"

It is more justifiable to think that Ivan was defeated not
so much by Batory's "genius" as by the devastation that was
wrought within Muscovy as a result of the oprichnina and the
disorderly land arrangements it provoked. There had been a
great outflow of population from the core of Muscovy
toward the east and south. Ivan suffered defeat at the hands
of Batory because he had had no home front to support him,
and because his base of operations had collapsed. In 1562 the
tsar could throw against Polotsk such a mass of field forces
that it "swept everything from its path." But by 1579-1580
he had no field army at all and avoided encounters with the
enemy in the open field. Prince Kurbsky maliciously pointed
this out to Ivan, saying: "Having assembled your host and
having taken refuge in the forest like a coward and a
runaway, you tremble and hide, though nobody pursues
you."[2] Kurbsky realized that Ivan's entire "host" was so
paltry in number that the tsar felt himself almost alone ("a
coward and a runaway") and had to flee and hide. Kurbsky
explained that Ivan "utterly ruined and drove everyone away
before the end." But, of course, this ought to be explained by a
more elemental cause: Ivan simply no longer had the men
and means for the struggle.

Peace with his enemies was concluded not long before
Ivan's death (1582-1583), and the tsar ended his earthly
sojourn with the bitter awareness of one who has suffered
defeat.[3] Boris, who shared this awareness, took power upon
the death of Ivan. Responsibility for the possible cushioning
of the consequences of the great political fiasco and for
restoring the prestige of Muscovy's power and enterprise,
which had been shaken by war, fell on Boris's shoulders.
Similarly, the burden which had been created by domestic
crisis devolved upon Godunov. He had to think about
rejuvenating the economic pulse of Muscovy's heartland,
abandoned by its working population, and about restoring

there the service and fiscal institutions that the crisis had enfeebled. Consequently, Boris's executive energy was expended chiefly in these two directions.

II   RELATIONS WITH THE POLISH-LITHUAN-
      IAN COMMONWEALTH, SWEDEN, THE IM-
      PERIAL COURT AND ENGLAND. GENERAL
      CHARACTERISTICS OF MUSCOVITE POL-
      ICY DURING THE TIME OF BORIS

It is not especially necessary to delve deeply into the details of the diplomatic relations which were carried on between the governments of Tsar Fedor and King Stefan Batory. According to one of the most serious historians (K. N. Bestuzhev-Riumin), these were "the most difficult" relations of that time. The king dreamed, after his victories, of a further triumph over Muscovy, even of its full submission to him. In his grandiose plans the seizure of Moscow was just one step on the road to the conquest of Turkey. "By his reasoning," F. I. Uspensky has said, "the solution of the Eastern Question was supposed to begin with the subjugation of Muscovy. The war with Muscovy could be finished in three years. After Muscovy would come the conquest of the Transcaucasus and Persia, an advance against Constantinople from Asia Minor, and capture of the Straits."

Materials discovered by Father Paul Pierling reveal these plans of Batory. It seemed to the king that operations against Muscovy would not present any difficulty. Muscovy was governed by a sick and weak sovereign. Indeed, power had shifted to the boyars, who were fighting among themselves for predominance. Supposedly the people were dreaming of the selection of a new tsar. Batory's plan, communicated to Rome through the Jesuit diplomat Antonio Possevino and other diplomats, evoked there the sympathy of Pope Sixtus V.

This sympathy in its turn inspired the king's policy and made him arrogant and pretentious in relations with Muscovy. Had the king felt himself on sure ground in the Polish-Lithuanian Commonwealth, Moscow might perhaps have been faced with the prospect of a new struggle with Batory and — who knows! — a new defeat, and subjugation to the king. The king's chancellor, Zamoyski, sympathized with Batory. The former's plans attracted the celebrated Possevino and other Jesuits. But the Polish nobility and gentry were not devoted to the visions of Batory and were weary of his wars. They did not wish for a new war and feared various political complications. This circumstance tied Batory's hands and made him wary.

On the other hand, Muscovite policy did not satisfy Batory by its tone and behavior. Moscow feared Batory. His ambassador, Leo Sapieha, expressed this fact many times in letters from Moscow just after the death of Ivan the Terrible. The Muscovite government was ready to make every kind of concession, even to face humiliation, if only to achieve peace for a time, "to take a truce." For example, the government released Lithuanian prisoners without receiving compensation, and at the same time agreed to pay for the release of Russian prisoners. The government gave its ambassadors an order to be compliant and to demur gently from everything which might seem to them unacceptable in the conduct of the king and the nobility, not causing a break in negotiations. But at the same time the government ordered its ambassadors to mention at every opportunity that circumstances in Moscow had changed, and that Moscow was ready not only for defensive but for offensive action as well.

Many times the Muscovite ambassadors spoke in their

negotiations as follows. "Moscow is not now as she has been
in the past. The tsar will not sue for peace with Lithuania.
The tsar is ready to stand against the king. Our tsar will not
yield the roof-tiles of a single town." "Moscow is not now as
she has been in the past. Neither Polotsk nor the lands of the
Livonians need beware of her, but Vilna must needs beware
of her." When the Polish nobility tried to refute this boast,
they heard it persistently repeated. The nobility would say:
"We too know what goes on in Moscow. There are no people,
and those there are, are poor and have no dwellings. There is
dissension among all the people."

In reply the Muscovite diplomats would remark, and not
without venom: "We do not see any sin over our state, only
prosperity and the grace of God. You have not yet talked
with God, and it is not given to man to know what lies
ahead. . . .Our sovereign is stately (that is, stalwart, stout,
handsome); our sovereign is wise and fortunate. He sits in his
states with the blessing of his father and rules the land himself
(in contrast to Batory, who was elected and whose power was
limited). . . . He has many people, twice as many as of old,
for he is gracious to the people and gives them the means
whereby to live, not sparing his own treasury. And the people
serve him with great zeal and wish so to serve in the future,
and in defense against his enemies they are willing to die.
There is no dissension whatsoever among the people."

Just as the Polish noblemen knew about Muscovy's
weakness, so the Muscovite boyars knew that in Lithuania
there was no unity between Batory and his nobility. In
conformity with this knowledge, the Muscovite diplomats
received the following order: if there be dissension between
the king and the Polish gentry, then the tone should be
sharpened. "If the Polish lords begin to speak in a
high-handed manner, then make answer to them in the same

way." "If you sense that there is no great dissension between the King and the nobles," then "in ultimate necessity" you should be conciliatory in order to conclude without fail an armistice "even for a short time."

Thus Muscovite diplomacy displayed considerable flexibility and changed tone and behavior according to the extent of its information. Thanks to these circumstances, that is, internal opposition in the Commonwealth and the evasiveness of Moscow, Batory did not resolve to go to war. Instead, in February, 1585, he lay claim before the Muscovite ambassadors (the princes Troekurov and Beznin) to Smolensk, Seversk Land, Novgorod, and Pskov. He threatened to break off negotiations but still agreed to extend the peace agreement for two years (until June 3, 1587). And subsequently Batory himself sent his ambassador Mikhail Haraburda to Moscow with a proposal of eternal peace and dynastic union between Muscovy and the Commonwealth. Haraburda's mission (in 1586), which was surrounded by the usual demands for concessions and threats of a break in relations, was unsuccessful. But it did lead to further talks of peace and union between the two states. Moscow maintained its policy of concessions at the decisive moment and threats at the first opportunity. From Batory Moscow decided even to claim Kiev, Polotsk, Vitebsk, Toropets and Livonian towns, agreeing to talk of eternal peace only on this condition. Of course, both sides understood that mutual requests of immoderate territorial concessions were but a well-known method of starting real negotiations and therefore, having hastily "spoken many unseemly and reproachful words," they conceded nothing to each other and ultimately arrived at the following result: to extend the two-year truce for two more months (until August 3, 1587).

This agreement was achieved by the embassy of Prince

Troekurov and Pisemsky in August, 1586, but on December 12 of the same year Batory died. With his death his ideas of conquering Muscovy and Turkey went out of political circulation, and the dreams of Possevino and Pope Sixtus V of turning Muscovy into a weapon of papal policy faded for a time. Into the life of the Commonwealth came a dark period of interregnum with the usual intrigues and party struggles that accompanied the election of a king. The idea of union between the Commonwealth and Muscovy continued to crop up in the diplomatic negotiations of those years. Lithuania broached the idea of union in Moscow. There they wanted Tsar Fedor as Grand Duke of Lithuania — chiefly because of his passive and meek nature, and secondly because they feared a Catholic candidate and his possible persecution of Orthodoxy.

Moscow answered the call from Lithuania and decided to take part in the election, placing in candidacy Tsar Fedor. Evidently the Muscovites feared more than anything else the election of the Swedish Prince Sigismund who had been placed in candidacy by Chancellor Zamoyski. Sigismund was feared because he could unite the Polish-Lithuanian crown with that of Sweden. At the beginning of 1587 Elizari Rzhevsky was sent to Lithuania with letters to the Polish and Lithuanian nobility. In the letters Tsar Fedor explained that, having heard of the death of King Stefan, he had decided to show "the sovereignless" his benevolence and good will, and for this reason he sent his nobleman "to visit you in your adversity and present to you our benevolence and favor." "And that you noblemen of the Council [of Lords], both secular and religious, who have talked among yourselves and with all the land about our Christian goodness and favor to you, might desire us for the Polish crown and for the Grand Duchy of Lithuania." In the event of his election the tsar promised much. "We wish in no wise to disturb the affairs

and freedom of the noblemen and knights of the land of the
Polish Crown and the Grand Duchy of Lithuania. We wish,
by our favor, to increase and enhance the ranks and lands
you have had previously and what you have now."

But Muscovite manners and conceptions were so unlike
those of Poland-Lithuania that Moscow was unable to adjust
to the conditions of an election, and did not know how to
carry out quickly and artfully all that was required in the
campaign. Moscow did not divine soon enough the need to
promise and to give money, commitments, or presents.
Moscow did not display the proper flexibility and tact.
Delicate questions about the religion and place of residence
of the future king and grand duke were bluntly posed. It
transpired that Tsar Fedor would not change his religion or
live in Poland or Lithuania; nor was he inclined toward
generous expenditures. Under such conditions the candidacy
of the Muscovite tsar became unattractive even to those who
sincerely desired it. "All of Lithuania and the greater part of
Poland have hungered and thirsted for your tsar" (said the
noblemen to the Muscovite ambassadors), "but it has become
obvious that your sovereign will not come soon." Fedor, by
his conduct, had become an awkward candidate. And so the
matter fell apart. Sigismund's party prevailed and he was
crowned in Cracow in December, 1587.

For Moscow the end result of Fedor's candidacy was
material losses, and only one gain. During the interregnum
the Polish government concluded a fifteen-year armistice
with Muscovy (from August, 1587 through August, 1602). At
the beginning of 1591 this armistice was confirmed by a new
treaty completed in Moscow with the embassy of King
Sigismund after the most unpleasant wrangling customary in
meetings between Muscovite and Lithuanian diplomats.
Moscow, it seemed, could now be calm about its immediate
future. At least the danger of attack from the

Commonwealth had passed for the next ten years. Now
Moscow was not alarmed by the fact that Sigismund as heir
to the Swedish crown could bring about a union of its
enemies — Sweden and the Commonwealth.

Muscovy was fighting with Sweden while generally
remaining aloof from the intervention of Sigismund in
Muscovite-Swedish relations. Moscow was ready to accept the
mediation of Lithuanian diplomacy only in the matter of
concluding an "eternal peace" with Sweden. Such foresight
and steadfastness was a credit to the Muscovite negotiators.
They soon sensed that Sigismund's personal characteristics
would undermine his popularity both in the Commonwealth
and subsequently in Sweden (where he had received the
throne at the end of 1592). As early as the end of 1589 (or
the very beginning of 1590) a Muscovite messenger, one A.
Ivanov, had transmitted to Moscow news from Lithuania that
the new king, Sigismund, had no support because he had no
enterprise, was not considered wise, nor was he liked by the
people. This news led Moscow to reassuring conclusions —
and Muscovy went to war with Sweden.

The relations between Muscovy and Sweden after the
death of Ivan the Terrible were different from the relations
between Muscovy and the Commonwealth. King Stefan
Batory had been feared in Moscow; Sweden, evidently not.
War with Sweden, according to S. M. Soloviev, "was
considered a necessity. Controversial Livonia had been ceded
to Batory during the reign of King Johann. But in the hands
of the Swedes remained age-old Russian towns whose return
state honor demanded." Besides, the internal condition of
Sweden was such that its enemies were given hope. According
to G. V. Forsten, "year in, year out, the situation in Sweden
grew gloomier. For several years in a row there had been crop
failure; the people were hungry, and whole villages had died
out. To cap all these woes, infectious diseases had broken

out. The mortality rate was approaching unprecedented heights."

King Johann had depleted the finances of the country and strained his relations with the aristocracy. The Muscovite diplomats were able to observe this situation and to draw the correct conclusions. In 1585, after quarrelsome negotiations, the Muscovite ambassadors Fedor Shestunov and Ignaty Tatishchev "in ultimate necessity" concluded a treaty with the Swedes in which the existing armistice was extended for four years, for Moscow did not yet see an opportunity to draw the sword with promise of success. It was proposed only that the Swedes agree to give up for ransom to the Russians their towns of Ivangorod, Yam, Kopore, and Korela. The Swedes were not enticed by the proposal of ransom, and Moscow decided to wait for a more opportune time. Within four years, in 1589, when domestic disorder in Sweden remained still unresolved, Moscow began to sing another tune. The Muscovite ambassadors were ordered "to speak with the Swedish ambassadors about great and high measures, including the most extreme measure: transfer to the sovereign's side of Narva, Ivangorod, Yam, Kopore, and Korela without payment, without money."

Had the Swedes agreed to this "final measure," the Muscovite ambassadors would have been permitted to agree to an "eternal peace." But the Swedes did not agree, and the Russians threatened them. "Why should our sovereign, not having regained his own patrimony, the towns of Livonia and of Novgorod Land, become reconciled with your sovereign? It now behooves your sovereign to return to us all our towns and to make any and all reparations that our sovereign might indicate." Such speeches could lead only to rupture and to war.

The Muscovite government began military operations immediately upon the expiration of the armistice — in

January, 1590. The Russian forces were directed against
Narva. They took Yam and Ivangorod, stormed Narva itself,
but did not capture it. An armistice, quickly concluded in
February, 1590, allowed Moscow to retain the occupied
lands for one year. In the years following (1591-1593),
hostile clashes were resumed, but they were not decisive in
nature. In 1593 a new two-year armistice was reached; and in
1593 both sides finally arrived at peaceful agreement. The
ambassadors gathered near Ivangorod in the village of Tiavzin
and began their negotiations with the usual polemics, advising
each other to abandon unseemly words and "to search in
themselves for the road to good deeds." Such a road was
found. The Russians retracted their pretensions upon Narva,
and the Swedes ceased holding Korela. Peace was concluded
on the grounds that the old Russian lands from the Narova
River to Korela remain under Muscovite control.

There is reason to think that this age-old Novgorod
borderland was of little use to the Swedes. Control of that
region, it is true, cut Russia off from the sea, but it cost the
Swedes dearly. The unfertile land required the import of
grain and forage of which the Swedes themselves had no
surplus at that time. The difficulties of provisioning the
region were so great that the Swedes, at the time of their
greatest triumph over Russia under Gustavus Adolphus, easily
conceded to Moscow the Novgorod lands in the Treaty of
Stolbovo in 1617, mainly because they did not have the
strength to organize provisioning. These difficulties were felt
all the more at the end of the sixteenth century when
Sweden itself was starving. Moscow recovered the old Russian
towns on the shore of the Gulf of Finland. She negotiated
some freedom of transit through Swedish lands to Europe —
for merchants going with goods in the tsar's name, for
doctors and technicians going to the tsar, and for the tsar's
ambassadors. But trade in Narva remained exclusively in
Swedish hands.

Moscow was satisfied with the "eternal peace" of 1593 because it had made territorial acquisitions — a mark of victory and military triumph. The dependence upon the Swedes of Russian trade on the Baltic coast did not disturb Moscow, for trade on the White Sea, in Arkhangelsk, guaranteed free commercial ties with the West. The German Hansa suffered more from Swedish control than did Moscow. The Swedes, too, were quite satisfied with the "eternal peace." G. V. Forsten has said that "everyone rejoiced when the thirty-seven-year war ended. In the churches they sang a *Te Deum.* Everyone exchanged congratulations upon the fortunate day." The king's ambassadors, upon returning from Tiavzin, were met in Reval with an extraordinary celebration. "For this great blessing be given praise and glory to the most high God!" exclaimed a Swedish contemporary.

The personal participation of Boris in Muscovy's relations with Lithuania and Sweden was entirely imperceptible. His role can be evaluated only in connection with a general appraisal of the expediency and farsightedness of Muscovite politics. In essence, one should say the same of relations with the court of the "tsesar" (as the Imperial Hapsburg Court was called in Muscovy). From the pertinent documents it is possible to extract two or three minor traits characterizing the personal conduct of Boris in relations with the "tsesar" and his ambassadors but even these traits permit varied interpretations.

Diplomatic relations between Moscow and Vienna at the end of the sixteenth century were in general indefinite and complex. The subjects of these relations were varied; motives and goals were not always clear. Evidently Emperor Rudolph II was certain of the possibility of dynastic union with Muscovy. In 1588 he pointed out to his ambassador, Warkotsch, in an official instruction, that there was evidence (which has "reached us from afar," and which has "otherwise reached us circuitously") of the alleged existence of a last will and testament of Ivan the Terrible, but that it was kept in great secrecy. In this will "it is stated that should the Grand Prince (Fedor) die childless, then preferential attention will be turned to our venerable house. Anyone from our house could be chosen ruler." It is impossible to ascertain definitely on what basis such evidence and hopes arose. But it can be suggested that the grounds for these lay in the circumstances of the Polish-Lithuanian election.

In the election campaign of 1587-1588 Moscow was ready to support Archduke Maximilian, brother of Rudolph II, in the event Tsar Fedor was not elected. Moscow informed Emperor Rudolph that the Muscovite ambassadors were operating in Warsaw with this policy in mind. Moscow said that the Polish nobility was "to elect us" [Tsar Fedor] as their great sovereign and to live under our tsarist hand. . . . But if they do not elect us as their sovereign, then they might choose your brother Maximilian, the Austrian archduke. . . [They must] not elect someone of low rank, a son of Sweden or another of the Baltic princes, for those sovereigns are unworthy to rule great states. They do not care about Christianity, but only desire the spilling of Christian blood, and that makes the Besserman [Muslim] rulers happy. If your brother Maximilian succeeds to the Crown of Poland and the Grand Duchy of Lithuania, it will be just as if we were on the throne in those states."

The agents probably accompanied this forthright declaration, written in letters, with more in words than was required or permitted in the official orders. In Vienna the conviction could have developed that in view of the childlessness of Fedor, Moscow, obsessed with the idea of union, would prefer the House of Hapsburg to "unworthy sovereigns" "of small stature." This fact caused Rudolph and Maximilian to turn their attention to Moscow and to send frequent diplomatic communiques there. But it is impossible to say what was the origin of the legend of the secret will of Ivan the Terrible.

For its part, Muscovite diplomacy was very interested in the emperor — and not only in dealings with the Commonwealth, but also for a possible alliance against the Turks and Tatars. Both sides suffered from the "Bessermen," and were seeking more reliable allies and instruments to carry on the struggle against them. Both sides could offer little to each other and in general sought more than they could give. Therefore there was much feeling, compliments, and promises in these relations, but little practical dealing. These exchanges acquired concrete expression only to the extent that Moscow forwarded personal gifts to the emperor, sending him sable furs to the value of 44,000 rubles. When, in 1597, the emperor requested money, not furs, Moscow declined for, in the words of K. N. Bestuzhev-Riumin, "they were not satisfied because the emperor said much about his alliances, but in actuality nothing was seen."

In relations with the emperor, whose title raised him above all other Western kings and princes, Moscow was especially sensitive to maintain the appropriate protocol in order to emphasize the equality of "the most-beloved brothers" — the Muscovite tsar and the Holy Roman Emperor. And Boris, personally, as ruler, saw to it especially that he himself appear worthy in the role of first person in the land, at the tsar's court as well as in his own boyar court where he gave audiences to the ambassadors. The accounts of the emperor's ambassadors and the "itemized lists" of the Muscovite state secretaries paint splendid pictures of meetings and receptions at the tsar's court and at Boris's court, but do not at all reveal their practical or important consequences.

Relations with England were another matter. Here there was little pomp and circumstance. Instead, in everything the tone was very business-like, and Boris's personal participation in these relations is quite clear and comprehensible. England had only trade interests in Muscovy, and Moscow for the time being occupied no place in the foreign policy of England. The circumstances of the appearance of English seafarers at the mouth of the Northern Dvina in the sixteenth century and of grants to them of exclusive rights to use the mouth of that river for trade with Muscovy are very well known. The English merchants and government had only this market in mind and wished to make it more favorable and lucrative for themselves.

In 1569 the English ambassador Thomas Randolph gained a "privilege" from Ivan the Terrible, according to which the commercial "Muscovy Company," which had been formed in England, received the exclusive right of trade, and furthermore duty-free trade, within the entire Muscovite state, as well as the right of trade through Russia with the East. The English were taken into the oprichnina, which was considered both by the English and by Ivan as a special honor and convenience for the foreigners. Ivan demanded his own kind of payment for so many privileges and honors. He wanted Queen Elizabeth to enter with him into an alliance against common enemies. He wished her to give comparable privileges to Russian merchants. And he desired the right to asylum in England in the event of personal adversity (the same asylum Ivan was ready to grant Elizabeth in return.)

But when Elizabeth, who did not see the necessity of entering into such obligations and of binding England with risky alliances, answered evasively, Ivan became upset, sent her a reproachful letter, and imposed his disfavor upon the English merchants. Relations later on were smoothed out, and the tsar, in 1572, returned the English to his favor and restored their "privileges and freedoms." He made the stipulation, nonetheless, that they pay half duty on their goods. The restoration of the privileges of 1569 turned out to be incomplete. And several political complications which followed shortly thereafter deprived the English of many other advantages.

The Muscovite government greatly valued English trade in the North; but it equally valued other opportunities to communicate with the West and to acquire European goods. While Ivan had held Narva, he had encouraged in every way possible trade with merchants of all nationalities — with whomever found the way to the harbor of Narva. Despite the monopolistic right of the "Muscovy Company" of English merchants, Ivan patronized other Englishmen, too. He granted the Company the northern route and a monopoly at the mouth of the Dvina. But at Narva he was ready to grant rights to other English entrepreneurs, although the Company protested most energetically. The competition of Narva did not diminish until the transfer of that port to Swedish hands in 1581, whereby the monopoly of the Northern trade route was in practice restored to the Company.

At the same time that Narva was lost, Moscow experienced difficulty in the North. Besides the English who were carrying on trade on the Dvina, seafarers of other nationalities visited the Muscovite North in the sixteenth century. They did not penetrate into the White Sea but put up at the shore of Murmansk, where were located the "district of Kola" and the "Kola harbor." "Frenchmen, Danes, Netherlanders, Brabanters" and other merchantmen came there, and at Kola (around the 1560's) trade sprang up. This trade could have created competition for the English who controlled the mouth of the Northern Dvina. Moscow understood completely the importance of the Murmansk trade, and was ready to encourage it. But the intervention of the Danish-Norwegian government spoiled the arrangement.

The Danes considered as Norwegian all of Lapland. They accused the Russians of coercion and seizure, and themselves ravaged and blocked trade on the Kola Peninsula. "They fell as brigands upon the Germans·4 who were coming to us and to our state at Kola and at Kholmogory." The Kola "harbor" lost its security, and the Muscovite government was inclined to transfer all trade and all "German" traders to the Dvina where, of course, it would be more secure. Such a decision was bound to abolish the exclusive rights of the English to the Dvina havens, whether or not Moscow favored these rights. The general conditions of maritime trade demanded this, and in 1583 Moscow began to build a town on the Dvina at the Arkhangelsk Monastery, as a shelter for ships. An exchange center for all the overseas "Germans" was to be formed there. In the middle of these undertakings, Ivan the Terrible died.

The matter did not stop with his death. Tsar Fedor explained to the Danes (in 1586) that "we have now transferred trade from all the Pomorie⁵ and from our own patrimonies, the Dvina lands, from Kola, and from other places, and have established trade in one place — at the mouth of the river Dvina in the new town of Dvinsk, and trading people without exception from all your maritime states are allowed to go to that place, to the town of Dvinsk, with all sorts of goods."

The English who belonged to the "Muscovy Company" evidently were not informed of the motives which guided Moscow. It seemed to them that with the death of Ivan the well-spring of favors at the court of Moscow had run dry. The English ambassador, Sir Jerome Bowes, was severely angered by the fact that his treatment in Moscow changed upon the death of Tsar Ivan. The state secretary, Andrei Shchelkalov, maliciously pointed out to Bowes that "his English tsar had died," and Bowes was held under house arrest. The expression "English tsar" was, of course, highly improper. It hinted that the English who had been taken into the oprichnina were far too honored and intimate with Ivan, and that this favor had to end together with the oprichnina. As regards the confinement of Bowes and his staff within the walls of the ambassadorial compound, this was the usual precautionary measure taken by Moscow during an interregnum and was directed not only against the English. Bowes should not have been angry, but he could not restrain himself and saw in everything that occurred only evil tricks directed against him personally. He accused Nikita Romanovich [Yuriev] and Andrei Shchelkalov of being "self-styled tsars." They in turn became angry with Bowes. Sir Jerome was released from Moscow without special honors, and in the process he himself outraged the Moscow authorities by his rude complaints. An English witness exclaimed bitterly that "it would have been better had Bowes never come here at all!"

Boris alone appeared to Bowes as a protector in this deplorable misunderstanding. In the words of Bowes, only Boris was "a well-born and honorable courtier." He invariably rendered every respect to the envoy and "willingly would have done him more favors, but he did not have the power." Boris sent Bowes a farewell gift — brocade and sables — and informed him that he desired friendship and brotherhood between their sovereigns and between themselves. This was the beginning of Boris's relations with the English. Boris had immediately shown himself to be their friend, in contrast to other powerful grandees. He unfailingly retained his friendly manner in subsequent years. Through his agent, the Englishman [Sir Jerome] Horsey, Boris eased the displeasure evoked in England by Bowe's skirmishes and paved the way for friendly relations later. In 1586 the English were given a "charter of favor from the sovereign" or "privilege" whereby their right of duty-free trade was restored ("but they were not to bring others' goods with them nor to sell these goods in our states.").

Boris changed nothing in the general direction of Muscovite trade policy. The trade monopoly on the White Sea was not returned to the English. The "harbors" on the White Sea were divided among merchants of various nations and all could trade directly with Moscow. The advantage of the English was limited only to customs privileges. The charter of 1586 was reaffirmed in 1596 on the same basis. Thus the English could only long for the first blessed years of their operations in Muscovy when Ivan the Terrible had sanctioned their unusual privileges.

Boris Godunov was not about to abandon the interests of the state to English gain and profit. However, he was very gentle with the English. Ignorance of Russian customs and procedures sometimes led the English government into unnecessary "mistakes." For example, Elizabeth received the Muscovite emissary not at court but in the garden, which was called by the Muscovites "a kitchen garden." She sent Tsar Fedor unusually insignificant "remembrances." She long detained in England a Muscovite interpreter, a "young worker," and then dismissed him without a personal audience. All this evoked reproofs and complaints from Moscow, which never missed a single such opportunity to teach Elizabeth the necessary rules of diplomacy, according to Moscow's understanding of them.

English merchants and stewards swindled and cheated in their trade dealings, misused credit, quarrelled with the Muscovites, "wrangled" among themselves, and then complained to England, asking for relief and intercession. This behavior on the part of the English merchants stirred the Muscovite officials to protest and restraints. But Boris invariably brought all misunderstandings to a happy conclusion and arranged for the tsar to render various favors to the English. "[We] love you, our dear sister," Boris wrote to Elizabeth, and [you have] our honor and concern." It must be said that the English, who in general were dissatisfied with the rigidity of the Russian authorities in the question of the freedom of foreigners to trade with Muscovy, always acknowledged Boris's attention and kindness to them.

There is no need to linger over the relations of Muscovy with other Western states during the time of Boris Godunov. These were incidental and fragmentary. In such relations Moscow played a passive role. When Moscow was approached, usually it sought either opportunities to gain new allies against its long-time enemies, or to obtain new suppliers or buyers for its markets. Muscovite diplomats did not look beyond or higher than these goals. Yet they were able to comprehend these immediate aims and to achieve them through directness and persistence. The government in Moscow never lost its courage and will, although Muscovy had experienced a series of grave military and diplomatic setbacks, had lost conquests of many years standing, and had grown weak from domestic strife. The government displayed readiness to embark on new struggles immediately upon termination of old ones. It vigilantly observed and accurately appraised the internal difficulties of its neighbors and knew well when it was time to yield, and when it was time to strike the enemy. Though the Moscow policymakers did not master the art of converting instinct and alert daring into logical political procedure and principle, they did remain firm and consistent in their methods and operations. Thanks to its ingrained suspicion and caution, the government did not permit anyone to toy with it. These broad characteristics — boldness and activity, caution and perspicacity, consistency and independence — received due recognition from abroad. Moscow was cursed and sometimes ridiculed,

but it had to be reckoned with. As the chartmaker of
Muscovite foreign policy, Boris could boast that he had
compelled his neighbors to recognize the rebirth of Muscovite
political power after the defeats it had suffered.

III   RELATIONS WITH THE EAST, THE TURKS,
       TATARS, AND THE CAUCASUS. SIBERIA

In his relations with the Turko-Tatar peoples, Boris
Godunov's policies were a direct continuation of the policies
of Ivan the Terrible. Fate had placed the Russian nation in
tight contact with all the groups of Tatar tribes. As regards
Muscovy's relations with the European group of Tatars
during the time of tsars Fedor and Boris, the Muscovite
conquest of Kazan and Astrakhan served as the point of
departure. Having come down the Volga as far as the Caspian
littoral, and having seized the middle and lower Volga,
Moscow had once and for all liquidated Tatar rule in these
localities, and created a threat from Astrakhan to the Tatar
peoples of the Caucasian group.

The Turko-Tatar world could not react neutrally and
calmly to such political success on the part of Moscow. Ivan
had received claims and demands from the Turkish sultan and
the Crimean khan. Moscow was threatened with war and
retribution. From the Sea of Azov to the Don the Turks
assembled their forces to gain the "portage" of the Volga
(near present-day Tsaritsyn[6]), and to capture Astrakhan; but
this complex scheme failed. The Crimean Tatars had
threatened Moscow itself. Several attempts to reach the city
were made during the 1570's. Only once (in 1571) was the
enemy able to get as far as the Russian capital, to burn
settlements and kill many people. "The streets of Moscow

were filled from end to end with people slashed to pieces," according to Palitsyn's account. But the citadels of Moscow were not taken and the Tatars departed.

This was the most terrible attack on Moscow during the reign of Tsar Ivan. The other assaults did not pierce the southern borders to reach far into the state. Taught by bitter experience, Moscow strengthened greatly its southern boundaries and settled the "Wild Field"[7] along the southern borderlands. We shall relate later how systematic and real was this strengthening and settling of the South. It reached the point where Tatar attacks on Moscow itself were no longer feasible.

The Crimeans came close to reaching Moscow for the last time in 1591, but immediately fled in shameful disorder. They were met under the walls of Moscow by a whole army standing in a mobile field fortification, a "walking-citadel." It prevented the Tatars from reaching the walls of the city and itself threatened them with attack. The khan remained near Moscow less than twenty-four hours and then "fled" straight away home, not once turning aside for plunder. "He returned by the same road as he had come." Pursued by the Russians, only one third of the Tatars returned to the Crimea. The khan himself arrived in Bakhchisarai ignominiously — at night, wounded, and in a wagon. His left arm was seen in a sling.

Godunov transformed the repulse of the khan from Moscow into a mighty victory. Boris, himself sharing leadership of the army with Prince Fedor Ivanovich Mstislavsky, received an extraordinary reward — among other things, the Vaga region and the title "servant," which was considered "more honorable than boyar." Other commanders were abundantly rewarded. At the site of the "walking-citadel" the so-called "Donskoi" Monastery was established. Although a year later (in 1592) the Tatars

brutally plundered the Riazan and Tula lands, the over-all
character of relations with the Crimea remained in Moscow's
favor. Muscovy did not fear the Crimea. The Muscovite
government turned its back on that area and freely launched
undertakings against the other Tatars. Thus the Nogais[8] were
subjected to the rule of Moscow, admitting themselves that
they fell "under the will of the Muscovite sovereign, to whom
belong Astrakhan, the rivers Volga and Yaik, and also all the
Nogai horde." No less decisively, Moscow ventured to attack
the Tatars of the Caucasus, although at first stinging failure
awaited it there.

Access to the Caspian Sea gave Muscovy an opportunity
for direct relations with the Caucasian and Persian shores,
and with the Central Asian khanates. In the 1550's, at the
very time of the conquest of Kazan and Astrakhan,
operations of Muscovite detachments had begun in the
northern Caucasus. At that time the Kabardinians had
become dependent upon the Muscovite tsar. Georgia had
already turned to Moscow for aid. In 1567 the Russians built
a town on the river Terek — Fort Tersky. It was to serve as a
base of operations in Kabardia on behalf of the Kabardinian
Prince Temruik (whose daughter married Ivan the Terrible).
The town did not last, was abandoned, reappeared in 1578,
and again did not last. "The tsar, out of love for his brother
Selim-Sultan (of Turkey), ordered the voevoda and his people
to leave that town." The Turks jealously protected their
sphere of influence in the Caucasus. They not only demanded
that the tsar's people leave the Terek, but complained to the
tsar about free Muscovite Cossacks who "were roaming" and
"plundering" along the Terek. The Cossacks were there in
significant numbers and harassed all the local ruling princes
with their plundering and pillage.

But these free Cossacks on occasion also served the great

Muscovite sovereign and his allies, the Georgian rulers. For example, in summertime "they stood guard in the land of Tsar Alexander (of Kakhetia)[9], in the mountain passes against Shevkal (of Daghestan)." Therefore Moscow continued to deal with the Cossacks in its customary manner. It scolded them and referred to them as "brigands" in diplomatic relations with the Turks and with the Caucasian princelings. But Moscow did not in fact "expel" the Cossacks but prepared to use them for its own purposes of conquest and colonization.

Boris began diplomatic relations with the Caucasus and the Turks through negotiations concerning the Terek and the Terek Cossacks. "No Cossacks may live on the Terek; not one Cossack may remain on the Terek and on the Don at the Sea of Azov." The sovereign "shall order the town on the Terek to be swept away, and the voevoda and all his people to be removed." Muscovite emissaries made all of these promises. But the Muscovite officials did not intend to carry out any of them. On the contrary, the Muscovite government augmented its ties with the Christians of the Transcaucasus with a view to gaining a firm foothold in Georgia, where Muscovite, Turk, and Persian influences contended.

Evidently Boris intended to take advantage of the struggle between the Persians and the Turks for Persia. By aiding the Persians he intended first to weaken the Turks, then to deal with the Persians themselves. The intervention of Moscow in Caucasian affairs was formally justified by the fact that Orthodox Georgia had sought protection from Moscow against its enemies. In 1586 the "prince" or "tsar" Alexander of Kakhetia sent word to Moscow saying that he would be "happy to put himself and all of his land under the roof of the tsardom and under the hand of the tsar." Moscow answered that Tsar Fedor "wishes to take Prince Alexander under his tsarist hand and defense." Thenceforth the defense and strengthening of the route from Astrakhan to Georgia openly came under the care of the Moscow government. On the river Terek, besides the old hamlet "at the mouth of the Suncha River," a new town was built "at the mouth of the Terek." The garrison of this town was to guard the road from Russia to the Transcaucasus and, in addition, to prevent the Turks from crossing the Terek against the Persians.

The contacts that were begun with Georgia demonstrated that the closest enemy of Muscovy and Georgia was not so much the Turks themselves as the local Muslim ruler "Shevkal" or "Shamkal" of Tarki, whose domain in Daghestan closed the road from Astrakhan to Georgia. Twice Boris equipped an army against him. In 1593 the voevoda Andrei Ivanovich Khvorostinin was sent to see to it that "in the land of Shevkal" two towns were built and fortified. The first town, on the river Koisu, was completed; the second (further south, in Tarki) "was not allowed to be built." The Russian army was smashed, and upwards of 3,000 men were left behind on the battlefield. "The voevody themselves escaped together with their remaining men." In 1604 the attempt to gain a foothold in the land of Shevkal was repeated, but it ended even more sadly.

The voevoda Ivan Mikhailovich Buturlin conquered and occupied the town of Tarki. But in the spring of 1605 he was besieged by Turkish forces and Shevkal. Buturlin surrendered on the condition that he be allowed free return to Russia. However, the condition was not honored. The Russian detachment was massacred as soon as it left the fort. More than 7,000 men perished, and in their number was Buturlin himself. The civil strife that subsequently ensued in Moscow temporarily brought a stop to relations with the Caucasus. Both on the Terek and in Astrakhan "came a great

disturbance from the Cossack brigands," and Muscovy lost its
friends in the Northern Caucasus.

With respect to the Siberian Tatars the government of
Boris Godunov had to begin anew the task of subjugation
which had fallen into abeyance with the death of the
celebrated and "most shrewd ataman," Yermak. After the
death of Yermak, the Khanate of Siberia, which he had
seized, regained its independence. In August, 1584, the
Russians abandoned the town of Sibir, and the khans
returned to it. It seemed that the Cossacks' Siberian
adventure had passed without a trace. But Moscow decided
not to let Siberia escape its hands. In that same year, 1584,
the government communicated the following statement to
the Holy Roman Emperor. "The sovereign's people dwell in
Siberia. All the land of Siberia, Yugra, and the princes of
Pelym and Kondin, the Voguls and the Ostiaks, and along the
Ob, the great river, have prostrated themselves before the
sovereign and agreed to give him tribute — sables and black
foxes."

When Moscow learned that Siberia had been abandoned,
it decided to recover it. At the beginning of 1586 a
detachment was sent there. According to Muscovite custom,
a country was subdued by means of "towns," that is,
fortresses. Arriving there by the summer of 1586, the
voevody began to set up towns: on the river Tura, the town
of Tiumen; on the river Irtysh, Tobolsk. Tobolsk was located
near the town of Sibir. From Tobolsk the voevody "gained"
Sibir, seized the khan, Seidiak, and devastated his town
(1588). From then on (says the chronicle) "Tobolsk was the
oldest town and there was victory and conquest over the
accursed Bessermen. Instead of Sibir, Tobolsk was the ruling
town." For some time around this "capital town" of Tobolsk
there was a contest with the Tatars, who dreamed of driving
out the Russians.

But this struggle soon disclosed that the balance of
power had shifted finally to the side of the Russians. Russian
towns sprang up almost yearly. At important strategic points
along the route to Siberia stood Pelym (1593), Fort Narym
(1596), Fort Ket (1596), Verkhoturie (1598), Fort Turin
(1600), and Tomsk (1604). North of the main route of
Siberian colonization materialized at that time the towns of
Berezov (1593), Obdorsk (1593), and Mangazeia (1601).
Moscow guarded its new colony, the Khanate of Siberia,
from foreign exploitation. When the English requested
permission to go by sea to the Pechora and the Ob (1584),
the Muscovite officials answered: "There are no harbors in
those places, and it will not be worthwhile to anchor there.
There live only sables and gerfalcons. Such valuable wares
would go to the English land. How could our government get
along without them?" This rhetorical question explains best
what Muscovy valued and sought in Siberia.

IV   THE QUESTION OF THE
        MOSCOW PATRIARCHATE

Relations with the Orthodox East occupied a special place in
Boris's policy. The Muscovite authorities firmly upheld the
"chief idea of that age, that the Russian tsardom, the
only independent Orthodox realm, must replace the fallen Byzantine Empire" (in the words of K.N. Bestuzhev-
Riumin). Fancying itself to be the "New Israel," in which
the true faith and piety were preserved, the Muscovite
secular officials acted both for themselves and for the Muscovite church and hierarchy in relations with the Orthodox
churches of the East.

The tsar, and not the metropolitan of Moscow, wrote letters to the Eastern patriarchs. The tsar permitted the representatives of the Greek clergy entry into his state and into his capital. The tsar displayed charity to the Greek churches and clergy. The tsar interceded for the Greeks with the Turkish authorities. As soon as they stepped upon the soil of Muscovy, the Greeks immediately became subject to the fullness of the power of the Muscovite monarch in whatever affairs that might interest them. They therefore looked habitually upon His Tsarist Majesty as the sole well-spring of charity and favor. They promised to pray to God for him day and night "in order that he perform daily good and worthy deeds, for he is disposed so to do."

The internal state of the Muscovite church, its relations with the temporal authorities, and the degree of its independence and autonomy, remained unclear to the Greeks. They had neither the opportunity nor the need to delve into this side of Muscovite life. Official meetings with the Muscovite hierarchy exhausted the entire range of necessary contact with the local ecclesiastical community. Therefore, the Greeks were everywhere confronted by a state secretary or some other official of state service acting in the tsar's name.

The question of the establishment of a patriarchate in Moscow was raised, discussed, and decided under conditions such as these. This issue, which might seem to be purely ecclesiastical and canonical, became largely political in nature and was construed by contemporaries to be the first important political success of Boris Godunov. "This establishment of the patriarchate was the origin of his pride," noted Ivan Timofeev. The role of the secular authorities in the matter of the patriarchate even has caused several historians completely to lose sight of the ecclesiastical and

historical significance of the event. Thus N. I. Kostomarov
ventured that "in internal affairs Boris had his own personal
ends in mind. He always did that which would bring
brilliance and prestige to his government. The transformation
which he brought about in the ecclesiastical hierarchy had
just such a purpose. Boris had the idea of establishing a
patriarchate in Muscovy."

Several other historians (even Karamzin) were inclined
to construe Godunov's active role in the establishment of the
patriarchate as a self-interested design to further his personal
political career. Such a view of the affair is, of course,
unacceptable to the serious investigator acquainted with the
basic currents of Muscovite social thought in the sixteenth
century. Not only Boris but all those high in Muscovite
society dreamed of the establishment of a patriarchal see in
Moscow. The vision, created in Byzantium, of a single
Orthodox Christian state led to this dream. The ideal
demanded that tsarist and patriarchal honor be inseparable,
each one supporting the other. This ideal did not take
immediate hold in Russia. Tsarist authority, created during
the reign of Ivan the Terrible, had not been crowned by a
patriarch. In theory it should have been so crowned, and that
is why a patriarch was desired in Russia. The initiative and
authority in this affair lay, therefore, with the tsar.

Professor A. Ya. Shpakov, one of the more recent
investigators of the establishment of the Moscow
patriarchate, has noted the predominance of the offices of
secular authority in dealings with the Greek clergy
concerning the patriarchate. However, he did not deny the
national and ecclesiastical significance of the establishment of
the patriarchate. In negotiations with the Greek hierarchy
Boris appeared as a clever and winning representative of the
Moscow government. By no means did he act on his own or

for himself, but for all the Muscovite tsardom and for all the people of the "New Israel."

Tsar Fedor had inherited from his father the desire to have a patriarch by his side. During the reign of Ivan the Terrible the idea had matured that once the Muscovite sovereign had assumed the Greek role as "Tsar for all Orthodoxy," he ought also to have next to him a patriarch, as had the Byzantine emperor. In the words of Professor Shpakov, "the flourishing state and high position of our church, and its relationship to the patriarch of Constantinople, made the establishment of the patriarchate inevitable." It remained merely to find a pretext to raise the matter.

Such a pretext appeared in 1586 when the patriarch of Antioch, Joachim, came to Moscow. This was the first visit to Muscovy of an Eastern patriarch. Until that time only lower-ranking Greek hierarchs had been there. The Greeks in Moscow sought subsidies (or, as was said then, "alms"), and also intercession with the Turkish authorities. Joachim was seeking the same. This high-ranking guest was received solemnly in Moscow. He was honored with "audiences," presented with gifts, and given a week's rest from his long journey in the palace of Fedor Ivanovich Sheremetev. There, however, he was surrounded by "attendants" and kept in complete isolation, as was customary. The tsar received the patriarch with the most "solemn" ceremony. The honored guest was brought to the Kremlin seated in the ceremonial sleigh of the metropolitan, despite the fact that it was summer (June 25). After the tsar's reception, a meeting with the patriarch and the Muscovite Metropolitan Dionisi took place in the Cathedral of the Dormition of Our Lady, the *Uspensky Sobor*.

During this meeting the patriarch experienced an

unpleasant moment. In violation of accepted Eastern
protocol the metropolitan, upon meeting his guest who was
vested in the robes of his high office, blessed him first, not
waiting to receive the patriarchal blessing. Joachim protested
and, according to an official Moscow record, "said simply
that it would have been more seemly had the metropolitan
received blessing from him first, and then ceased to speak
further of it." The humble suppliant did not dare to instruct
his benefactors and accepted the role that his patrons gave
him. In return he was quickly supplied with the tsar's alms
and gently sent home.

No precise official testimonies have been preserved of
the negotiations with Joachim concerning the establishment
of a patriarchate in Moscow. In their later records and
speeches Muscovite officials were contradictory in their
recollections of what was actually said and done in this
matter. Tsar Fedor allegedly spoke secretly with his wife and
closest boyars about establishing a patriarchate, and
communicated his ideas to Patriarch Joachim through Boris.
The patriarch then "promised to consult with all the
patriarchs, archbishops, and bishops — with all the Holy
Council." What was actually agreed between Boris and the
patriarch cannot be ascertained in the absence of records. But
if Joachim promised anything at all to Boris, he did not live
up to Moscow's hopes and aspirations. Evidently Moscow had
clung fast to the hope that through Joachim the cause of the
patriarchate would gain support in the East. For this reason a
Muscovite herald was sent along with Joachim to consult
with the other patriarchs. Secretly this agent was to request
that the patriarchs establish a patriarchate in Moscow.
Nonetheless, no answer was forthcoming, for the East was
not anxious to fulfill the wishes of the Muscovite sovereign.

Yet the East wanted and needed Muscovite alms. That is

why in 1588 Jeremiah, patriarch of Constantinople, suddenly
appeared in Russia (but not, perhaps, without some
connection with the question of the patriarchate). Moscow
expected letters and ambassadors from the East, whereas a
patriarch came in person, and not one of the lower-ranking
ones, but the presiding patriarch of the East. Muscovite
politicians, of course, remembered that in 1561, when the
ecumenical patriarch had sanctioned the title of "tsar" for
the Muscovite grand prince, he had written that the
coronation of the tsar is the exclusive right of two patriarchs
only, the patriarch of Rome and the patriarch of
Constintinople (and because of the apostasy of the former,
this right belonged to the patriarch of Constantinople
alone). [10] And now this especially competent ecclesiastical
personage had himself come to Muscovy.

It was natural to suppose that such a rare and
unprecedented event would signify a new phase in the cause
of the Moscow patriarchate. The ecumenical patriarch, it was
thought, would establish a patriarchate in Moscow more
quickly than would anyone else. Despatching his emissaries
to meet Patriarch Jeremiah, the tsar ordered them above all
else to find out from the patriarch and his suite "by which
custom and with what is he coming to the tsar?" "Has he
come with the agreement of all the patriarchs, and does he
have with him some order for the sovereign from all the
patriarchs?"

Trying to ascertain the reason for the patriarch's visit,
the Muscovites also attempted to determine the legality of
Jeremiah himself, to find out if he was truly patriarch.
"Where is Theoliptos, who was patriarch before this one
(Jeremiah)? When Jeremiah returns to Tsargorod
[Constantinople] will he still be patriarch, or will
Theoliptos?" The Muscovites conjectured that Theoliptos,

Jeremiah's predecessor, had not died but had "gone off"
somewhere. They wished to learn what had happened to him
(he had been dethroned by the Sultan), and whether
Jeremiah was firmly established in his place. Thus, excited by
the arrival of an important and indispensable guest and
expecting substantial benefits from him, the Muscovites
hurried to find out to what extent he could be believed.

Evidently the findings of the investigations were
satisfactory, and Jeremiah was received in Moscow as the
authentic ecumenical patriarch, with much respect. But
expectations were not fulfilled and hopes were not realized.
It turned out that Jeremiah brought with him no decision
concerning the question of a patriarchate. He only requested
"alms" and reported political news from the East and from
Lithuania, through which he had passed.

Then in Moscow a plan matured whose executor, if not
creator, was Boris Godunov. The plan was not to allow
Jeremiah to leave Moscow without some sort of a decision
concerning the establishment of a patriarchate there. It was
decided to persuade the ecumenical patriarch either to place
a patriarch in Russia on his own initiative, or to pursue this matter
at the Ecumenical Council which was to be convened upon
his return to his homeland. Adroitly flattering him, they
prepared him for compliance and agreement. As soon as the
first signs of compliance appeared, Boris himself came
regularly to the patriarch's Moscow residence to talk secretly
with him. Jeremiah's travelling companions, the Greeks who
comprised his suite, remarked with bitterness that apparently
"the patriarch had a disposition never to listen to advice from
anyone, even from those devoted to him." That is why "he
suffered much, and also the church during his days."

Being presumptuous in his discussions with the clever
Muscovites, Jeremiah spoke too freely. He well understood

that he could not personally create a Moscow patriarchate; but, desiring to please Moscow and to remain on cordial terms there, he thought to solve the problem by remaining in Moscow himself as patriarch. "If they wish, I shall remain here as patriarch," he commented to one of his Greek companions, Metropolitan Herotheus. Herotheus retorted sharply that this was not possible. "You do not know the customs of this country. Things are done differently here. The Russians do not wish you for their patriarch. Take care that you do not bring shame upon yourself."

But the patriarch remained deaf to all objections and warnings. Even in conversations with the Muscovite attendants he expressed his readiness to remain — and therein he was trapped. According to Professor Shpakov, "from the moment of his pronouncement 'I am staying,' the negotiations quickly moved forward, and we can find an official description of this in Russian memorials." Boris Godunov received the tsar's order "to counsel with the patriarch and see if it be possible that he remain in his state, in the Russian tsardom, in the capital town of Vladimir." Having received a general expression of agreement from Jeremiah, the Muscovites cleverly desired that he agree to live not in Moscow, but in Vladimir.

Shabby Vladimir frightened Jeremiah. He had in mind Moscow, the glittering palace of the Muscovite tsar, and the splendid "rank" of the metropolitan's court in the Kremlin (the future patriarch's court). Instead, the tsar proposed to him a town with three or four hundred houses and a crumbled, desolate and neglected fortress on the high banks of the quiet Kliazma River. One of Jeremiah's companions said of Vladimir that it was "worse than Kukuz," the little Armenian town where St. John Crysostom had been confined. Understandably, the patriarch refused. He answered Boris as follows: "I will not reject remaining in His Majesty's realm. But it is not possible for me to be in Volodimer [Vladimir]. Patriarchs always remain with the sovereign. What sort of patriarchate is it where the patriarch does not live with the sovereign? Under such conditions I can in no wise stay here!"

The Muscovites also understood that patriarchs always remain with their sovereigns. If they intended for Jeremiah to live in Vladimir, then it was only to get him off their hands. The Greek, not understanding Russian and having come uninvited to Moscow, presented no great fascination to Moscow, especially while there was another living patriarch of Constantinople (Theoliptos) whose fate was unknown. Jeremiah had done what was required of him. He had agreed in principle to the establishment of a patriarchate in Moscow — and he could leave. Cleverly Boris had led him to refuse to settle in Vladimir, and had taken the matter even further. At a church council Tsar Fedor publicly expressed regret that Jeremiah had refused Vladimir and had desired instead to live in Moscow. The tsar said: "And this cannot come to pass! But how could we do more? How could we separate. . .Most Reverend Job, Metropolitan of All Russia, from [the churches of] the Immaculate Virgin and the great saints [that is, from Moscow] and replace him with a Greek patriarch? He does not know our customs and language, and cannot speak to us of spiritual things except through an interpreter."

Only one alternative remained: "to take counsel" with the patriarch and request that he make Metropolitan Job patriarch of Moscow. Boris Godunov and the ambassadorial state secretary Andrei Shchelkalov "took counsel" with Jeremiah so persistently that it appeared to the Greeks to be a demand. The patriarch, who had hastily and thoughtlessly admitted the possibility of a Greek patriarch in Moscow, reluctantly agreed to a native patriarch and begged leave to go home.

There remained the ceremonial part of the matter. Jeremiah pointed out the necessity of selecting a patriarch by a church council. A church council was convened in January 1589, and consisted of the highest level of the Russian hierarchy. Only then, six months after the arrival of Jeremiah in Russia, did the Muscovite clergy join the cause of the establishment in Russia of a patriarchate and enter into contact with the visiting Greek hierarchs. By order of the tsar the council selected three candidates each for the patriarchate and for the two newly-established metropolitanates of Novgorod and Rostov. From the three candidates for the patriarchate the tsar, of course, chose Job. Moscow requested from Jeremiah the Greek rite of investiture and changed it, making it more solemn. Then the celebration of the nomination and installation of the new hierarchs began, with the participation of Jeremiah and his suite. On January 26, 1589, Moscow finally received a patriarch. Job was solemnly consecrated in the Cathedral of the Dormition.

The matter was done; it remained to formulate it in writing. Jeremiah was detained in Moscow until the solemn charter of the establishment of the Moscow patriarchate was prepared. The ecumenical patriarch signed this charter together with the Russian hierarchs and three of his own suite (a Greek metropolitan, archbishop, and archimandrite). Then, graciously, the Greeks were allowed to depart for home (in May 1589) with the stipulation that they formally register in the council of the Eastern churches the act that they had completed in Moscow.

Jeremiah reached Constantinople only a year later (in the spring of 1590) and immediately convened a council of the highest ranking Eastern hierarchs. The council began to consider the propriety of Jeremiah's acts in Moscow and, of course, not everyone recognized them as canonically correct. Nonetheless, the Moscow patriarchate was recognized by the council and the patriarch of Moscow was assigned fifth place among the Orthodox patriarchs. A letter informing Moscow of this action was sent from the council. The Muscovites were offended. They wished at least third place for their patriarch, for Moscow had become the third tsardom after the old Rome and the new Rome (Byzantium). But the East would not yield.

At a second council early in 1593, in Constantinople and in the presence of the Muscovite emissary, state secretary Grigori Afanasiev, the question was re-examined. The matter was left unchanged chiefly as a result of the influence of the learned patriarch of Alexandria, Meleti Pegas. But Moscow persisted. The Muscovites defied the council of 1593 and stubbornly continued to consider their patriarch third — below the patriarchs of Constantinople and Alexandria and above the patriarchs of Antioch and Jerusalem.

Moscow placed extraordinary value on its success in the matter of the patriarchate and celebrated, among other things, the fact that it had raised its many bishoprics in the hierarchy. To the two metropolitanates (Novgorod and Rostov) were added two more — Kazan and Krutity, the latter in Moscow itself. Six archbishoprics and six new bishoprics were established. Thus the Muscovite hierarchy grew. Metropolitan Herotheus, the learned Greek who had critically observed Muscovite ecclesiastical events, attributed all this flowering to the energy and abilities of Boris Godunov. "Tsar Fedor," he wrote, "was a humble man, simple and pacific, and in all things similar to the young Emperor Theodosius. But the tsar's brother-in-law, Boris by name, was in all things able, intelligent and cunning. He managed everything and everyone obeyed him."

V   THE CONSEQUENCES OF BORIS'S FOREIGN POLICY

Men of that time generally ascribed the leadership of Muscovite foreign policy to Boris. The achievements of this policy must also be credited to his account. According to the circumstances of the time, the direction of Moscow's foreign policy was aimed toward softening the grave effects of Ivan the Terrible's wars, causing the defeats and failures suffered by Muscovy to be forgotten, and restoring its lost international position.

Boris was successful in doing much toward the revival of Moscow's international political power. The victim that Batory envisioned slipped from the mesh of Catholic policy and, instead of further subjugation thereto, began itself to threaten the Commonwealth with aggressive action. Taking advantage of the weakness of the new monarch of the Commonwealth and of the internal disorder of Sweden, Moscow openly attacked Sweden and regained by force of arms the lands that Ivan had forfeited. As concerns the improvement of its trade, Moscow carried out a number of steps along its northern seacoast. These measures were directed toward the organization to Muscovy's advantage of the trade exchange that had grown up there. These actions annulled the exclusive privileges given by Ivan to the English trading company. In the East and South Moscow continued to exploit the military and colonial successes gained through the subjugation of Astrakhan and Kazan.

The movement into Siberia and into the Northern Caucasus was a direct consequence of these gains. This

advance was not accomplished without some setbacks and
losses, but in general it was a movement forward which was
not interrupted by frequent failures and which did not
undermine the gains already made. Moscow displayed no fear
of Turkey and the Crimea. It was reaching out for Georgia
and subduing the Nogai tribes and the Siberian Tatars. It
rendered assistance and support to the Greek hierarchy,
which was subject to the Sultan. From that hierarchy it
demanded recognition of its spiritual primacy, openly
declaring itself the inheritor of the Byzantine Empire and
claiming the formation of a patriarchate in Moscow.

In all manifestations of Muscovite political life, and in all
relations with Europe and the East, Boris's reign generated an
upsurge of executive energy and a rebirth of political power.
It may be said that he gained his ends, and compelled his
neighbors to regard Muscovy as they had during the best
years of the reign of Ivan the Terrible.

The foreign policy of Boris Godunov therefore may be
termed successful. Not so his domestic policy. However great
Boris's administrative talent may have been, it was
insufficient to save him from ruin. The complexity of the
internal crisis with which Boris had to deal proved as
invincible for this practical statesman as it seems inscrutable
to the inquiring historian.

VI   BORIS'S DOMESTIC POLICY. THE "RE-
     MOVAL" OF PEASANTS AND THE SHIFT
     OF THE LABOR FORCE TO THE OUT-
     LYING DISTRICTS OF MUSCOVY. THE
     "EMPTY LANDS" AND THE ECONOMIC
     DECLINE OF THE CENTRAL LANDS. THE
     LANDOWNER'S SEARCH FOR WORKERS

Muscovite society at the close of the sixteenth century had
been shaken to the roots by the crisis of the time of Ivan the
Terrible. Several aspects of this crisis are already known to
us. The system of terror directed by Ivan against the
hereditary aristocracy, "the princes," destroyed not only
them but also the whole social structure of the central
Moscow regions. It was not just the princes who had been
torn from their old dwelling places by the oprichnina, and
scattered about the borderlands of the state. The whole mass
of people connected with the oprichnina, all of the
land-owning class of princes and fallen boyar aristocracy also
had been set adrift. The "lord-prince" or "lord-boyar" (as he
was then called) disappeared — and with him his "court,"
that is, his "servitors," his "servants," his "people," his
"slaves." In a word, the entire clutch of persons with whom
the lord served, ruled, and operated his patrimony, vanished.
The more fortunate servitors followed their lord to his new
place of residence; the less fortunate perished with their lord
or were set free from his service and condemned to vagrancy.
     In Muscovite custom, when the sovereign's disgrace
befell a lord, not only was his estate confiscated, but also his
documents — his "letters and deeds of purchase." These
bonds ceased to have any effect, the obligations lost their

force, and the serfs, "the servants of the disgraced boyars,"
received their freedom, sometimes with a prohibition to enter
any other household. They were thereby doomed to hunger
and usually they fled to the southern borderland. There, by
the end of the sixteenth century, they had formed a large
"assemblage of miscreants," according to the expression of
that vivid writer of the time, Avraami Palitsyn.

Furthermore, with the destruction of a large boyar or
princely household, its patrimonial economy was also
destroyed. A princely or boyar patrimony that had been
taken into the oprichnina was usually broken up and
distributed as pomestie estates. Such a patrimony was split
into small portions and came under the control of petty
pomeshchiki[11] with whom the peasant had a harder life than
with a boyar or prince.

With the latter the peasants of large patrimonies enjoyed
the benefits of communal organization and self-government,
comparative economic prosperity, and the legal protection of
an influential master. Petty pomeshchiki could not provide
such protection by virtue of their insignificant social
position. Because of their precarious situation, they squeezed
the peasants more than did rich landowners. And peasant
self-government was unthinkable on a pomestie with five, ten
or fifteen peasant households all managed directly by the
pomeshchik.

The pomeshchik himself, and not an elected peasant
"elder" [starosta], collected state taxes from the peasants
along with his own private quit-rents. Taking upon himself
the functions of those who formerly had been elected by the
peasant "mir" [commune], the pomeshchik naturally turned
these functions into one means of binding the peasants under
him. It is understandable that such a change was looked upon
by the peasants as a loss of civil autonomy, as "enserfment"

and "bondage," which were intolerable. The ruined and deprived peasant "could not endure" his situation. He attempted to escape — legally or illegally — from the old but now hateful "hearth" to new and happier places.

This same feeling and desire for flight also must have possessed the peasants on the crown domains, the "sovereign's," "palace," and "black lands."[12] Here they fell directly under the sovereign, and were caught in the process of distribution of pomestie estates. Here, too, the pomestie with its distressing dependence of the peasant on the pomeshchik drove the working populace away from the yoke of serfdom toward lands where the old and customary relationships remained legally in force.

In this manner was generated a general "exodus" of peasants and enserfed people, and slaves, from Muscovy's core area. The "exodus" was one of the consequences of the revision of landownership through the oprichnina and of mass distribution of pomestie estates in the central regions of Muscovy. The authorities noticed this exodus in the 1570's and thought to explain it by "pestilential infection," "crop failure," "ravages by Tatars," and "operations of the oprichnina." But these were all contributing factors. The chief cause lay in the fact that the working population was losing its personal freedom and with it the customary privilege of using and disposing the lands on which it lived and worked.

The Muscovite officials were actively engaged in consolidating the conquests of Ivan the Terrible. In the conquered lands of the former Khanate of Kazan, numerous towns with garrisons were organized and service landowners settled there. Along with them, by grant of the sovereign, monastery patrimonies also sprang up in the new lands. Monastic landownership required peasant labor no less than the new towns required military and industrial personnel. Abandoning their old nests on the upper Volga and the upper Oka, peasants and slaves knew well where they might go. The government itself was calling on these "migrants from the Upper Reaches" to settle the new towns and the fortified border "line" in the Lower Reaches (along the Volga) and in the "Wild Field" (to the south of the middle Oka in the black-soil region). The new areas lured settlers by their wide-open spaces, attractive climate, and richness of soil, forests, and rivers. Some of the measures employed by the central authorities drove, as it were, the people away from the state's axial regions. Apparently other actions by the authorities also drew the people into the borderlands, which were tempting enough already without any invitations from the government.

Finding a new way of life, the settlers did not always remain in the towns and on the land. They pushed further on beyond the "line" in search of "new lands" in the "Wild Field." There they "lived like Cossacks," beyond the reach of the state. Free colonization outstripped official colonization. It created an array of Cossack freemen, dangerous to state order, just beyond its borders. A contemporary, Avraami Palitsyn, said sternly that Ivan and his disciple Boris had encouraged this liberty-seeking colonization of the South. "Following the manner and style of Tsar Ivan Vasilievich, Tsar Boris filled the borderlands with the military and built there strong fortresses and towns against the enemy. . .and the snake who should be put to death for his crimes, if he escape to these towns, will there escape death." In the words of Palitsyn, Tsar Ivan had kept these "criminal snakes" in fear through his "wit and cruelty;" Tsar Fedor, "through prayer." But during Boris's reign these "snakes" began to band against the state, and "more than twenty thousand such

brigands" gathered in the borderlands. A real danger to
Muscovy burgeoned through migration of unfortunate and
discontented peasants who found a life for themselves
beyond the boundaries of the realm.

The exodus of crowds of peasants and slaves from their
former hearths was accompanied by striking consequences
not merely in the borderlands whither they wandered, but
also in the centers which they had abandoned. In these latter
areas a severe economic crisis emerged because of a shortage
of labor, and a fierce struggle for workers ensued. The loss of
peasants brought on economic desolation. Land registers of
the sixteenth century mentioned a great many "wastelands"
— empty patrimonies grown over by forest; villages
abandoned by the population, churches "without
singing;"[13] deserted, overgrown lands standing idle. In some
places the departed proprietors were yet remembered, and
the wastelands still bore their names. In others the lords had
passed from memory, and "there is no one to find their
names."

The estates of the petty service people were usually
completely ruined. The holder of a small pomestie found no
wherewithal to support his service and "nothing to look
forward to." He himself went "to wander from household to
household," that is, to live by begging, and willed his
deserted estate to the mercy of fate. But large and important
landholders, both lay and monastic, enjoyed greater
economic stability. The legal tax privileges which they
usually enjoyed attracted workers to their lands. The muzhik
knew well the advantages of working for these landowners.
Besides, a chance to preserve the peasant "mir" and an
opportunity for a measure of self-government bound the
peasants to these large estates.

Finally, it was not so easy for a peasant to leave a large landlord. The men who supervised the large patrimonies had experience, influence, and means enough to retain not only their own peasants, but as well "to call" still others to the estate from elsewhere. While ruin threatened the petty proprietors, the large and aristocratic landlords held their own and even sought to buy up deserted and depopulated lands and to restore them. The mighty landowners had well-tried methods for preserving their own estates and for establishing new ones. In the first place, they resorted to the transfer of other peasants to their own lands. Secondly, these lords devised various forms of economic enslavement for their own peasants as well as for any other "working" people within their economic grasp.

The "transfer" of peasants became a social calamity by the end of the sixteenth century. The Muscovite law codes [of 1497 and 1550] decreed that "peasants are prohibited from renouncing, that is, moving from district to district and from village to village except at one period of time during the year: in autumn, from a week before St. George's Day [November 26] through the week following St. George's Day." Late every year during this period, a peculiar campaign of "renunciations" began. Special agents, or "renunciators" [otkazchiki] were sent out by the rich landowners. These agents would appear on the estates of other landowners, and luring the peasants to leave, would "renounce" them and "transfer" them to the estates of their own principals and proprietors. But the peasants were not released from their places easily and without struggle. According to V. O. Kliuchevsky, "in the second half of the sixteenth century 'renunciators' often complained that peasants who had renounced were not allowed to leave, that they were held in irons. The landowners, though agreeing to removal, would plunder the property of the peasants and impose on them inflated exit-fees."

But if those who lost peasants committed willful acts of violence, those who removed the peasants behaved no better. The "renunciators" enticed and transferred not only those peasants who had a right to leave, but indiscriminately took all peasants whom they could extract from other proprietors. In the process they operated "violently," in flagrant violation of government decrees and private interests. The "exodus" of the peasants, therefore, usually took place "amidst quarrels, fights and violence which were repeated every year in November and which filled the courts with captious lawsuits" (the words of V. O. Kliuchevsky). The endless "violence" caused the government to become concerned. At the time of Ivan the Terrible certain steps, not exactly known to us, were taken with reference to the removal of peasants, and some sort of "code" was issued which provided that peasants were not to be removed by force, or that during certain "forbidden years" peasants were not to be removed at all.

These periods were precisely defined in advance by the government. What sort of a "code" this was is difficult to say. But in any case the Muscovite government under Ivan had already found it necessary to intervene in the matter of transferring peasants in order to protect its own interests as well as those of the petty service landed gentry. The migration of peasants subject to taxes deprived the government of regular revenue and the landowner of a lawful income and service on the deserted land.

If by means of "renunciation" and "removal" landowners managed to replenish their work force, other measures allowed them to bind permanently the workers they had obtained. These steps usually amounted to the economic enslavement of the peasant. Many methods were available to accomplish this. Though by law the rates of peasant land rents were not tied to the other liabilities of the peasants, severing those rent payments by "exodus" naturally liquidated other monetary accounts that the peasant had with the landowner. The proprietor would not release a peasant without a final settlement, and the more the peasant was obligated, the more firmly he was bound to remain on the land. That is why the landowners were very willing to give their peasants economic assistance — "loan money" — and to lend them "silver," that is, to give them tools and grain for planting and for sustenance, or simply money on credit.

Although neither loan money nor silver involved "debt servitude," that is, turned a peasant into a slave, they nevertheless furnished good pretexts for arbitrary detention of a peasant. The loans weighed upon the consciousness of the indebted farmer, morally obligating him to remain with the lord who had helped him in time of need. The extraordinary development of peasant indebtedness in the second half of the sixteenth century is attested in many documents, and it is explained by the fact that extending credit to peasants was useful and convenient for the landowners.

A peasant's debts did not by themselves make of him a slave, though in fact they bound him to the landowners. In order to become a slave, that is, to lose civil autonomy and become unfree, a peasant had to sell himself formally. "To sell himself from off the field to someone into full slavery," read the Code of Laws. In many instances this actually happened. In the registry books of service bondage of the sixteenth century, one can read dozens of entries showing that poor landless peasants and the children of peasants were entering debt bondage. In the pursuit of workers the landowners were happy to take "into the peasantry" or "into the household," into slavery, anyone who offered his labor or waived his freedom. It was necessary only to decide in a given instance whether there was greater advantage in placing a newcomer on the land "in the peasantry," or in taking him into bondage and making him a slave. A worker could be an independent tax-payer on a peasant "plot." Him it was better to place on the land with the other peasants, advancing him a loan, or silver. Another, because of his youth and weakness, would not be placed on the land; it was more worthwhile to make him a debt-slave.

From the registry books it may be seen that the majority of those who entered bondage were single and homeless persons, orphans and vagrant peasant youth. They as yet had no part in the running of the peasant household, but they were useful as household servants and day laborers. In other cases the workers themselves actually preferred service "in the household" to work in the fields. Thus, for example, a landless peasant and a wandering skilled worker, a tailor or cobbler, might find it more comfortable and pleasant in household service than living in his present impoverished state or maintaining a poor itinerant trade.

Such were roughly the conditions which created bondage or slavery. These conditions contributed to the binding to the landowners of landless elements of the peasant community, those who were more mobile, even vagrant. While diverting people from land cultivation and from paying state taxes, bondage did not remove them from the landlord's husbandry. Therein lay the advantage of bondage to both sides. The slave was relieved of the burden of paying taxes, while his "sovereign" owner secured for himself a stable work force.

Cases did arise, however, when this work force was willing for household service but had no desire for formal serfdom. The itinerant peasant might seek work and shelter but not feel the need to sell himself completely. He would agree to private service, but without bondage. He was willing to be a "slave," but a "voluntary" or "free" one, with the option to leave whenever he wished. For want of workers in general the landlords gladly kept such "voluntary" servants.

From the governments's point of view, "free slaves" were undesirable. They were not firm in their loyalty to their lords, for they could forsake them with impunity. They were of no use to the state, for they neither served it nor paid taxes. They were a bother to the administration because of their elusiveness. Persons escaping from the tsar's service could easily hide among them. These escapees could then avoid paying taxes and "pledge themselves" to influential lords in order to avoid responsibility for offences and crimes.

Muscovite officialdom did not encourage the "voluntary" service of a laborer without executed deeds of enserfment. Many times the government censured whoever "believed the volunteer and retained him without securing him as a serf." "Free" service and work, nonetheless, continued to exist in various forms. Under the names "mortgagors," "depositors," "housekeepers," or "free slaves," servants without deeds of enserfment lived and worked freely on patrimonies and in urban households. They were considered outside the law and embarrassed the Muscovite administration, which sometimes simply did not know what to do with them. For example, during the census of the population of the town of Zaraisk up to 200 "mortgagors" were detected who neither served nor paid state taxes. The "scribes" were puzzled and wrote their superiors as follows: "Altogether, of house servants, skilled

persons, and all those who live in servants' quarters, but make
their living by begging and hiring themselves out, there are
198 souls. And henceforth how does the Sovereign Tsar and
Grand Prince of All Russia, Boris Fedorovich, wish us to
deal with these people?"

VII   ADMINISTRATIVE MEASURES – PEASANTRY, SLAVES, AND FUGITIVES

By the time of Boris's rule a series of grave problems had
appeared in Muscovite society. These demanded
extraordinary attention and active intervention on the part of
the government. The exodus of the working populace from
the heartland of Muscovy to the borderlands created a crisis
in land tenure. Petty landholders who lived only by the labor
of the peasants under them were brought to utter ruin by the
flight of the people. Many hardships and complications fell to
the larger and more well-to-do landowners as well. Concern
for the need to hold the work force in the emptying lands
produced a struggle among landowners for workers, and led
to the desperate "renunciation" and "removal" of peasants
by landowners from one area to another. In the struggle for
peasants the landlords resorted to all sorts of contrivances
and to infractions of the law. Open violence and evasion of
the law gave the advantage in the struggle to the rich and the
powerful. Petty proprietors lost their peasants. But through
enserfment to the rich, the peasants lost their civil rights.
They "departed" from the peasantry and became "bonds-
men," slaves.

Together with formal enslavement flourished, a
"voluntary" slavery beyond all government control which
deprived the state of much service and tax income while

diverting taxpayers into illegal private vassalage. To this disorderly state of affairs still· a further evil was added. Fugitives living in the "Wild Field" gradually gathered into sizeable Cossack bands and filled the authorities with misgiving and alarm by their "brigand-like" inclinations. Boris was confronted by a drastic need to regularize the relationships of the peasants and slaves to their "lords," the landowners, and to the state. What would be the government's attitude toward the problem of the great and petty landowners both in the matter of peasants and of general land relationships where the decline and desolation of pomestie estates and the excessive growth of church ownership of land in comparison to secular ownership had become serious? Such was the setting in which Boris must act.

It would be grievously mistaken to imagine that Boris's government grasped the course and significance of the social crisis with the same force that historical science understands it today. At that time it was easy enough to become confused in the maze of complexities and multi-faceted social relationships and clashes. A cautious, indecisive and timid approach to the solution of the vexing economic and legal problems was unavoidable. The government must observe the movement of interrelationships among classes, guard the weak and defend the downtrodden. Yet it must safeguard state interests when social disorder threatened them. The latter problem was considered the most important. For the most part, it dominated the consciousness of the government and determined official policy in social affairs and with respect to the landowners' pursuit of a work force. In general, this struggle was leading to the ruin of small service landholding, to the personal enslavement of peasants, and to the development of serfdom. All of this was disadvantageous to the government for it deprived the state of taxpayers and service people. The indebted and enslaved peasant ceased to pay his taxes; therefore the government was prepared to come to the defense of his civil autonomy to preserve him from ruin and exploitation.

Once his peasants were gone and his pomestie desolate, the petty servitor did not remain in service and no longer maintained a household. To prevent this the state authorities were willing to help him retain his peasants and secure his lands. In both instances the central government sided with the muzhik and with the petty servitor against the great landowners, both lay and clerical. Serving its own ends, the state administration upheld the interests of the lower social strata by defending their labor, their people and their lands against the encroachments of the powerful. Boris's administrative decrees concerning peasants, bondmen, and volunteer serfs must be viewed in terms of the government's desire to safeguard its sources of taxation and military manpower.

Even under Ivan the Terrible, the Muscovite authorities considered it essential to intervene in the "transport of peasants." Ivan issued some sort of "code" (exactly what kind is not known) against the removal of peasants and established "forbidden years" during which the removal and departure of peasants and *posad* [14] taxpayers were prohibited. What period (or periods) was envisaged in Ivan's "code" is unclear. It was operative in 1584. The Riazan landowners alluded to it, complaining to Tsar Fedor that the influential state secretary Sherefedinov "is forcibly transporting peasants from small servitors in Your Majesty's villages against the code of your father and our sovereign."

"Forbidden years," in which the posad population and the peasantry could not leave, were also in force in

1591-1592. At this time mention was made of both past and future "years." Decrees prescribed the return of those tax-bearing people who "had left the posad during the forbidden years," and it was prohibited thenceforth to remove "peasants during the forbidden years until our decree." Consequently, the "code" of limitation established under Ivan the Terrible was acknowledged to be temporary ("until our decree"), but it was extended and remained in force for a whole series of years.

The halt of "peasant transport" was generally intended to hold the working, tax-bearing population in place and to curtail its massive migration. Subsequently, the interdict was intended to secure a work force for the small pomestie estates of "military servitors" and to prevent the peasants from migrating to the lands of large and privileged landowners. From such migrations "will come a great wasting away of the military servitors."

Boris's government inherited from Ivan the latter's restrictive measures and expanded their application. But Boris's administration also introduced several new measures. In 1597 was issued the celebrated decree concerning the establishment of a five-year period for the recovery of "fugitive" peasants. The government ordered that "runaway peasants" "be tried in court" and "after trial and investigation" be returned "back to where they were living." This applied only to peasants who "had escaped within a period of five years prior to the present year" (1597). For those peasants who had escaped "six, seven and ten and more years" before 1597, there was no directive to try them except for those who were "attainted," that is, whose court cases had begun. These cases it was necessary "to complete after trial and investigation."

This decree obviously softened the application of the

measures established by the "forbidden years." The peasant who had violated the "interdiction" and who had escaped during "years" other than those specified, might remain in his new place if five years had elapsed since the time of escape. In 1601 and 1602 new decrees were issued apparently limiting the "forbidden years." Tsar Boris in 1601 and 1602, at the very time that peasant removals and transfers were usually completed (at the end of November), granted permission for an "exodus." "It has been ordered in all our tsardom to grant 'exodus' to peasants [freed] from tax [arrears] and from sale." This privilege, however, was not given directly to the peasants but to their lord-landowners. "The gentry may renounce and remove peasants," said the decree, and it enumerated various ranks of servitors — "common" gentry.

Although the decree permitted the common service landholders to transfer peasants, it forbade such transfer to the large landowners — to high-ranking clergy and monasteries, boyars and "grand" gentry. The tsar himself refused to transport peasants "into crown villages and black [that is, tax-bearing] districts." Only on small pomestie estates throughout Russia, except in the district of Moscow, did the landowners receive the prerogative of exchanging certain peasants in certain instances. These landowners were not permitted to turn "renunciation" and "removal" into a systematic economic operation. The decree stated: "Whoever transfers peasants in the 110th year [1601] may transfer, one person to another, only one or two peasants, but the transfer of three or four will not be permitted."

The mitigation of the "forbidden years" turned out to be incomplete. In granting peasants freed "from taxes and from sale" restoration of the right of exodus, Tsar Boris was clearly striving not for freedom of peasant movement but for

the convenience and advantage of the pomestie service class.
He was safeguarding the labor force of this class against
inroads by the large and powerful landowners and also from
the vagabondage of the peasants themselves. In this instance
the interests of the pomeshchiki coincided with those of the
government, and Boris supported them for that very reason.

For Boris the peasant "exodus" itself was in no wise
desirable. Rather, the attachment of the working people to
the land and their registration by state financial agencies or
through an agreement with a landowner were very much
desired by the government. The authorities, without a doubt,
wanted the peasants to be bound to the land, and while that
had not yet occurred, it strove to direct their migration in
conformity with its objectives. But officialdom had not
resolved upon a full and categorical declaration of peasant
bondage, for it did not wish to hand over the peasants to
private ownership and to lose them from the tax rolls.
Therefore the authorities did not abolish the right of
"exodus," but attempted in their own way to regulate and
direct it.

The same goal of regulation and direction is found in
the attitude of the government toward the matter of slaves.
Its attention was drawn to this question because "fully
bonded and indentured men, women, and children were
running away" from the boyars (that is, the lords). In order
to provide the "boyars" with a means of combatting the
widespread flight of their "people," the administration in
1586 ordered that thenceforth each entry into slavery be
registered in government offices. Each person who "petitions
to enter [someone's] service" had to furnish a "service
indenture" [kabala]to his "sovereign." In Moscow this was
done at the chancery of the Slavery Court, and in other
towns "with the knowledge of the chancery officials." Such

officials were obliged to "register those service indentures in
the Moscow registry books and in the towns." In this way
was introduced the obligatory registry of all those persons
newly entered into slavery. And in 1597 such confirmation
of slavery became mandatory for all slaves. Their owners
were required to present to the authorities documents for
their own domestics and to register in "the books of bonded
persons" all "old obligations, whether full [ownership],
registered, or purchased, and all obligations and indentures."

Apparently a general census of slaves was contemplated.
At the same time, as concerns "free" slaves who were serving
"voluntarily" without agreements, it was resolved to ask
them "whom they had served voluntarily and how long, and
whether they had not given an indenture for themselves." If
they had given an indenture, they became ordinary bonded
people. If not, they still did not remain "free servants." Those
having served less than six months were allowed "to go free."
Those having served six months or longer were ordered to
enter slavery and were registered as bondmen without their
consent. So it was that the status of "free" servant was
formally abolished and the ruling introduced by a decree
with these words: "Do not keep a slave without an indenture
for a single day. Whosoever does so, and feeds him, he will
lose him."

The law of the year 1597, which founded a uniform and
compulsory system of strengthening slavery, further defined
the position of bonded persons. From that time on (speaking
in the words of V. I. Sergeevich) "all bonded persons, both
new and old, became provisional slaves and forfeited the right
to end their dependent status by paying off their debts. But
the moment the creditor died, they would all receive their
freedom without paying for the indenture." The law of 1597
concerning slaves pursued the interests of the state even more

clearly than had Boris's decrees concerning peasants. With
equal force the law subordinated the interests of the "lords"
and those of the "slaves" to the government's purposes. The
relations among "lords" and "slaves" must be so fashioned
that the government might account for the labor force, that
the labor force might be sufficiently "bound" to the lord,
and that bonded persons not become "full" slaves upon the
death of their lords. All this preserved the requisite social
order, as the government understood it, and guarded the legal
interests of both parties.

Thus it is impossible to say that Boris was the
"founder" or "perpetrator" of the enserfment of the
peasants and the creator of bonded dependence for "free"
persons. If it is found that in the sixteenth century general
measures were instituted which hampered the peasants'
freedom of movement, the beginning of these measures
should be traced to the "forbidden years" of Ivan the
Terrible, not to the laws of Boris's time. Moreover, should
the measures of 1586 and 1597 concerning slaves be
considered the first constraints on "free" service, it should be
remembered that these constraints applied equally to lords.
Boris made it incumbent upon the landowners to register
their workers, thereby limiting arbitrary rule and the
possibility of illegal transactions at the expense of the system
as decreed by the government. The rules concerning the
"registration" of serfs were accompanied by enactments
clearly tending to the latter's advantage.

On the other hand, Boris's government was not at all
inclined to protect and to treat gently fugitives who fled
Russia for the Cossack lands. There is evidence that Boris did
not look kindly upon the Cossacks of the "Wild Field," that
he cruelly punished contacts with them (for example, Zakhari
Liapunov), and that he overburdened the working populace

on crown lands in the "Field." From land belonging to the
great sovereign he organized in the new, recently settled
southern localities *"desiatinnaia* ploughland"[15] of sizes
clearly beyond the strength of the local people. About
twenty years after Boris's death the Moscow government, in
negotiations with the free Cossacks, reminded them "how
unfree they had been under the former Muscovite sovereigns
and especially under Tsar Boris." "Not only were you not
free to come at liberty to Moscow but also to the borderland
towns to see your families. Everywhere it was forbidden for
you to buy and sell." If the authorities failed to hold the
peasant on the land and if they were unable to return the
fugitive "to the old hearth," they tried to overtake him in his
new place of residence and to attach him to a newly-built
town or to the sovereign's *desiatinnaia* ploughland on the
borders. When this failed, the free man was treated very
badly indeed.

The authorities inclined to consider such a free man a
"brigand," in legal terms or in more ornate language, a
"mischievous viper" from whom only evil could be expected.
Thus was defined the general attitude of Boris's government
toward the "working people" — the peasants and slaves.
Obviously, the peasantry as a group did not enjoy the special
protection of Boris. He protected and defended them only
insofar as he considered it essential for the general welfare of
Muscovy.

VIII   BORIS, THE ARISTOCRACY AND THE
CLERGY. GENERAL APPRAISAL OF
BORIS'S CLASS POLICY

Concern for the tax-paying and working people sometimes
placed Boris in a position opposed to that of the Muscovite
landed aristocracy — the "boyars." Though he belonged to

this caste by ancestry and personal ties, Boris nonetheless found enemies in this patrician group. It was not merely that his personal ascendancy created such enemies. Rather, the old high-born princely aristocracy saw in Boris a supporter of Ivan the Terrible's policy. To these nobles Boris was an oprichnik who pursued the earlier policy of destruction of the princes. Systematically he placed at the top of the Muscovite administration persons who were non-aristocratic — "commoners" unaccustomed to leadership. Boris's contemporary, the state secretary Ivan Timofeev, who was close to the establishment of the very aristocratic princes Vorotynsky, devoted an entire article in his *Annals* to this one administrative policy of Boris. Taking the point of view of the boyar-princes who were reared and educated in the tradition of ruling, Ivan Timofeev with disgust condemned Boris for patronizing the "low-born" and raising them above all "measure and time" to "the rank of the high-born."

In Timofeev's opinion Boris's policy caused suffering not only among the neglected aristocracy, but throughout the whole of the Muscovite state, which he likened to a ship guided by an unskilled helmsman. As a ship steered by an "incompetent" sinks, as a flock perishes while the shepherd dozes, as a monastery "grows weak because the monks are poor providers," a city also is ruined — "and [it] cannnot be otherwise" — by bad rulers who are greedy and mercenary, yet ignorant and clumsy. More than once Timofeev compared such "low-born" rulers to swine. As "swine are seen with rings in their noses, so power and authority appear in the hands of the unworthy. They behave in the manner of mindless swine." "Unaware," they devour all that is given them, "all that is animal and liquid." For the sake of bribes and profit they connive and close their eyes to everything.

Unknown to them is the evil they wreak upon the "city," that is, the state.

This was the way the supporters of the old aristocracy and the admirers of the old customs appraised the administration of the Godunovs. Not only did they complain that the aristocracy had been shunted aside, they also charged Boris and his close associates with first-hand persecution. Evidently there was a general feeling that Boris held the aristocracy in no high favor. In 1608 the Polish ambassadors recalled that under Boris "it had been hard for the boyars." The Dutchman Isaac Massa, a contemporary, wrote that "Boris removed all the eminent boyars and princes, thereby completely depriving the country of a high nobility and of staunch patriots." The Englishman Fletcher was convinced that the oprichnina of Ivan the Terrible and all the steps that he took against the princely aristocracy was the inheritance of the government of Boris Godunov, and that the Godunovs tried in every way to annihilate or to demean the most distinguished and most venerable nobility. These opinions lend some weight to the words of Avraami Palitsyn, that Boris "greatly" plundered "the houses and villages of boyars and grandees."

If the matter was not so crude and vulgar as Boris's ill-wishers have expressed it, it is still clear that the hereditary aristocracy played no role under Boris either in the state or at court. The high nobility had conceded the throne to Boris upon the death of Tsar Fedor. There is no difficulty in understanding that the author of the chronograph of 1616 was correct when he said that Boris "evoked the indignation of all the high-ranking leaders of all the Russian land." Boris needed to employ neither disgrace nor execution in order to call forth and feed this sharp indignation on the part of the aristocracy. The sum of his activities, alien as they were to the old court traditions of the days before the oprichnina, and also he himself — reared in the bosom of the oprichnina — were loathsome and unacceptable to all who remembered the flowering of the princely Muscovite aristocracy and who supported and admired it.

The Muscovite clergy are usually considered to have been friendly to Boris. Patriarch Job, indebted to Boris for his office, is portrayed as his most loyal friend. In his writings Job always eulogized Boris and depicted himself as his supporter and admirer. During the election of the tsar in 1598, Job and "the holy sobor" (that is, the patriarch's council and suite) took leading roles. Job first named Boris tsar and led all the clergy, the members of the Zemsky Sobor, and a mass of the populace to Boris at the Novodevichi Convent, where they requested Boris to take the throne. Job lost the patriarchate simultaneously with the deposition of the Godunovs and thus shared the fate of the dynasty which he himself had chosen and crowned on the throne of Muscovy.

Among the remainder of the clergy no movement against Boris is discernible after the unsuccessful intrigue of Metropolitan Dionisi and the princes Shuisky. Boris, first as regent and then as monarch, knew how to get along with the servants of the church. Upon the easing of discord in Muscovy, evidently, he found it possible to revive the "immunities" (privileges) of the clerical landowners which had been temporarily abolished "until the land settles down" by the sobors of 1580 and 1584. This was an exceptionally gracious measure which returned to the monasteries and sees the unusually privileged position forfeited during the days of crisis. Boris therefore had grounds to boast that he "had given them all their lands."

But this kindness on Boris's part certainly did not mean

that the state had been conciliatory in all matters concerning the property interests of the clergy. In the matter of peasants, Boris's decrees prohibited the patriarch, metropolitans and other church authorities, as well as the monasteries, from "removing peasants" just as were the boyars and "grand" gentry. Peasant renunciation and "removal" were permitted only among the petty "bureau officials" of the patriarch and other hierarchs, as among the corresponding small lay pomeshchiki. Church lands, in consequence, were placed on the same footing with other lands, without any privileged exceptions. Boris's government subsequently undertook steps to survey the patrimonial rights of monasteries and to eliminate possible misuse of them.

In 1590 a novel decree excised the right of monasteries to "deposit" their lands for personal possession and use. Persons holding monastery lands must return them to the monastery, which was to return the deposits if the parties wished their money back. This procedure ended the practice of leasing monastery lands into private lifetime possession in return for payment of a "deposit," and also the transfer of lands from the pomestie system to the monasteries with the right of life use of those lands. The latter option was a convenient means for landowners to take land out of service without losing actual possession of it, and as a result become "non-service deti boyarskie."

In upholding the principle of keeping land in service, the government in 1593-1594 began a general review of monastic landownership and surveyed the rights even of the most prominent and richest monasteries (the Trinity—St. Sergius, Spasso-Efimiev). At that time, as a result, many monastery patrimonial estates were reclaimed "for the sovereign" when the monastery could not document and justify its right to them.

In clashes of interest between state and church landholding, Boris preserved the interests of the former, and as in much else, remained a faithful servant of the state.

A survey of Boris's social policy confirms the conclusion that he served no private or class interests. The goodwill of the princely aristocracy could in no way accrue to Boris, for the whole story of Boris's climb to power underlines the mutual dislike of Boris and the princes. The desires and needs of the working masses who had escaped the yoke of serfdom Boris sacrificed to governmental advantage, which in this instance he united with the economic needs of the service class. Because of his concern for the productivity of the service lands, Boris aided the petty landowning "gentry and deti boyarskie." At the same time he demanded from "the great sovereign's pomeshchiki" and from the patrimonial landowners a full measure of service. In order that the lands remain in their hands, he mounted the same strict watch over them as always practiced heretofore by the Moscow authorities.

It is literally impossible to name a single social group for which Boris would have created an especially privileged position or which he would have particularly patronized. The times were so troubled and difficult, and the crisis had generated such social tension, that the government found no opportunity to permit privileged conditions for anyone at all. The situation allowed no one to be fully pleased with or satisfied by the social climate. The natural antagonism of the landowning classes and working masses could not be assuaged by official wisdom and dexterity alone.

However, Boris's adroitness and perspicacity enabled him to define sharply what was essential to his goal of calming the country.

IX   THE STRUGGLE AGAINST THE SOCIAL
       CRISIS AND STEPS TAKEN TO BRING
       ORDER. FINANCIAL PRIVILEGES. CON-
       STRUCTION. FOREIGNERS AND ENLIGHTEN-
       MENT. THE GENERAL TREND OF BORIS'S
       POLICIES

Power came into Boris's hands at the very moment when the
government realized the magnitude of the social crisis which
weighed upon the country and grasped the necessity of
fighting it. Boris had gained deep insight into the situation
from his predecessors, Ivan the Terrible and Nikita Romanovich
Yuriev, and from such administrators as state secretaries
Andrei and Vasili Shchelkalov. In no real sense was Boris the
creator of the idea of a policy of social reconciliation. Yet he
was its champion and demonstrated through his personal
qualities that he was a man capable of dealing with the social
paralysis. Gentle and kind, he inclined to affability in private
life. An "enlightened" man (by contemporary definition), he
was as sensitive to good and evil as he was to truth and
falsehood. He abhorred oppressors and bribe-takers, just as he
did drunkards and libertines. Distinguished by his generosity
and "love for the poor," Boris willingly came to the aid of
the destitute and down-trodden. So it was that men of the
day spoke of Boris Godunov.

       Testimonials bespoke that Boris, who had grown to
manhood among the oprichniki, was in no way like them.
From the notorious "court" of Ivan the Terrible with its
orgies and its lewd and bloody "cruelty," Boris had learned
only disgust and loathing and had gained an awareness of the
harm Ivan provoked. Boris succeeded in rejuvenating court
life and governmental practice by injecting a completely
different tone. In him administrative talent and a piercing
mind were joined to worldly wisdom and native shrewdness.

Close scrutiny of the documents of that period reveals in this respect a great difference between the time of Ivan and the era of Boris. Under Boris the Muscovite court grew sober and moral, quiet and good, and the government waxed peaceful and shed its wrath. The people found "justice" and "order" in Tsar Fedor and in the "kindly rule" of Boris, not the "dread" and "executions" typical of Tsar Ivan IV. "His order in the land was such that there was no suffering," said officials of Boris. "Not one great, not one powerful person nor a single weak orphan suffered." It was quite in the character of Boris that he set great store in humanity and justice. But this did not mean that he was weak. When necessary, his hand was no less strong than that of Ivan. Whereas Ivan could not manage without the executioner's block and the hangman's rope, Boris was never quick to employ them. Intrigue he answered not with bloodletting but with banishment. Not until after investigation and trial did he resort to execution. "The sovereign's disfavor," when it befell a man without trial and investigation, did not go hand in hand with open bloodshed. Contemporaries not numbered among Boris's friends accused him of resorting to denunciation, of encouraging informers with rewards, and of commanding the attendants of persons in disgrace to "take them away" — to kill them secretly in exile.

But in the Muscovy of that time the practice of denunciation did not indicate personal weakness on the part of Godunov; rather, it was a sad custom which in time would be replaced by "secret agents." Clandestine executions (if we wish to believe that they happened) were shrouded in mystery and were rare, one may say, isolated occurrences. The strength of Boris's government lay not in terror, of which there was none under Boris, but in other attributes of his authority.

The government knew the techniques of winning popularity. Unquestionably Boris succeeded in pacifying the country in the aftermath of the oprichnina and unfortunate wars, as was attested by all men of the time. Under his administration the country experienced a real sense of relief. Russian writers have said that during the reigns of tsars Fedor and Boris, God "granted a happy time" to the land of Rus. The people of Muscovy "began to be comforted from their former grief and to live quietly and serenely," "brightly and exultantly," and "Russia flowered with all blessings." Foreigners also testified that the situation in Moscow appreciably improved under Boris. The population was quieted and even multiplied. Trade, which shrank under Ivan the Terrible, revived and grew. The people rested from the wars and brutalities of Ivan the Terrible and felt that the style of authority had changed sharply for the better.

These conditions were brought about, insofar as one can judge, by a direct lessening of the tax and service demands made by the government on the people. The steps by which Boris sought to improve the well-being of society are roughly these: the restoration of immunities revoked during the latter years of Ivan's reign; the reduction in rates of "impost," that is, direct taxation, and an attempt to switch to a system of tax farming (especially a monopoly in the production and sale of spirits) for the replenishment of the "money treasury of the great sovereign;" the awarding of privileges to people of various estates; the stimulation of trade, notably foreign trade. In the hyperbolic statements of Muscovite officials these measures acquired the character of universal liberation from all payments and obligations. It was as if Godunov "placed in privilege all the lands of the state which were under the plow of the working man; no tributes of any sort were demanded, all things were done on hire from the treasury." In the official version, at Boris's accession "he suddenly commanded that three payments a year be given" to the servitors. "He demanded no other payments than the taxes and imposts on the land." "He established freedom of trade for the *gosti* 16 and trading people of all Russia."

In addition to granting privileges, Boris exhibited a broad philanthropy which revealed his personal generosity and kindliness. Boris liked to be thought of as a "lover of the poor" and a "generous giver." To the payment of money he added his concern for the rights of the people and for the defense of the interests of the poor and weak. He punished offenders and bribetakers. He paraded his "justice" and hatred for "bribery." Public works (if this term is applicable to that time) was a particular form of his philanthropy in domestic affairs. He resorted to them in various forms and at every opportune moment.

During all his years in power Boris displayed an extraordinary love for building and left after him many remarkable structures. He began his public works with the wall of Moscow's "white" city *[Belyi gorod]* which followed the course of the present-day city boulevards. This wall, or "city of stone near the great suburb along the side of the earthen embankments," was completed in seven years. The "master" of construction was the Russian "church and palace master builder" Fedor Saveliev Kon (or Konev). The wall was a grandiose and decorative structure for that time. It was shielded from the outside by a new fortress — "the wooden city," which followed modern Sadovaia Street "around Moscow near all the settlements."17 A stone fortress was built at approximately the same time in Astrakhan by the same Fedor Kon. In 1596 work began on the famous walls of Smolensk, engineered by the same "city master," Fedor Kon.

The walls of Smolensk, which measure more than six

versts[18] in length and contain thirty-eight towers, were built in less than five years. "All the towns of Muscovy" took part in the construction. "Stone was brought from all the towns, and they had stone from towns in Staritsa and in Ruza. Lime was burned in the Belsky district at Prechistye in the Upper Reaches." Thus the building of the walls of Smolensk was quite an elaborate undertaking. "Stonemasons and brickworkers" were summoned from various towns. Even "potters were rounded up" and sent to Smolensk for the building of the fortress. Boris himself went there for the laying of the foundation stone. He took along "great wealth" and made his entire journey, as it were, a continuous ceremony. "Whosoever petitioned for something, he gave unto him. And thus did he appear kind to all men."

In his report to Tsar Fedor on the construction at Smolensk, Boris wished to say that the new walls of that city would become a model for all the towns of Muscovy. "This city of Smolensk will be as a necklace to adorn all the towns." The boyar-prince Fedor Mikhailovich Trubetskoi, who was in attendance, maliciously commented "on Boris's speeches." He noted that "even the lice which will infest that necklace will not be able to survive." The chronicler who recorded Trubetskoi's words found them to be prophetic. "These words," he said, "came true in the painful years that followed. Many people from both lands [that is, Muscovy and Poland-Lithuania] perished under those walls." But Boris's "necklace" was nonetheless essential to the Russian state and proved its value during the Time of Troubles, when King Sigismund was long detained "under" Smolensk.

Finally, on the southern borders of Muscovy, Boris continued the construction program of Ivan the Terrible with unusual energy. During the 1570's a plan was developed in Moscow for the colonization of the "Wild Field" through fortresses, and the construction of towns was begun. But the major work of fulfilling this plan fell to Boris. Under him Kursk and Kromy were built. The line of the river Bystraia Sosna was occupied, and the towns of Livny, Elets, and Chernavsky Gorodok were founded there. Further, the course of the Oskol River was also settled by means of the towns of Oskol and Valuiki. "On the Don on the Voronezh" sprang up the town of Voronezh, and on the Donets stood Belgorod. Finally, even further south the town of Tsarev-Borisov was built. This network of fortifications, systematically placed in the steppes "on the Tatar trails," won for Muscovy an enormous expanse of the "Field" and closed to the Tatars the road to Moscow and to central Russia in general.

Within the limits of the city of Moscow itself, besides the "white stone" walls of the "tsar's town" and the wooden walls of the outer city, Boris laid numerous buildings and churches. According to the words of praise of Patriarch Job, Boris "rules the holy city of Moscow as if she were his bride, and adorns her well. He has created many beautiful churches of stone and has built great palaces, marvelous to behold. He has built halls and chambers for the shelter and provision of the merchants." In addition, to Boris belongs credit for the erection of the famous "Bell Tower of Ivan the Great" in the Kremlin. Boris was also responsible for a massive structure to house the administrative bureaus. It was located in the Kremlin by the Cathedral of the Archangel. He also built large stone halls (the "reserve court"). In the Walled City [Kitaigorod], [19] after a fire in the trading "stalls," Boris set up new stone stalls for the merchants — "merchant chambers." Further, Boris erected a "large bridge," containing many shops, across the Neglinnaia River.

In various quarters of Moscow Boris constructed new

and richly decorated churches of stone. Many old churches were renovated. Boris planned as well the construction of a new cathedral in Moscow. The people of that time said that this new house of worship would be an extraordinary structure. It would overshadow and replace the presiding Cathedral of the Dormition, "that ancient building of Holy [Metropolitan] Peter, the Church of the Dormition of the Mother of God." Many "tools" and materials were collected for the new church — "many and in great numbers." But the edifice was never built. The materials for it were sold later by Tsar Vasili Shuisky [1606-1610] for use in other structures, even "in plain chapels."

Another undertaking experienced a similar sad fate. Boris erected some kind of special catafalque of Christ or, according to the precise expression of Ivan Timofeev, "a sepulchre of Christ the Lord God, a receptacle for His divine Relics," after the pattern of the one in Jerusalem "in measure and likeness." Evidently this was an imitation of the catafalque and pall in the Church of the Holy Sepulchre in Jerusalem, with representations of Christ and the Blessed Mother, archangels, apostles, Joseph of Arimathea and Nicodemus. The "likenesses" or "wrought images" so glistened with gold, pearls, and semi-precious stones that, when beholding them, it was hardly possible "to remain standing." At Boris's death this work of art for some reason aroused the scorn of the rabble who massacred the Godunov family. "In hatred and in enmity did they smash it. Piercing it with lances and boar-spears and raising it on high, they paraded shamelessly throughout the city, forgetful of the fear of God." (This statement was officially recorded in February, 1607.)

Since Boris was possessed by this passion for building and construction, at every appropriate moment he naturally used this as a means of employing the people and giving them wages. During the years of famine (beginning in 1601), in addition to a dole of money and bread, the government gave work to the people. A foreigner (one Thomas Smith) noted that during what seemed a general famine Boris undertook, for example, to reinforce the outer walls of the city of Moscow. "He ordered that galleries (battlements) be built around the outermost walls of the great city of Moscow."

A curious feature of Boris's activity in government was his kindness toward foreigners. Contemporaries reproached Ivan the Terrible for his inclination to receive foreigners and the non-Orthodox. In the *Annals* of Ivan Timofeev one finds remarkable lines on this subject. In place of the grandees whom he banished and slaughtered, Ivan supposedly grew fond of "those coming from neighboring lands." He took foreigners into his confidence and shared with them his "most secret thoughts." He entrusted his health to them, listening to their "medical cunning." In this lay the source of "the harm to his soul and also of his physical illness." Unhesitatingly he placed his own head "in the mouths of asps." In this way "he placed himself into the hands of barbarians." Foreigners did with him whatever they wished. Timofeev attributed all the misfortunes of the time of Ivan the Terrible to the hold of foreigners over him. Such was the national opposition to the Europeanism of Ivan.

Boris was like Ivan in this respect. He did not fear the charges which befell his political mentor. In his *History*, N. M. Karamzin diligently collected evidence of Boris's fondness of European culture and enlightenment, and for "the Germans." "Boris surpassed all the ancient crowned heads of Russia in his ardent love of secular education," said Karamzin. Boris dreamed of establishing European schools (even universities, supposedly) in Russia. He ordered that scholars be sought abroad and brought to Moscow. He received with extraordinary graciousness those foreigners who either by need or by good will had come to Moscow for service, for industry, or for the purpose of trade. He conversed often and at length with his foreign physicians. He allowed the construction of a Lutheran church in an area of the Moscow posad. Moreover, he was obsessed by the desire to give his daughter Ksenia in marriage to some reigning European prince.

Twice Boris attempted to realize this wish. First, marriage was proposed between Ksenia and the exiled Prince Gustavus of Sweden. Gustavus was invited to Muscovy, "to an appanage," and was shown much kindness. But Gustavus did not wish to change his religion for Ksenia's sake nor to give up his morganatic wife who had followed him to Moscow from Danzig. The affair went no further than matchmaking, and Gustavus was banished from the tsar's sight to Uglich. There he was kept in the event that his name and person might be used to bring influence to bear on the Swedish government. Gustavus, however, did not prove useful even against Sweden. In Kashin he died peacefully in 1607.

Another attempt at matchmaking grew from Boris's close relationship with Denmark. In [August] 1602, Duke Hans, brother of King Christian of Denmark, came to Muscovy as the fiance of Tsarevna Ksenia. The affair progressed better with Hans than with Gustavus. But it was God's will that Hans fell ill and died in Moscow a month and a half after his arrival. A most curious diary of the Danish ambassador, Alexis Guldenstern, who accompanied Hans to Moscow, offers the reader many details not only about the proposed marriage, but also about Muscovite life in general and about Muscovite political figures, including Boris.

Boris visited Hans several times during the latter's illness. This was a breach of tsarist custom, according to which all who were ill were denied the right "to see the eyes of the tsar." Boris displayed much attention and kindness at the bedside of the duke. He sighed and even wept. With his usual propensity for gesture "he pointed with both hands to his breast, saying: 'Here are Duke Hans and my daughter.'" When Hans died, the Danish ambassadors were told that in grief the tsar was forced to take to his bed. Personally the tsar accompanied the body to the grave and bade a touching farewell to the deceased. Boris insisted upon full pardon for one of the Danes who had been arrested for attempted murder and awaited severe punishment. Obviously the death of the betrothed son-in-law truly grieved Boris. With tears in his eyes he lamented at the graveside: "Alas, Duke Hans, my light and my consolation. Because of our sins we could not keep him!" "The tsar (said an eyewitness) could hardly pronounce the words for weeping."

During Boris's reign the Moscow authorities first resorted to an enlightened step which later, from the time of Peter the Great, would become a lasting Russian custom. The government sent several "Russian youths," young gentry, abroad for study. They were to study "thoroughly the grammar and language" of the country to which they were sent. Documentary evidence shows that five were sent to Lubeck and four to England. According to the testimony of one contemporary, a German, in all eighteen persons were sent to England, France, and Germany.

Not one ever returned. Some died before finishing their studies. Some fled from their instructors "for unknown reasons." A few remained abroad for good, possessed by love of new-found cultures. One of these latter, Nikifor Olferiev Grigoriev, became a priest in England, "a noble member of

the Episcopal clergy." At the time of the Puritan movement
(1643) he even suffered for his steadfastness in his new faith,
losing his parish in Huntingdonshire. Muscovite diplomats
abroad sought in vain for the return of these youths. But
neither the "youths" themselves nor the governments of
their new homelands would agree to their return to Moscow.

A sketch of Boris's political activities does not disclose
any "system" or "program" in his policies. Muscovites of the
time were not in the habit of raising the motives for their
actions to abstract principle or moral postulates. If they gave
this or that reason for their opinions, it meant that "thus it
was done" or that "it was unseemly." Why one thing "was
done" but another "unseemly," they did not explain. Nor
did Boris explain his actions and intentions as governed by
any comprehensive idea, except to indicate broadly their
benefit to the state and to the general welfare. For this
reason it is difficult to outline the aims and plans of Boris as
politician and administrator. There remains only speculation.

Yet certain known facts allow one dominant tendency
to emerge as characteristic of Boris's policies. Without doubt
he acted in the interests of the middle classes of Muscovite
society at the expense of those of the aristocracy and of the
enserfed masses. At least it was this middle social strata
which looked upon him with favor, recognizing the benefits
he wrought and the "good deeds" he performed. The
common people (not the enserfed masses but its free strata,
pospolstwo in Polish) greatly loved and esteemed Boris.
"They looked on him as on God," according to one
contemporary, and were happy "to stand up" and serve him.
Russian writers of the time generally acknowledged that
Boris "was loved by everyone because of his popular deeds."
The populace, "perceiving his reason and judgment," his

"just and strong rule" and his "great kindness to the people," in 1598 favored Boris for the throne.

Boris's great popularity during his lifetime is beyond question. "Boris brought so much favor upon himself that they spoke of him everywhere," notes one who even despised him, the Dutchman Isaac Massa. There can be scarcely any doubt that behind the simple desire to be liked and the quest for popularity lay hidden a deeper and more serious goal — the transfer of the fulcrum of power from its former base, the land-owning aristocracy, to a new and more democratic foundation, and the creation of an order of government resting on the support of the petty service class and the free taxpaying populace. Boris's political reckoning was farsighted, one which was justified by the entire course of public life in the eighteenth century. But Boris himself was unable to taste the fruits of his own vision, for while he lived the middle layers of Muscovite society had not yet organized and had not grown conscious of their social strength. They were unable to save Boris and his family from misfortune and ruin when the upper and lower levels of Muscovite society took up arms against the Godunovs. These were the old aristocracy, inspired by its long-standing enmity toward Boris and his family, and the enserfed masses, drawn by their hatred of the entire Muscovite social order.

CHAPTER THREE

THE TRAGEDY OF BORIS

I   THE DEATH OF TSAREVICH DMITRI IN UGLICH. VARIOUS REPORTS CONCERNING HIM. THE NAGOI FAMILY IN UGLICH. THE TSAREVICH'S ILLNESS. MAY 15, 1591. THE "INQUEST" AND TRIAL

"But the time was drawing near," says Karamzin about the end of Boris's reign, "when this wise ruler, worthily praised in Europe for his judicious policies, love of enlightenment, zeal to be a true father of the fatherland, and good conduct in public and private life, would have to taste the bitter fruit of lawlessness and become one of the astonishing victims of divine judgment." Karamzin considered the "lawlessness" of Boris to be that crime which contemporaries had attributed to him — the murder in Uglich of Tsarevich Dmitri. Karamzin did not believe in Boris's other "crimes." This historian, however, did not dare to discredit the murder for it had been confirmed by the church. Boris's misfortune lay not only in the fact that he had fallen prey to scandal and calumny, but also in the fact that this slander and calumny had received the indisputable (for that time) sanction of government and church. Simple suspicion turned into official truth, ecclesiastically confirmed.

Murmurings of envy and malice accompanied Boris's every step on his road to power and to personal supremacy at court and in the state. His success was explained not so much by his intelligence and good fortune as by cunning, "pushiness," and "villainy." Boris's struggle with the boyar-princes for supremacy at court led to the exile of boyars (certain of them died in exile), and even to the execution of some of their supporters. All of these troubles were attributed to Boris's "lust for power" and were charged directly to him. The entry of "the tsar's brother-in-law" into the regency was accompanied, in the eyes of Moscow, by many "sacrifices," and herein the rumor concerning the favorite's insatiable lust for power found sufficient ground.

If Boris was about to use the feeble-mindedness of Tsar Fedor to become ruler of the state, then it was natural to expect that this ruler would take advantage of the tsar's childlessness to inherit the tsardom and to seize the throne for himself. Boris's personality and place aroused such suspicions and assumptions. They seemed incontestable. It was impossible to refute them through arguments. How could Boris convince anyone that he did not desire power when he had been the leader of the power struggle for several years? And indeed, did he not desire power? Once one believes in the "insatiable powerlust" of Godunov, then how can one not be tempted also to believe that the untimely death of Tsarevich Dmitri was the fruit of that same lust for power? The death of the tsarevich coincided with Boris's victory over his rivals at court. He stood by the throne itself as the "bold ruler" and "close friend" of Tsar Fedor. Those who hated the fortunate court favorite plausibly said that it was time for

Boris to eliminate the last person who stood between him and the throne, namely the tsar's [Ivan's] son who was growing up in Uglich.

There is no need to expound again all the details concerning the death of Tsarevich Dmitri after all that has been printed about the affair. There is also no necessity in reviving the old and hopeless polemics on whether the tsarevich died in Uglich or whether he was spared from an attempt on his life; and if he died, whether he stabbed himself or was stabbed; and if he was stabbed, whether or not Boris had a hand in the crime.[1] Our account will not dissuade those who are convinced that the tsarevich escaped from Uglich and in 1605 came to Moscow to the "ancestral throne." Nor will our account dissuade those who hold that the tsarevich was silenced by command of the "cunning slave," Boris Godunov. We have another aim in mind — to present the affair as it is explained by the texts of surviving documents to the reader who is not inclined toward preconceived accusations against Boris, and who does not rely upon this or that interpretation of "evidence" or notorious "lives" and "legends."

It is known that the tsarevich died in Uglich on May 15, 1591, from a throat wound which evidently severed the carotid artery. His death became known in Moscow within two days, and an investigatory commission was dispatched to Uglich on the same day. The commission arrived in Uglich on May 19. It held an inquest which determined that the tsarevich had stabbed himself with a knife during a fit of the "black" illness [epilepsy]. The documents of this inquest, pasted together into one "column," have been preserved. More than once they have been published under the name "investigatory proceedings." In 1913 the "proceedings" were published *facsimile.* [2] Hence all the evidence is now accessible for review and thorough analysis.

When in 1605 the self-styled Tsar Dmitri appeared in
Moscow, the inquest of 1591 was considered refuted, and the
tsarevich was believed to be alive. But when in 1606 this
Dmitri was killed and the remains of the true tsarevich were
brought to Moscow and ceremoniously placed "at the
right-hand pillar" in the Cathedral of the Archangel, the truth
of the investigatory proceedings was still not confirmed. The
people were informed officially that Tsarevich Dmitri
"through the envy of Boris Godunov, as a gentle lamb was
laid to rest." An inscription was engraved on the tsarevich's
grave to the effect that the boy had been killed "by
command of Boris Godunov." In the life of the new saint it
was written that he had gained immortality and the gift of
miracles through his innocent suffering, for he had been
slaughtered "by his cunning slave Boris Godunov." The
government of Tsar Vasili Ivanovich Shuisky [1606-1610]
and also the church made this same charge against Boris. But
the charge was in no way documented and remained
unsubstantiated.

In various redactions of the "life" of Tsarevich Dmitri
and in legends about the pretender [the false Dmitri],
individual authors recounted varying versions of the stories.
These accounts were about how, at the instigation of Boris,
all sorts of attempts were made on the life of the tsarevich
until finally one of the murderers "slit his throat." These
versions are at variance with one another. They are generally
untenable and can by no means serve as documentary
evidence. Arranged chronologically, the lives and legends
present a curious pattern of the gradual accumulation of
fanciful details upon an epic subject. The later they appear,
the more detailed they become. In this sense they have some
value for the literary historian; but for the historian who
relies on facts they are of no worth at all. Far more important

for the historian of this description are those opinions on Dmitri's death found in contemporary writings on the troubles of the seventeenth century. Their writers had no wish to describe the event at Uglich, mentioning it only in passing.

Employing all the material listed above — the investigatory proceedings, legends, lives, and the opinions of contemporaries — we shall attempt to analyze the events at Uglich, which are essential to the further understanding of the tragedy of Boris.

First of all, very curious relations existed between the court in Moscow and the exiled family of the tsarevich — Tsaritsa Maria Fedorovna and her brothers, the Nagois. On the surface, mutual good will reigned supreme. For example, according to the custom of the time, *pirogi* [meat pies] were sent to the sovereign in Moscow on the name-day of the tsarevich (October 19). These pirogi were sent in memory of the martyr Uar (the tsarevich's baptismal name was Uar; Dmitri was his "secular" name). In return the tsar sent furs to Tsaritsa Maria, and money and Chinese silks to her messenger, Andrei Andreevich Nagoi. But good will was limited to like tokens of attention. The Nagoi family was being held in Uglich "on appanage," but under surveillance. This surveillance was entrusted to a special official, the state secretary Mikhailo Bitiagovsky. He had been sent to Uglich by the Moscow government.

The Nagois disliked this Bitiagovsky as well as the other agents sent from Moscow, and quarrelled with them. For example, "they quarrelled about the fact that Mikhailo Nagoi had requested treasury money from Bitiagovsky over and above the tsar's order. Bitiagovsky refused saying that he could not give out money without an order from the sovereign." On the very day of the tsarevich's death, Mikhailo

Nagoi and Bitiagovsky "quarrelled violently because Mikhailo Nagoi had not released the *posokha*," that is, persons summoned to bring transportation for the sovereign's army. Hatred of Bitiagovsky resulted in his being the first killed during the massacre which the Nagois committed in Uglich after the death of the tsarevich. Another Muscovite official, the "town prefect" named Rusin Rakov, was also threatened with murder. He had been sent from Moscow to Uglich to muster the posokha. He was told that he "had not been sent for the posokha, but to gain information on what was occurring there." He was driven out of Uglich and threatened: "Why do you want to perish here? Do you desire the same treatment as those who have been slain, Mikhailo Bitiagovsky and his friends?"

The Nagoi family nourished similar feelings for the high-ranking officials of the Moscow administration, for that government had deprived them of their courtly honor and the comforts of the capital city, and had banished them to a shabby town. Although cautious in his comments, Avraami Palitsyn was resolved to reveal to his readers that Tsarevich Dmitri was far removed from his "close ones," that is, relatives. The tsarevich "was confused and troubled that he was not with his brother," in other words exiled from Moscow. Thus "he often spoke in childish mockery and acted in an absurd manner with respect to his brother, Tsar Fedor, and even more so with respect to this Boris (Godunov)." The young boy's "absurd" actions are described by a foreign contemporary (Bussow). Having noted that the tsarevich generally displayed "his father's cruel-heartedness," Bussow related that once Dmitri commanded his young gentry friends to make several figures of snow. He called them by the names of the well-known boyars, placed them in a row and began to hack them up, saying again and again: "That is how it will be for them when I reign."

Of course Moscow received secret reports about the attitude of the Nagois toward the boyars. Palitsyn, with his usual subtlety of expression, said that enemies (of the Nagois) and "admirers" (of the boyars) appeared. "They plotted trouble, concocted lie upon lie and with these lies approached great men, even Boris himself. And from the great turmoil they seduced them into sin, and that most handsome youth (Dmitri) they sent unwillingly away into eternal rest."

Rumors in Moscow about the wicked disposition of the tsarevich and about the possibility of attempts on his life were circulating even before the tsarevich's death. The Englishman Fletcher, who left Moscow in 1589 and who published his book about Russia in London in 1591 *[Of the Russe Common Wealth]*, set down therein the following portentous lines about Dmitri. "The emperours younger brother of sixe or seven yeares old. . .is kept in a remote place from the Mosko, under the tuition of his mother and hir kindred of the house of the Nagaies: yet not safe (as I have heard) from attempts of making away by practise of some that aspire to the succession, if this emperour [Fedor] die without any issue. The nurse that tasted before him of certaine meat [as I have heard] died presently. That hee is a naturall sonne to Joan Vasilowich [Ivan Vasilievich], the Russe people warrant it, by the fathers qualitie that beginneth to appeare already in his tender yeares. He is delighted (they say) to see sheepe and other cattel killed, and to looke on their throtes while they are bleeding (which commonly children are afraid to beholde), and to beate geese and hennes with a staffe till he see them lie dead."

Understandably, such rumors and opinions about the tsarevich could not promote the establishment of agreeable and trustful relations between Moscow and Uglich. Both sides

feared the other and nourished mutual enmity. According to
contemporaries, in Moscow they wanted the tsarevich dead,
while in Uglich there were dreams about the early death of
Tsar Fedor. Bussow states that many boyars saw in the
tsarevich a strong similarity to Tsar Ivan Vasilievich and were
extremely anxious that the son quickly follow his father to
the grave.

Mikhailo Bitiagovsky's "bitter widow," Avdotia
Bitiagovskaia, in a petition to Tsar Fedor, mentioned that her
husband (killed in Uglich) "spoke much and quarrelled often
with Mikhailo (Nagoi) because he (Nagoi) constantly brought
sorcerers and sorceresses to Tsarevich Dmitri. The sorcerer
Andriushka Mochalov constantly lived with Mikhailo and
with Grigori and with Andrei Nagoi's wife, Zinovia. And
Mikhailo Nagoi commanded the sorcerer to foretell how long
you, Sire, and the tsaritsa (Irina Fedorovna) have to live."

Apparently it is possible to determine the source of the
belief that Tsarevich Dmitri had the same temperament as his
father. The child suffered from a serious disease. This disease
was epilepsy, with the basic characteristic of that illness —
periodic seizures along with epileptic psychosis — rage. Many
witnesses confirm this. Some said that "the falling weakness"
or "falling ailment" was the chronic illness of the tsarevich.
"That sickness was on him for months on end." Others
determined more precisely that the interval between seizures
was nearly a month. The tsarevich, they said, had the disease
"during Lent," then immediately before Easter (which in
1591 was celebrated on April 4), then again on May 12.
During the seizures the boy would throw himself on the
ground. When people tried to pick him up, he would fight
and bite them on the arms and hands.

Eyewitnesses described his last seizure, and the onset of
his disease generally, in the following manner. "The tsarevich

was playing with a knife," said his nurse, "and there he was stricken by the black illness and thrown onto the ground. He stabbed himself in the throat with the knife and beat himself so long that he was no more. And before that, during the Great Fast of this year that disease was upon him, the falling sickness, and he stabbed himself then with a (large nail) and also his mother, Tsaritsa Maria. The disease also came to him suddenly before the Great Day [Easter], and the tsarevich gnawed the hands of Andrei Nagoi's daughter so badly that they almost had to cut them off."

Andrei Nagoi himself testified that the tsarevich "chewed his and his daughter's hands during a seizure, and also the hands of those living there, and of those in bed. When the illness comes upon him, they lay hold of the tsarevich. At those times he is totally unaware that he is being restrained." Bitiagovsky's widow wrote in her petition to the tsar: "During the Great Fast he was taken in his room (that is, in the palace) by that sickness, Sire, and he stabbed his mother, the tsaritsa. Then, Sire, much happened. He started to beat himself, and Andrei Nagoi and his wet-nurse, and the boyar ladies all tried to hold him. But he, Sire, bit them on the hands and arms or whatever parts he could grasp with his teeth." This grave heritage damaged the health of the child. The tsarevich with his frenzied fits appeared to contemporaries as some sort of monster, similar to his father in spirit, thirst for blood, violence and evil.

Such were the setting and conditions in Uglich for the events of May, 1591. The drama began at noon on May 15, when "the tsarevich was walking in the rear court and playing with a knife with some children."[3] In this "rear" or inner courtyard of the palatial residence he received the mortal wound. In order to learn the topography of the "citadel" or kremlin of Uglich, it is necessary to study the accompanying

diagram, composed from data of the seventeenth century.
The "citadel" was located on the bank of the Volga and
surrounded by walls. Two gates led into it, the Spasskie and
the Nikolskie. A remote corner opposite the gates was
occupied by the palace, the courtyard of which extended to
the Church of the Transfiguration. The space located in the
farther acute angle of the citadel by the Naugolnaia-
Florovskaia Tower was the "rear court" of the palace. Churches
"on the blood" were later built on the spot where the tsarevich
had his accident and where his blood was spilled.

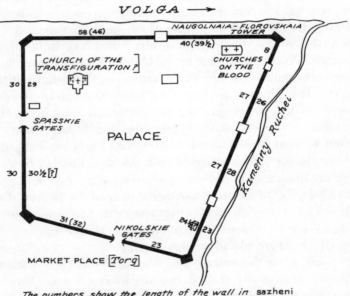

The numbers show the length of the wall in sazheni
[one sazhen = 2.13 meters]. One set of figures is from
a description of 1663, the other from a description
of 1674–1676. The reason for the discrepancy cannot be determined.

THE CITADEL OF UGLICH [4]

Thus it is established that at the moment of the catastrophe the tsarevich was far away from personal contact with outsiders. They were on the other side of the "citadel," passing through the gate near the "marketplace" and the "posad." They, of course, could not pass through the palace to its inner courtyard. At the dinner-hour on May 15, during the customary recess from service activities, when all the official personnel from the chief state secretary Mikhailo Bitiagovsky to the lowest "messenger" had dispersed from the citadel to the posad outside the walls, a tocsin sounded from within and an alarm was raised in the palace. A young court resident, one Petrushka Kolobov, ran up to the palace and reported that the tsarevich had stabbed himself with a knife.

According to Kolobov and his friends, other boys with him, "there were with the tsarevich only the four of them, his wet-nurse, and the chambermaid," at the time of the accident. There were no outsiders with him. The tsarevich's mother, however, upon running into the courtyard, immediately accused his nurse, Vasilissa Volkhova (longest in the tsarevich's service), began beating her, and cried that Volkhova's son and Bitiagovsky's son had "slashed" the tsarevich. At the sound of the alarm people came running from the posad: "many from the posad and the *sloboda* 5 and the fields, from [presumably] boats 6 (on the Volga), Cossacks (workers) with axes and pikes."

The tsaritsa's assertion that her son had been stabbed by the Moscow official, his son, and their friends, was quickly accepted by the crowd. The tsaritsa's brother, Mikhailo, long an enemy of Bitiagovsky and drunk after dinner, was instrumental in arousing the crowd. Under the influence of the tsaritsa's cries and Mikhailo's speeches a massacre began in Uglich. The crowd went after Bitiagovsky and his family, and also after others whom they suspected of having a part in the death of the tsarevich. Bitiagovsky ran into the palace grounds and tried to hide in the "log house," but the crowd found him. "They tore down the doors of the house and dragged out Mikhailo Bitiagovsky and Danil Tretiakov and killed them on the spot." They beat the son of the tsarevich's nurse, Osip Volkhov, and tortured him for a long time. Finally, they brought him, "barely alive, to the tsaritsa in front of the church." There, in front of the tsaritsa, they put him to death. Bitiagovsky's son was killed "in the state secretary's house" (he was not in the palace). His mother and sisters were taken in their home. The crowd "scourged" them, dragged them outside toward the palace, and "went to beat them, too." Only the intervention of the clergy spared them from death. But they were taken anyway and, like the nurse Vasilissa, "put under guard."

Bitiagovsky's home was robbed "clean." "To Mikhailo Bitiagovsky's house (said a witness) went all the people of the community, and they ransacked even the beverages from the cellar and cracked the barrels. And they took nine horses." They also plundered the "state secretary's hut" — the chancellery where Bitiagovsky worked. "At the state secretary's house they smashed the doors and passageways and knocked the windows out." A junior clerk, Tretiachko, said of himself: "And I, Tretiachko, went into the hut. My desk-chest was smashed, and taken from it were twenty rubles of the sovereign's money which had been prepared for the tsaritsa and for the tsarevich's expenditure."

The people of Uglich threatened Tretiachko and the other assistant clerks, saying that "it will be the same" with them as with Bitiagovsky. They "fled in fear in all directions and did not dare to enter the town." Several posad people also fled because of the same fear. "About twenty men

chased them, for they were friends of Mikhailo Bitiagovsky."
For several days the fugitives "wandered about in the forest,
but did not dare to enter the town."

Posad people of Uglich, not involved in the massacre,
said that "the whole community was killing." The entire
town rose up against the persons whom it thought to be
guilty of the misfortune and, from animal hatred, destroyed
persons known to be innocent, even those untouched by the
hysterical accusations of the tsaritsa and the drunken malice
of her brother, Mikhailo Nagoi. Such was the outcome of the
misfortune which befell the tsarevich!

The records of the investigation demonstrate how the
drama of Uglich appeared to the court of the Muscovite
government. The investigators in their "inquest" officially
established that the tsarevich had "stabbed himself" in the
throat with a knife during a seizure. His mother, in her grief,
had brought false charges of murder against several persons.
Her brother Mikhailo had aroused the crowd against these
persons. The crowd, "with all the mir," committed a
massacre and killed ten suspects. The crowd also destroyed a
good portion of the palace. The "inquest" in Uglich was first
and foremost reported to the patriarch's council or "sobor,"
which had sent Metropolitan Gelasi to take part in the
investigation.

The council found that "Tsarevich Dmitri's death was the
result of God's judgement" and that the Nagois were guilty of
"high treason." "There has never been" such evil, such murder and spilling of blood, as "was done by Mikhailo Nagoi and
his men." The council therefore turned "that affair" over to
the will of the sovereign. "All is in his Majesty's hands — punishment, disfavor, [or] mercy." The tsar ordered the boyars
to "complete" the Uglich affair, that is, to carry out the appropriate investigation and trial.

Unfortunately, the pertinent documents have not survived. We know only from private reports that those who took part in the massacre were severely punished. A chronicler, presenting the penalty of the court as part of a personal vendetta on Boris's part for the ruin of his confederates, reported that he commanded Tsaritsa Maria to take the veil and sent her "to a desolate place beyond Beloozero." All the Nagois were sent to dungeons in different towns. The people of Uglich were dealt with severely. "Some were executed, some had their tongues cut out, others were thrown into dungeons. A multitude was sent to Siberia to the town of Pelym where they lived and worked.[7] And thus Uglich grew empty." Legend has it that even the bell of Uglich, which sounded the tocsin on May 15, shared exile in Siberia with the people.

The work of the investigating staff was correct and legal. Its findings are also irreproachable from the paleographic point of view. The Muscovite authorities received unimpeachable material for the prosecution of the Nagois and the "muzhiki" of Uglich. But this material evidently was not published by the government for public consumption. This evidence would not, of course, dissuade those who believed that Bitiagovsky murdered the tsarevich, and that Boris, by the principle *cui prodest*, was the prime culprit behind the evil deed. Thus, for example, several of the Nagois held onto this belief all their lives. Those who hated Boris in general wished to think this way. Moscow rumor, which gleaned every sort of scandalous gossip, whispered the same. The basic similarity of the interpretations of the Uglich drama hostile to Boris accounted for their persistence and diffusion.

II CONTEMPORARY ATTITUDES TOWARD
THE EVENTS OF MAY 15, 1591

When in 1606 Tsarevich Dmitri was canonized, church
custom demanded that his "life" be written. It is believed
that his "life" was written in the Holy Trinity-St. Sergius
Monastery. It was composed in a high literary style. Since the
biography of the little tsarevich could not have much
substance (essentially the tsarevich had not lived a conscious
life), the martyrology was not constructed from biographical
material. It places before the reader the devouring image of
the power-crazed Boris Godunov, whose lust for power
pushed him from crime to crime. In his drive for power and
the throne, Boris had ruined the Shuiskys, then Tsarevich
Dmitri, then Tsar Fedor. He was elected to the throne
through his own design and contrivance. By his own crimes
he called down upon himself the wrath of God. His
punishment came in the form of a pretender to the throne.
Like God's own flail, this pretender was successful, and
destroyed Boris and all his family. The pretender, upon
fulfilling his purpose, was in turn crushed by the pious Tsar
Vasili Shuisky, whom the Lord considered worthy to find the
relics of the righteous tsarevich and to install them in
Moscow.

The tragedy of Boris, who supposedly fell victim to his
own criminal passions, received literary expression for the
first time in this "Tale of 1606." The wondrous appearance
of the remains of the tsarevich was explained as a reward
from on high, given to the innocent who had suffered from
Boris's lust for power. The "Tale," however, was not
accepted in ecclesiastical circles because of its political
attacks. For hagiographic purposes it was shortened and
reworked. But it set the tone for all the subsequent "lives" of

the tsarevich composed in the seventeenth century and during the time of Peter the Great (the Tulupov and Miliutin Lives of St. Dmitri of Rostov). Though all versions followed this pattern, not one introduced anything of historical value.

On the other hand, the "Tale of 1606," understood by contemporaries to be an historical chronicle of events in Moscow, was studied by chronographers and "chroniclers." Largely through their compilations this text received wide distribution in the writings of the seventeenth century. There appeared a legend based on the "Tale." According to Karamzin, this legend was a "curious, although dubious" tale "about the reign of Tsar Fedor Ivanovich," in which the fate of the tsarevich was set forth in completely incredible, naive and fairytale-like details. This cluster of works, springing from one source, is of value to the historian solely as an example of historical-literary fiction. This literature is curious not so much for its factual data as for the examples it provides of the views of the respective authors and of the evolution of a theme.

Aside from this group of "lives" and tales there are several special stories about the assassination of the tsarevich. For an example, in the official "New Chronicle" of the seventeenth century there is a detailed narrative of the events at Uglich. As a piece of literature it is original. Still another account is recorded in one of the articles of the famous archeographer, P.M. Stroev. This narrative probably dates from the eighteenth century. Of these texts, the story of the "New Chronicle" is the most detailed and has provided critics with much material. Such historians as S.M. Soloviev, N.I. Kostomarov, and Archbishop Filaret considered it the most weighty testimonial against Godunov. But their arguments have met with strong objections from, for example, E.A. Belov and A.I. Tiumenev, who have studied the Uglich affair closely.

The closer the researcher's contact with the aggregate
of text relating to the death of Tsarevich Dmitri, the
more negative becomes his attitude toward the memorial in
question [the New Chronicle]. "The story of the New
Chronicle," said A.I. Tiumenev, "does not withstand even the
condescending criticism which Soloviev applies to it. In the
text itself are found many features which force us to suspect
it. A number of legendary insertions and fairytale-like turns
of speech, a number of pieces of information of very
doubtful nature or deliberately false — prevent us from seeing
in the author an eyewitness, a contemporary, or one writing
on the basis of contemporary sources." Actually, the New
Chronicle was written only in 1630 (about forty years after
the death of the tsarevich), and its story about the Uglich
drama by this time had, in many respects, acquired the
nature of epic tradition. In composition and structure it
resembles the "lives."

The starting point of the narrative is Boris's criminal lust
for power. This powerlust leads him to make a number of
attempts on the life of the tsarevich. Poison, administered
many times to the boy, is ineffective, for God does not allow
a secret death for the tsarevich. "His righteous soul and
innocent blood will be declared before the whole world."
Persons assigned to attempt the life of the tsarevich refuse to
do so (Zagriazsky and Chepchugov, whose actual roles are
quite unknown to historians). Finally, the executors of the
plot are found — Klesnin (one of the investigators sent to
Uglich in 1591 by Tsar Fedor), Bitiagovsky, Kachalov, the
Volkhovs (victims of the massacre at Uglich). During a walk
Kachalov and two youths wound the tsarevich. The two
youths are the son of Volkhova, the nurse, and the son of
Bitiagovsky, the diak. The older conspirators remain on the

side. In fear the murderers flee "twenty versts" from the
scene of the crime; but the blood of the righteous victim cries
out to God and "not in vain." The perpetrators return and,
together with the other "conspirators," are "stoned to
death." Then follows a prejudiced and deceitful investigation
by Boris, together with persecution of the tsarevich's family,
the Nagois. Such is the content of the New Chronicle which,
unquestionably, is similar in character to the "lives," and to
the legends related to the "lives."

Stroev's narrative is more original. It resembles a
detailed diary of the events of May 15, 1591 and describes
hour by hour the tsarevich's life on his last day on earth. It
gives the details of the attempt on his life with minute
precision. The tsarevich was attacked when he was "opposite
the Church of Constantine the Great;" his wet-nurse was
"bludgeoned with a cudgel;" and the tsarevich had "his
throat slashed with a knife." However, close study of the
structure and content of this account raises doubts as to
whether the author knew the topography of the town of
Uglich (the existence of a Church of Constantine the Great in
the "citadel" is not mentioned in census registers), and
whether he lived at the time of the events. It is probable that
this text is no older than 1606. The text known to us bears
traits of the eighteenth, not the seventeenth century.

If one does not go beyond these works and neglects to
examine the entire Muscovite literature devoted to the Time
of Troubles, the general impression will be that all the people
of that troubled era truly believed that Boris was a criminal and
that the tsarevich was murdered. Yet such an impression
would be completely untrue. All evidence indicates that
many contemporaries questioned Boris's guilt in the death of
the tsarevich. Their doubts lingered even though later
governments, the church, and the literary works cited, all

loudly and persistently pointed to the villainy of Boris, the man who loved power. The conscience of the people of Muscovy was not always stilled by official assurances. The more daring and candid writers tried in one way or another to circumvent the unwritten but nevertheless persuasive and powerful demands of Muscovite censorship. In another place the author of these lines has shown how these writers accomplished this.[8] "The attitude of seventeenth century Russian writers toward Boris was most curious. They set down their comments at the time when a shrine containing the remains of the tsarevich was placed at the 'right-hand pillar' in the Cathedral of the Archangel. This was also the time when the government of Tsar Shuisky, having dared to interpret the ways of Providence, declared that Tsarevich Dmitri had gained immortality and received the gift of miracles through his innocent suffering and death at the hands of his cunning slave, Boris Godunov. The government declared Boris a murderer of saints; the church composed prayers to the new martyr who had met his death thanks to Boris. Which ordinary Russian of the seventeenth century would doubt what was written in the 'life' of the tsarevich and what was heard in the church services dedicated to the new miracle-worker? In contrast, modern criticism can explain that the later 'lives' of Tsarevich Dmitri derived from the earlier 'Tale of 1606.' Furthermore, today's criticism can trace the road traversed by a political pamphlet gradually transformed into a historical source for hagiographic writing. But in the seventeenth century the keenest and most courageous mind was not in a position to separate fact from fiction in the life of the saint.

"Today we can identify two aspects of the question of the transfer of the tsarevich's body to Moscow in May, 1606. More than a peaceful church ceremony was involved.

Actually, a definite political maneuver is also indicated. It may be surmised that for Shuisky the political aspect of the affair was far more important and valuable. But seventeenth century Russians, even if they understood that Tsar Vasili played with a holy object, dared neither to reject his precedent nor even openly to discuss it in their works. Only Ivan Timofeev, the state secretary, ventured directly to turn his readers to the question of Boris's guilt in the death of the tsarevich, and then only because he was certain of Boris's guilt and was ready to prove the latter's criminal nature.

"Timofeev argued with those who did not wish to believe Boris guilty. 'Do they speak only of Boris's innocence in the slaughter of the tsar's little child?' he asked as he collected evidence about Boris. But Timofeev was an exception among the literary fraternity of his day. He was the most outspoken chronicler of them all — bold, sincere, and loquacious. The others tried to disguise the meaning of their words, preferring rather to remain silent than to speak out carelessly."[9]

Two features stand out in the accounts of Boris's affairs voiced by those seventeenth century writers of a dispassionate and independent stamp. These features are important and significant for the historian. If partisan authors such as Patriarch Job and the author of the "Tale of 1606," who eulogized the Shuiskys, are set aside, the following observation applies to those remaining. In the first place, they were most reluctant to connect Boris to the murder of Tsarevich Dmitri. In the second place, they praised Boris as a man and as a ruler. Their vision of Boris usually rested on an elegant antithesis comprised of virtue which brought good fortune and peace to the Russian land, and of a fatal thirst for power which brought ruin down upon Godunov's head and upon the heads of those close to him.

A few examples can be cited. The chronograph of 1616-1617, the author of which is unfortunately unknown, contains samples of historical observation and literary art. Only one phrase concerns the death of the tsarevich, namely that he was killed "by Mitka Kachalov and Danilka Bitiagovsky. Many spoke of how the righteous Tsarevich Dmitri Ivanovich of Uglich was murdered by command of the Muscovite boyar Boris Godunov." A rhetorical passage follows on the "wicked voluptuousness of power," which brings people to ruin. The next chapter of this work includes a most favorable appraisal of Boris as man and statesman. After he brought peace and established his tsardom, this "bright-spirited and gracious" sovereign flowered "in virtue as does the date tree." Godunov could be likened to the ancient tsars who shone in piety, and whose "virtue was not clouded by wicked and envious malice."

Pointing to Boris's fatal weakness, the author noted that "no one who boasts is free of the snares of that hostile and wily enemy," that is, the devil. Boris's participation in the Uglich murder is mentioned guardedly by this writer. It is his contention that Boris's role was surrounded by rumor at the expense of hard fact. Yet he dared not ignore the rumors, and hence he treated Boris as a victim of "the enemy" who overcame him "with the evil voluptuousness of power." The author of the chronograph of 1616-1617 attached more weight to Boris's "cunning and intrusive" nature than to his guilt in the tsarevich's death. Thus Boris's guile helped him prevent the Romanovs from taking the throne in 1598. In relating the "envious wickedness" of Godunov, the author emphasized especially his obtrusive character. The remaining portions of the chronograph present Boris as a virtuous hero.

The famous Avraami Palitsyn is no less guarded in his statements about the role of Boris in the Uglich affair.

According to Palitsyn, the little tsarevich spoke and behaved
"absurdly" with respect to the Muscovite boyars and
especially Boris. People appeared "who plotted great
troubles." These persons lied and exaggerated, and informed
Boris and other important officials in Moscow of the
tsarevich's behavior. "By the many troubles they caused,"
these enemies and flatterers "brought this sin down upon
him, this most beautiful youth, and dispatched him
unwillingly into eternal peace." Thus Palitsyn finds the cause
of this sin not in Boris himself but in those persons who
disturbed and troubled him. Nothing further was said by this
monk about the Uglich affair, even though he did not
number among Boris's most ardent admirers.

Meanwhile Palitsyn pursued his first vocation — exposing
the sins of Muscovite society punished by God through the
Time of Troubles. In following this theme, Palitsyn also
pointed to Boris, but the Uglich affair played no role in his
accusations. Palitsyn attacked Boris for his arrogance,
suspicion and violence, and for his disrespect for ancient
customs and sacred objects. Yet Palitsyn disregarded
completely the death of the little tsarevich and contended
that "the troubles of all Russia" began as the retribution for
the hounding of the Romanovs. "For the sake of the sons of
Yuriev and for all the world an insane silence was maintained
to keep truth from the tsar." At the same time the wise
monk, though he disliked Godunov intensely, did not hide
from his readers the fact that Boris from the outset knew
how to gain the love of the people through his benevolent
rule. "For the sake of all the people he was kind."

Prince Ivan Andreevich Khvorostinin, like Palitsyn, was
cold toward Boris. He called Godunov cunning and
power-hungry, but at the same time he composed a flowery
panegyric to him. Khvorostinin gives only obscure and

fleeting hints of the murder of Dmitri during a description of
the transfer of the remains of Boris from the Kremlin to the
Varsonofiev Monastery. On the other hand, Prince Ivan Mikhailovich Katyrev-Rostovsky, who occupied a high position in
Muscovite court circles, was a brother-in-law of Tsar Mikhail [10]
and therefore was obliged to show special discretion in
wielding his pen. He repeated the official version of the
murder of the tsarevich by the "secret agents" of Boris
Godunov, but this did not restrain him from otherwise giving
most enthusiastic praise to Boris.

Nowhere is there found such a detailed account of the
virtues of Godunov, such open praise of his intellect and even
of his appearance, as in the writings of Prince Katyrev. For
this prince, Boris was "a very marvelous man," and his
children, Fedor and Ksenia, wonderful offspring. Katyrev's
affection for the ill-fated Godunov family is extraordinarily
enthusiastic in tone. Otherwise the seventeenth-century
chronicles, containing extensive accounts of the murder of
the tsarevich by order of Boris, confirm that Boris was
elected tsar because of his "righteous and strong government
[the regency]," and "his great kindness to the people."

Thus all the literary works of the seventeenth century
not belonging to the hagiographic tradition, and which
describe the Time of Troubles, portray Boris without reference
to the murder in Uglich. That affair is either circumvented or
ignored completely. Ivan Timofeev, in his *Annals,* makes it
clear, nevertheless, that this murder deeply and poignantly
affected the conscience of the Russian people who lived
during the Time of Troubles. Boris's role in the affair, as well
as the tragic fate which befell him, also sincerely troubled the
minds and hearts of the people. Timofeev was beset by doubt
and confusion. He heard rumors from all sides about Boris.
He heard charges of villainy, violence, wickedness, and

intrigues inspired by lust for power. Boris's policies held no
mystery for him, and with some he sympathized while others
he condemned. His belief was that the miracles and holiness
of the new saint, Dmitri, were but divine reward for innocent
suffering. But he also understood that the suspected
"slave-tsar," Boris, was blessed with outstanding intelligence
and displayed many "good deeds to the world." No matter
how Timofeev sought to penetrate the opacity surrounding
Godunov, he recognized finally that he was incapable of
unravelling the riddle of Boris and understanding "whence
came his goodness." "Even at the very hour of his death,"
Timofeev concluded, "no one knew which side prevailed in
his affairs — good or evil . . . ."

After these and similar observations can it be asserted
that the society of that time did not question Boris's criminal
nature? Can it be maintained that the Uglich affair did not
confront Boris's contemporaries with the same obscure and
puzzling tangle that it presents to us? The canonization of
Dmitri in 1606 removed this question from the realm of
argument. But until the discovery of the remains of the
tsarevich, the attitude toward his relics and memory by the
authorities and people provided no grounds for added honor
and glorification of the tsarevich. Dmitri excited no special
attention or esteem. His death evidently passed without any
appreciable ripples in the usual current of Muscovite life. It
must be remembered that Dmitri was not considered to be a
legitimate child. He was born to Ivan the Terrible's sixth or
seventh wife. The church had not even sanctioned Ivan's third
marriage. "He is of the unlawful seventh wife," it was said in
official conversations between Muscovite and Polish
ambassadors.

Because of this point of view, Dmitri probably was not
always called "tsarevich." There is a curious entry in the

"cellerer's daybook" of the Monastery of St. Cyril which was compiled during the reign of Boris Godunov. The daybook enumerates a "requiem feast" which was set out by the brothers of the monastery in memory of various persons and events. For the eve of October 26 there is the entry — "for Prince Dmitri Ivanovich of Uglich." This prince — son of Ivan III and nick-named Zhilka — died in 1521. For May 15 (the day of the tsarevich's death) is noted: "for Prince Dmitri Ivanovich Uglet-sky holy day food." By this "latter Uglichsky" [11] Dmitri the Tsarevich is understood. He was not, however, called tsare-vich in this entry in the daybook. But when the canonization of Dmitri was completed, this entry was attached to the day-book by paper and on the fastening was written: "On the fifteenth of this month, in memory of the pious Tsarevich Prince Dmitri of Uglich, wonderworker of Moscow and all Rus-sia, a requiem feast." Thus the title was changed from "prince" [kniaz] to "tsarevich."

The tsarevich's funeral was held in Uglich immediately after the "inquest" of the commission of investigation. It was not considered necessary to transport the body to Moscow to the "burial-place of his fathers" in the Cathedral of the Archangel, as was done in the past for princes who died outside Moscow. For example, Dmitri Ivanovich (Zhilka), who is also mentioned in the daybook of the Monastery of St. Cyril, died in Uglich. He was buried in the Cathedral of the Archangel alongside the grave of Dmitri Donskoi. Another Prince Dmitri, called "Krasny," the brother of Dmitri Shemiaka, who died in Galich, was also taken to Moscow (in 1441), and the chronicler relates many curious things about the details of his death and about the difficulties of transporting his body, which "was twice dropped from the carriage." It seems that there was no obstacle to burying the "latest Uglichsky" prince-tsarevich in Archangel Cathedral. But he was not accorded this honor. In the words of the

chronicler, Tsarevich Dmitri "was buried in the Church of the
Transfiguration of Our Savior" in Uglich.

The grave itself was quickly forgotten. The tsarevich's
relatives who were sent away from Uglich did not, of course,
have a chance to care for the grave, and Tsar Fedor saw no
need for it. There exists a quite curious testimonial that in
1606 the inhabitants of Uglich were unable to point out the
burial site of the tsarevich to the clergy who had been sent
from Moscow to claim his body. The whole town searched
for the grave (it is not clear whether inside or outside the
Church of the Transfiguration). "For a long time they did
not find it and sang prayers. By these prayers they found the
body. A puff of fragrant smoke came from the side of the
ditch. Here they immediately found him." Removing the
hagiographic overlay from this story, we find an indisputable
fact — an abandoned, even lost, grave. What hindered the local
residents who honored his memory, if there were any, from
honoring his grave? Fear or persecution by Boris could have
stifled any desire to decorate the final resting place of the
disfavored tsarevich. But no one could have forbidden the
remembrance of the place of his rest.

Contemporaries of the events of 1591 have noted that
Tsar Fedor did not attend the burial of his brother in Uglich,
although he did visit the Holy Trinity-St. Sergius Monastery
that year on the Feast of the Holy Trinity (May 23). They
attributed this fact to the wiles of Boris, who was supposed
to have set fire to Moscow in order to distract Fedor from a
journey to Uglich. [12] However, the Moscow fire (1591)
occurred not in May but in June. For that reason the fire
could not have hindered the tsar's journey to Uglich where
the tsarevich was to be kept, probably, until Trinity Day. The
absence of Tsar Fedor must be explained otherwise. The tsar
could travel and evidently liked to do so. Other than the

11111

ordinary trips in the vicinity of Moscow, he made, for example, a winter journey to the area around Narva where he conducted military maneuvers (1590). In 1592 he made a spring tour of the monasteries at Mozhaisk, Vorovsk, and Zvenigorod. Three years later he again visited Vorovsk. But Tsar Fedor never once went to Uglich, for the burial of his brother or for the solemn church ceremony celebrating the discovery of the remains of Prince Roman of Uglich (1595). This was not because of any physical weakness of Fedor's. If the tsar's failure to visit Uglich was not accidental, then it probably stems from the fact that Uglich was then considered to be an "appanage" — a place apart from the territory of Muscovy and therefore foreign. Tsar Fedor's love for his brother Dmitri was not so strong that it would move him to visit an "appanage." Nor was brotherly love so binding that it would cause the tsar to honor the tsarevich's funeral by his presence in this "appanage," which had witnessed so much bloodshed.

Still another curious and significant detail must be added to those already cited. This detail was noted at the time by Polish diplomats. During negotiations in 1609, they pointed out to the Muscovites that the time and conditions of Dmitri's death had been thoroughly considered in Muscovy, and that when the Muscovite voevody were forced to reveal the designs of the pretender, they clearly were confused and mistaken. The voevoda of Chernigov, in 1603 or 1604, had written to the elder of Oster that the tsarevich was stabbed in Uglich in 1588 — "sixteen years ago," when it was actually in 1591, thirteen years before. The tsarevich was interred, according to the voevoda's report, "in the Cathedral Church of the Virgin Mother of God." But the Poles knew that there was no such church in Uglich. There was, however, a "Cathedral Church of the Holy Savior." Having discovered

other errors of a similar nature, the Poles justly reasoned that
the guilt lay not with the voevody themselves but with their
Muscovite superiors who had sent them false information.
"Boris and his state secretaries caused harmful misunderstanding, Your Majesty," they said.

III   TSAREVNA FEODOSIA, TSARITSA IRINA,
      AND THE QUESTION OF THE MUSCOVITE
      SUCCESSION

And so the "last Uglich" appanage prince, born "of the
unlawful seventh wife" [of Ivan the Terrible], was not
vouchsafed to be buried with his "illustrious" tsarist
"parents" in their Moscow tomb, but was forgotten in his
abandoned grave. Such was the fate of Tsarevich Dmitri until
his canonization, according to documents of that day. But
the death of the tsarevich, which excited no remarkable
interest among the Muscovite populace, turned out to be
fateful for Boris. It gave those who hated him a convenient
motive for slanderous charges as to the murder of the
tsarevich. They accused Boris of many things: of an attempt
on the life of Ivan the Terrible, of the murder of the
Shuiskys, of the fire of Moscow, and finally, among many
other things, of the deaths of Fedor and Irina. All of these
charges seem arbitrary and improbable. But the death of
Dmitri from a stab wound, together with bloodshed and
strident accusations against the government's agent,
Bitiagovsky, who was killed for his evil deed, actually created
suspicion against his master and mentor, Boris. The motive
for the crime also seemed clear — "an unslaked hunger for
power" and thirst for the throne. With Dmitri disappeared
the last representative of an expiring tsarist lineage, and the
end of the dynasty arrived. For whom could this situation be

more desirable than for Boris? Who, more than Boris, could dream of inheriting the throne? Who was closer to the rank of tsar than the ruler of the realm who in his hands held *de facto* power already?

Reasoning and reflection of this kind could kindle the certainty of Boris's criminal guilt among simple people not inclined to take into account all the aspects of the situation, or unaware of all the details. The researcher of today who wishes to consider the conditions of those years, certainly will take such details into account. He will assign significance to the fact that Tsaritsa Irina, at the moment of Dmitri's death, still had not lost hope of having children, and that all those close to her gave her comfort through this hope for tsarist offspring. And Boris, naturally, understood that the death of a doubtfully legitimate brother of the tsar would hardly pose any loss for the dynasty if only Fedor and Irina would have a child. In 1591 the murder of Dmitri did not signal the deathknell of a dynasty.

In May, 1592 the royal couple had a daughter, Tsarevna Feodosia, "a gift of God." [13] There grew a strong hope in Muscovy that the tsarist root would flourish through this new and "noble branch." While the tsarevna was still little, Boris said officially that she was both his "sovereign and niece." If later there were intentions in Moscow to search for foreign bridegrooms for Tsarevna Ksenia Godunova, then it is reasonable to assume that the same idea arose concerning Feodosia — to marry her in the future to a foreign prince and thus provide Muscovy with dynastic succession. How myopic Boris must have been had he timed an attempt on the life of Dmitri under such circumstances! Of course Boris calculated the possibility of dynastic issue. As a subtle politician he knew that it was necessary to do what he could to assure power for himself and for his sister, Tsaritsa Irina, even in the absence of the desired offspring.

One particular detail of court "rank" of the time is quite significant. For the first time in Moscow, Tsaritsa Irina Fedorovna, in the presence of her spouse, formally entered the sphere of government as the senior adviser to her husband and took part in discussions of state affairs co-equally with the boyars. Not only secular affairs, but even ecclesiastical business came under her advisement. The celebrated decision of the Moscow government to install the Greek Patriarch Jeremiah "in the first seat in Volodimir" and not in Moscow, was reached with the participation of the tsaritsa. Boris, in his deliberations with the boyars, included "his righteous and Christ-loving Tsaritsa and Grand Princess Irina." Had Tsarevich Dmitri lived, his right of succession would have been disputed by Irina. The legitimate wife and adviser of the sovereign, and his co-ruler, naturally would have had a greater chance of stepping into power than the epileptic tsarevich, begotten through an unlawful marriage. Muscovite attitudes toward illegitimate children, expressed in the Law Code of 1649 (Chapter X, Article 280), were scornful and severe, and it must be assumed that the tsarevich's rivals would have entertained similar attitudes toward him.

One more interesting detail of Boris's conduct deserves attention. Boris did nothing to display his dynastic ambitions until the question of the tsar's children became moot. When Tsarevna Feodosia died and the physical deterioration of the tsar ended his hope (but not the tsaritsa's) of having more children, Boris, as ruler of the tsardom, began to place his own son Fedor by his side. Fedor Borisovich became an active figure in Boris's court ceremonies and in his correspondence. Fedor Borisovich received ambassadors, sent personal gifts to important landowners, and "signed himself" next to his father in documents. The inclusion of his son in political affairs testifies to the subtle foresight of Boris

Godunov. Gradually he was preparing a successor. The debut
of Fedor Borisovich dates from 1594-1595; earlier would
have been futile and imprudent. Conditions in Moscow at
that time were such that not even the tsarevich himself could
have hoped to succeed to the throne. Athwart the road to the
crown stood the women — the wife and daughter of the tsar.
When the daughter died there remained the wife. Boris did
not expect that she would prove a hindrance and antagonist
for her brother and nephew. Hence he began to have his son,
the tsaritsa's nephew, "appear" in the realm and before
friendly governments.

The consideration of all these circumstances facilitates
the understanding that conditions were much more complex
than the public and private charges against Boris would
indicate. Rumor spread easily in a crowd, for as is said, a
crowd always "believes what it hears" and "is quick to spread
it," be it truth or falsehood. The aim of historical research is
to free the facts from the tendentiousness and biases which
might hide the truth. Because this is true, the historian has
not the slightest right to bring charges against Boris's
memory, charges lacking in objective proof and historical
meaning.

IV   THE DEATH OF FEDOR IVANOVICH.
      THE SUCCESSION AND ABDICATION OF
      TSARITSA IRINA. THE ROLE OF THE
      PATRIARCH IN THE PROVISIONAL GOV-
      ERNMENT AND THE ELECTION OF THE
      TSAR BY THE *ZEMSKY SOBOR*

At the beginning of 1598 the Muscovite dynasty came to an
end. Towards morning on January 7, "the torch of the

Russian land was extinguished; the Orthodox light died."
Tsar Fedor "received the invasion of the cloud of death,
abandoned his temporal realm and entered into eternal life."
Such words express the chronicler's sadness over the death of
the blessed fool of God, the tsar. The patriarch's narrative of
the life of Tsar Fedor, in describing the final hours of the
childless monarch, states that the tsar died, "having himself
handed the scepter of his righteous tsardom to his lawful
wife, his righteous Tsaritsa and Grand Princess of All Russia,
Irina Fedorovna." "The fair ruler Boris Godunov shortly
thereafter commanded the tsar's councillors to kiss the
lifegiving cross and to pledge allegiance to the pious tsaritsa
who reigns over them." The boyars' oath to Irina was made
in the presence of Patriarch Job and his council. "The most
holy patriarch and all the sacred council were at the kissing
of the cross."

Thus was Irina's accession to the throne accomplished.
The country tacitly recognized her authority. Prayers were
offered and litanies sung in Moscow and other cities for the
tsaritsa. Orders and decrees went out from the capital in her
name. Messages and dispatches were received from many
places in the name of Tsaritsa Irina — in the name of the nun,
Tsaritsa Alexandra, after she had taken the veil. In a word,
Irina reigned. Had she remained on the throne and had she
found it possible and proper to marry, her husband would
have shared her power and perhaps a new dynasty would
have been founded. Irina, notwithstanding, had no thought
of marriage. She mourned the fact that through her "the
tsarist root will come to an end." Immediately after the
burial of the tsar she decided to leave the world and to enter
a convent. Behind this public reason, as it were, for her
entering a convent there lies the hint of another motive. Irina
was ill. The tsaritsa suffered from consumption and chronic

hemorrhage from the throat. She went to an early grave in 1603.

The tsaritsa's abdication and her entry into the convent left Moscow "sovereignless" and created an interregnum. Power was temporarily placed in the hands of the patriarch. Attempts to prevail upon the nun Alexandra to remain "in the state and hold the scepter of the great state of the Russian tsardom" had no success, although the patriarch asked only that she be sovereign in name, and that she hand over power to her brother Boris. All requests that Irina "give her blessing" to Boris to rule "in her stead" were unsuccessful. Neither Boris nor the tsaritsa would agree to the simple procedure of succession by means of "blessing" from the tsaritsa. According to an official account, these requests came from the patriarch, the clergy, the boyars and all the people. Private reports related that, after the abdication of Irina the boyars thought to form a provisional government headed by the Boyar Duma instead of calling the former ruler, Boris, to power. But when state secretary Vasili Shchelkalov took this idea to the people, who were gathered in the Kremlin, supposedly they refused to swear allegiance to the Duma and reiterated that they had already sworn allegiance to the tsaritsa. They desired the immediate enthronement of Boris. Because Boris had not agreed to take the throne without formal election, the matter was postponed until forty days after the death of Tsar Fedor, and the patriarch remained at the head of the government.

The "forty-day period" ended on February 15, 1598. The official act of Boris's election — the "Charter of Affirmation" — relates that the patriarch supervised the entire procedure of the election of the tsar. He set the period of mourning ("forty days of blessed memorial"). During this period he "sent" after the hierarchs and the "entire holy sobor," after the [state] servitors, "the sovereign children of various great states," the boyars, and others who "usually attend great councils." He commanded that all the people "who are in Moscow" "ponder among themselves who will be tsar." Thus the patriarch prepared the convocation of the Zemsky Sobor for the election of a tsar on the very day that the "forty-day period" ended. He opened the Sobor immediately and "commanded that everyone be in attendance and agree together in the reigning city of Moscow."

The dominant role of the patriarch has troubled several historians. "By what right the patriarch took it upon himself to convene the Zemsky Sobor, we do not know," wrote I. D. Beliaev. "No one ever gave him this right." But the documents of those weeks during which Patriarch Job was at the head of the provisional government definitely state that authority was given to him by Irina. "By order of the tsaritsa" the boyars were to "discuss" affairs with the patriarch, and the patriarch was to execute the decisions by issuing decrees. The attempt by the boyars to arrogate plenary power to themselves and to gain for the Boyar Duma the allegiance of the people was, as has been stated, unsuccessful. For that reason the "primate," Patriarch Job, quite correctly considered himself to be the leader of the state.

The composition of the Zemsky Sobor which the patriarch ordered to convene before him on February 17 has also evoked bewilderment among researchers. They have considered the Sobor unfairly weighted in favor of Boris Godunov. "The Sobor of 1598," wrote I. D. Beliaev, "assumed merely the form of the Zemsky Sobor. Actually, it was but a cover for the intrigues of a well-known party and was designed for the advantage of Godunov." Rather than a

properly representative meeting, it was a caricature, a
"comedy." This view dominated the learned literature until
the publication of V. O. Kliuchevsky's remarkable work, *The
Composition of Representation in the Zemsky Sobor of Old
Russia.* In place of general and unsubstantiated surveys of the
composition of the electoral body of 1598, Kliuchevsky
provided a detailed account of the members of the Zemsky
Sobor.

In the "Charter of Affirmation" of the election of Boris
the list of members was repeated twice. Where the Charter
begins, starting with the clergy, there is a systematic listing of
all "who were at the Sobor with the primate, the most holy
Patriarch Job." Then, at the end of the text of the Charter,
the official signatures of the members of the Sobor are
affixed. "The difference between both lists," said
Kliuchevsky, "is that in each of them there are names which
do not appear in the other. In the list of those present at the
electoral Sobor there are many persons who did not sign the
charter. Several signed who are not mentioned in the list of
electors." If we count the names which appear in both lists
and those which appear in one list only, according to
Kliuchevsky's reckoning, there were 512 persons who
participated in the election of the tsar in 1598.

V. O. Kliuchevsky tried to collect information about all
of these persons. He arrived at the interesting conclusion that
the composition of the Sobor was completely regular and
that it conformed to the sixteenth-century notion of the
order of representation. This notion enjoyed a unique
interpretation in Moscow. Members of the Sobor attended
upon the invitation of the government and not by authority
of the electors. Members were chosen by the authorities, who
determined the representatives of this or that group. Thus the
nobles of Muscovy "were not representatives at the Sobor of

district noble societies, but represented the latter by virtue of
their official positions as marshals appointed by the
government from among the landowners of those districts."

This procedure achieved territorial representation
without the use of electors from the provinces. It did not
seem necessary to call representatives from all the towns of
Muscovy in order to record the voice of the whole country.
In defining who should be included in the Sobor of 1598,
the same rules were followed as in 1566. This is why the
Sobor of 1598 must be considered completely proper in
composition. There were in attendance some 100 clergyman,
some 50 boyars and members of the Duma, around 30 state
secretaries, about 270 gentry and deti boyarskie, and some
36 of the commercial class. "Thus (concludes Kliuchevsky) in
the composition of the Sobor of 1598 we can clearly discern
the same four groupings that appeared in the earlier Sobor:
the ecclesiastical administration, the government, the military
service class, and the commercial-industrial class."

The matter was irreproachable. The Sobor was lawful
and correct. Its leader, the patriarch, acted on the authority
of the sovereign, the tsaritsa. No "comedy" can be found
with respect to this Sobor. If any advantage accrued to Boris
(and, of course, there was), it was not because of any
distortion of the Sobor's membership. "The order of business
may have been contrived, but not the composition of the
Sobor," noted V. O. Kliuchevsky. "The plan of Godunov's
supporters consisted not in securing his election to the throne
by juggling the membership of the Sobor, but in forcing a
properly composed Sobor to yield to the dictum of a popular
movement."

V   THE ELECTION OF BORIS AND HIS
     ACCEPTANCE

The Charter of Affirmation relates the course of Boris's
election as follows. On Friday, February 17, the Sobor
opened under the chairmanship of Job with a ceremonial
convocation. Preceding the convocation were private
meetings among persons "who were in Moscow." In these
meetings "they reached an agreement on who should be
tsar." Job began the ceremonial convocation with a flowery
speech in support of Boris. His opinion and the sense of these
preliminary meetings "of all Orthodox Christians who were in
Moscow," was that "no one was searching for or desired a
sovereign" other than Boris. The whole meeting — the people
"who were in Moscow" as well as those who "had arrived
from distant towns to the sovereign city of Moscow" — agreed
with the patriarch and resolved to elect Boris without debate.
It is clear that the convention of February 17 merely
sanctioned a decision which had been made earlier.

Having thus completed the election, the Sobor decided
to meet again on Saturday, February 18, in the Cathedral of
the Dormition, for a service of public prayer. At that
gathering, Monday, February 20, was set as the day for a
ceremonial procession of the entire Sobor to the Novodevichi
Convent. The purpose of the procession was to secure the
assent of Tsaritsa Irina-Alexandra to the election of Boris, and
to gain Boris's agreement to accept the throne. However, on
February 20 neither the tsaritsa nor Boris agreed! This same
day the patriarch again convened the Sobor to discuss further
measures to be taken. Publicly the Sobor resolved to return
the next day to the Novodevichi Convent, this time in a
religious procession bearing the most holy relics of the
capital. A huge crowd of Muscovites accompanied the
procession. To Boris was presented a petition that he accept

the throne, and along with the petition a threat of excommunication should he refuse. Boris had no choice but to accept. On Shrove Sunday, February 26, he appeared for the first time in the robes of the tsar. But he postponed his coronation until September 1.

Such is the official account of the circumstances of Boris's election. Private reports of Russians and foreigners of that time portray the election in a different manner. With the exception of the "Tale of 1606," Russian chroniclers are laconic. "The New Chronicle" depicts the course of events much as does the Charter of Affirmation, though without sympathy for Boris. Its narrative is brief and restrained. It says of the Sobor that "from all the towns of the land people were sent to Moscow for the election of a tsar." It admits that the patriarch and clergy "took counsel with all the land" and unanimously elected Boris tsar, "seeing in him, during the reign of Tsar Fedor, a righteous and strong ruler over the land, demonstrating to the people [his] great kindness." The chronicler agrees with the Charter of Affirmation in depicting the course of the election and the petition presented to Boris. But in this connection he wrote that "the princes Shuisky did not wish Boris to be tsar. They knew that he would persecute them and the people. He would bring them much trouble and woe."

There is reason to believe that the chronicler substituted the name Shuisky for Romanov. The Romanovs suffered greatly at the hands of Godunov; the Shuiskys, not at all. Nevertheless, the Romanovs and the Shuiskys were united in their desire not to see Boris become tsar. The author of the "Tale of 1606" was clearly a supporter of the Shuiskys. He hated Boris. In his narrative apparently he combined all the malicious gossip which surrounded Boris's accession to the throne. He presented the matter thus — Boris crudely and cleverly paved the road to his own success with fear and flattery; he brought such pressure to bear on the people that "all the world begged Boris to take the throne."

Intimidated, the nobility remained silent. "The great boyars (the princes Shuisky) and those intimate with the Great Sovereign and Grand Prince of All Russia Fedor Ivanovich (the Romanovs), all of whom were worthy, were not wont to choose themselves, but gave in to the will of the people." Having deceived and cowed the nobles and having frightened and bribed the people, Godunov staged, with the help of the Moscow police, a scene of public supplication at the Novodevichi Convent. Those who were unwilling were forcibly brought to the convent. "Whoever does not come and beg Boris to take the throne will be fined two rubles." At the convent the crowd wailed loudly and entreated Boris. Police officers ordered the people to fall on their knees and then to stand up – to cry, to howl. They "beat and struck on the back of the neck those who hesitated." So it was, seemingly, that Boris's agents proved to the boyars and to Boris himself the desire of the people to see him on the throne. It would appear that there was no legality, no justice and not the slightest bit of decorum in the manner whereby Boris, the tsar-killer, seized the tsardom.

The slander of the "Tale of 1606" spread among those Muscovite political circles hostile to Boris. But this slanderous story also fell among the common people of the square. Various rumors circulated in Moscow, and often acquired the most improbable forms. One small incident particularly illustrates the growth of such rumors. Ivan Timofeev relates a curious story. A small boy appeared on the convent wall before the very window of Tsaritsa Irina's cell just at the moment when all Moscow was beseeching Boris to accept the crown. Timofeev believed that Boris or his "troublemakers" had engaged this "lad" with insidious purpose, for no one drove him away or stopped him, despite

his reprehensible behavior. "Needlessly and unceasingly" he
shouted into the tsaritsa's window that she should urge Boris
to comply with the wishes of the people and accept the
throne. Had this not "obliged" Boris, then the boy "would
never have dared appear in such a place."

Timofeev was not alone in mentioning this little
hooligan. Others spoke of him, too. The rumor about this
impudent, brazen and unpleasant petitioner took on various
textures. A foreigner then in Russia relates that, upon the
request of the electors, "two youths" sang "in a rather
unpleasant manner" in the hope of softening Boris's resolve.
Another version of this story recounted that a whole crowd
of boys sang, "and the group consisted of a large number of
young boys and youths." Finally, the most extreme version
of the rumor, now legendary, suggested that a special
procession moved to the convent from Moscow. This
procession was comprised of several thousand boys in tearful
petition to Boris ("They sent several thousand young boys
out"). It is in this form that this worthless episode was
recorded by Peter Petreus.

The student who trusts this kind of eyewitness report
will find a few curious and superficial items about the
election of the tsar, but he will not thrust to the heart of the
political game then taking place. From Timofeev, for
example, it may be learned how Boris behaved before the
crowd during the general public petition, how he went out
onto the porch of his cell and, with his usual habit of helping
his tongue with his hands, "put his handkerchief around his
neck." By this he meant that he would hang himself "if they
did not cease pleading." In this way Boris illustrated his
words to the people standing far away who could not hear
him. "The worst of them were able to understand" (in other
words, he made sure that even the dumbest understood).
Then he "escaped" into his cell where he finally agreed to

become tsar. Similar passages may be collected from chronicles and memoirs, but they neither refute nor clarify nor amplify the official reports of Boris's election. He was elected by a properly constituted Zemsky Sobor in ceremonial convocation on February 17 under the leadership of the patriarch. The patriarch had been placed at the head of the government by the tsaritsa. The election took place after preliminary conferences which were held with the knowledge and by the instruction of the patriarch.

VI   FOREIGN INFORMATION ON THE MOSCOW ELECTION

Foreign sources offer new and very valuable information concerning the events of the preliminary conferences in Moscow. They include documents relating to official Lithuanian administrative correspondence and to German merchants then trading in Muscovy. Moscow took every precaution to conceal from foreign eyes the events which occurred there after the death of Tsar Fedor. The interregnum and the election of the new sovereign were to proceed in utmost secrecy. No foreign influence could be tolerated. The borders were sealed upon the death of the tsar. No one was allowed to pass the frontiers. Guards were set on all the roads, even on the footpaths, so that news from Moscow would not pass to the Germans or to Lithuania. Foreign merchants were detained in Moscow, Pskov, Smolensk and other towns and placed under constant surveillance. Official messengers from neighboring states hastily were turned back from the frontiers of Muscovy. They were not allowed to communicate with the Russian people. The frontier fortresses were reinforced and strengthened in fear of attack by neighboring states.

Foreigners, seeing these precautions, intensified their efforts to follow events. In the town of Orsha, on the border of Muscovy (at Smolensk), the senior Lithuanian official, Andrzej Sapieha, upon learning of the death of Tsar Fedor, at once sent his spies to Muscovy's borders. They were able to procure a great deal of information despite Moscow's precautionary measures. The nature and extent of this intelligence indicates that it was collected not from the common people but from well-informed sources having connections with Moscow. Andrzej Sapieha reported his information to the Grand Hetman of Lithuania, Christopher Radziwill. These dispatches give considerable and curious evidence about events transpiring in political and court circles in Moscow during the forty-day period following the death of Tsar Fedor. This is the period in which, according to Patriarch Job, people "who were in Moscow" pondered "who would be their sovereign."

In January, 1598, three weeks after Fedor's death, Sapieha apparently knew that four candidates vied for the throne! Boris Fedorovich Godunov, about whom it was said that he was in mourning; Prince Fedor Ivanovich Mstislavsky, who was the presiding dignitary in the Boyar Duma; Fedor Nikitich Romanov, a relative by marriage to Tsar Fedor; and Bogdan Yakovlevich Belsky, who during the reign of the late tsar had been in disfavor, but who now reappeared in Moscow with a large retinue. He wished to become tsar. Sapieha thought that there might be bloodshed over the throne. He felt that, among the candidates, Romanov had the best chance, for he was the tsar's relative. About ten days from the time Sapieha wrote this letter, he received fresh news from Moscow. He relayed it to Radziwill in a letter dated February 5 (Old Style), that is, before Boris's election. This time the news was surprising. In the first place, it was said that during his last days Tsar Fedor had answered Boris's question as to who would reign after him by saying: "You cannot sit on the throne. You are not of high birth." Apparently the tsar had chosen Fedor Nikitich Romanov to be the new tsar.

In the second place, Sapieha learned an improbable and confused story concerning the death of Tsarevich Dmitri. "After the death of Fedor Ivanovich, Godunov had with him a friend who was very similar in looks to the late Prince Dmitri, brother of the Grand Prince of Muscovy, born of Piatigorka (Maria Temruikovna?),[14] who had been dead a long time. A letter bearing the name of this Prince Dmitri, sent to Smolensk, stated that he had become grand prince. All Moscow wondered whence he had come. The people supposed that he had remained in hiding until this time. When this news reached the voevody and the boyars, they began to make inquiries among themselves. One of them, a Nagoi, said that Prince Dmitri was not alive and that Mikhailo Bitiagovsky knew it. They immediately sent for Bitiagovsky and attempted to learn from him whether or not Prince Dmitri was alive. Under questioning, Bitiagovsky admitted that he had killed Dmitri himself at the order of Godunov, and that Godunov wanted this friend who looked like Dmitri to pass for the prince, and become tsar in the event that Boris was not elected. The steward of Astrakhan (Bitiagovsky) was executed and Godunov was reproached for being false to his sovereigns. He was accused of having treacherously murdered Dmitri, who was expendable, and of poisoning Fedor because he wished to become grand prince. In a quarrel Fedor Romanov drew a knife to kill Godunov, but others present stopped him. After this quarrel Godunov did not appear again in the Duma. He remained hidden with his supporters."

Sapieha's letter of February 5 (15), 1598 reveals startling facts. First of all, it shows that there existed a basis for the later legends about the transfer of the scepter of power from Tsar Fedor directly to the Romanovs. Legends have created the scene for us. Tsar Fedor, dying, offered the scepter to Fedor Nikitich Romanov. Romanov then yielded it to his brother Alexander. Alexander handed it to his other brothers who accepted it, but then Boris seized it. This legend proposed that at the very moment of Tsar Fedor's death the elder Romanov became a candidate for the throne. The letter of Sapieha testifies that the charge of the murder of Dmitri, together with the tale of the resurrection of the tsarevich, existed before Boris came to the throne.

The story was put into circulation as a means of waging an electoral struggle against Boris. An absurd and malicious rumor, it spread from Moscow throughout the countryside and reached the ears of Sapieha. Sapieha concluded his letter of February 5 with a postscript stating that, according to his latest intelligence, some boyars, all the streltsy and practically all the *posolstvo* [the free commoners] supported Godunov. The majority of the boyars upheld the Romanovs. It appeared to Sapieha that Boris's chances of election were growing. From the first Sapieha believed that Romanov would be elected, for he considered Godunov a man of low birth. Then he learned of Godunov's popularity among the masses and attached appropriate significance to this fact. In a letter dated February 13 (23) he stressed that the people and the streltsy desired Godunov very much, but that the boyars would have been more "pleased" with Fedor or Alexander Romanov. The situation in Moscow seemed to Sapieha to be one of "*zemeszanie,*" that is, rebellion or social disorder. He knew that the official "election" of the Grand Prince of Muscovy had not taken place, but was set either for forty days after the death of Tsar Fedor, or for the "first Sunday in Lent."

Regrettably, Sapieha's letters offering impressions of Boris's victory have not been preserved. His letter following that of February 13 bears the date June 6 (16) and speaks of later events in Muscovy. But in those letters concerning Moscow which have been preserved, the general course of the electoral struggle becomes clear. Of several candidates for the throne of Muscovy, two finally emerged: Boris and the elder Romanov. Apparently a sharp struggle took place between them. A rumor circulated telling of an attempt on Boris's life by Fedor Romanov. Revolt and bloodshed were in the offing. The mood of the people grew to favor Boris prior to the meeting of the Zemsky Sobor on February 17, and this led to Boris's election by the Sobor. But those opposed to Boris refused to lay down their weapons and acknowledge his victory. The struggle against him persisted even after the election. In a letter in German sent from Pskov shortly after the election and the oath of allegiance to Boris, there are curious hints that the aristocracy did not recognize Boris as tsar and that the oath of allegiance did not go smoothly in all places. The brothers of the Pskov-Pechersky Monastery had to be forced to swear allegiance, for the monks did not believe that Boris had been elected.

VII   THE OATH OF ALLEGIANCE TO BORIS.
      "TSAR" SIMEON BEKBULATOVICH. THE
      MARCH TO SERPUKHOV AND THE
      CORONATION OF BORIS

The information from abroad just cited is of extraordinary value. What was suppressed in Muscovite political writings was freely voiced in foreign documents. Outside information about the election, Boris's agreement to take the throne, and the aftermath of these events, explains a great deal. The people of those times were dissatisfied with the manner in which the oath of allegiance to the new tsar was performed in Moscow. For the sake of appearances, Boris wished to attach to the oath the greatest solemnity and moment. Rather than the palace and other official places where formerly the oath was given by kissing the cross, Boris ordered the people to swear allegiance in the churches and even in the Moscow cathedral — the Dormition. State secretary Ivan Timofeev figuratively described how the endless crowds swore allegiance there. For days on end the people loudly cried out the words of the ritual of the kissing of the cross like "a large bellowing herd of dumb animals," interupting and drowning out the church services. The patriarch as "pontiff," the clergy, and the boyars were obliged to attend, though without purpose and the performance of any related ceremonies. Thus the oathtaking gave the impression of a ceremonial parody. In the text of the oath of allegiance Timofeev found frightening, threatening and totally inappropriate words. "The oration was an apostasy," wrote Timofeev. "It was as if neither the grace of the Creator nor of His saints was with us." In the ritual itself were the following words: "if I fail to serve and obey the sovereign, and commit any evil after the kissing of the Cross, then may the mercy of God, the Blessed Virgin and all the saints be not upon me." In this manner, said Timofeev, Boris "placed an anathema on all."

Contemporaries condemned other measures undertaken by Boris to strengthen his tsarist "name" and dignity. During his rule Boris ordered the *Mnogoletie* [15] to be sung in the churches not only for himself but also for his wife and children. He ordered that his "full name" must always be written, in other words, his full title must be cited. Every year a ceremonial procession from Moscow to the

Novodevichi Convent celebrated the memory of Boris's election to the throne. The building of chapels in honor of the newly-installed sovereign's patron saint, Boris the Prince, was encouraged. Decrees of this variety were accompanied by ornate ceremonials. The Charter of Affirmation was composed in an especially florid literary style and signed in duplicate by all the members of the Zemsky Sobor.

Then arose the problem of where the document should be kept. "The members of the Sobor decided that it would be preserved. For the sake of posterity it must be preserved whole, and not an iota, not a dot must ever pass from it." Such great consequence was attached to the idea of the inviolability of the tsar's election in 1598 that the electors ventured to repeat the words of the Sermon on the Mount — that not an iota, not a dot would pass from the Law (Matthew V, 18). It was decided to keep one copy of the Charter of Affirmation "in the royal treasury together with other documents" and the other — "in the patriarch's sacristy in the Cathedral of the Dormition." But the fact remains that the latter copy was placed in the shrine of the relics of Metropolitan Peter in the Cathedral of the Dormition. It was placed in a reliquary to remain sealed in perpetuity, something which perplexed Ivan Timofeev. For him this act approached blasphemy.

Finally, the council of hierarchs, which formed a part of the membership of the Zemsky Sobor, entered at the end of the Charter a forthright "anathema" on all "who do not respect this Charter of Affirmation." "Whoever speaks spitefully and spreads rumor among the people" against the election of Boris "will be stripped of his rank and excommunicated." He will come under the judgement of the tsar's law and "will be damned now and in ages to come." Clearly, the causes for such extreme measures lay not only in

the pre-election agitation for and against Boris, but also in
the circumstances that followed his election between the
17th and the 21st of February, 1598.

Historians long have noted a certain oddity in the ritual
by which the oath of allegiance to Boris was taken. In the
first place, the text of this ritual dates from the 15th of
September, 1598. Although this date refers to a copy of the
ritual made in Solvychegodsk and not to the Moscow text
itself, it is a date considered too late to be a copy. It must be
supposed that this ritual was a second oath of allegiance to
Boris, repeated perhaps on the occasion of his coronation on
September 1, 1598. There was precedent for such repetition
of an oath of allegiance. The oath to Ivan the Terrible was
repeated after his well-known illness, when he was convinced
of the insincerity of his advisers. The chroniclers of Ustiug
noted then that "they kissed the cross to the sovereign" for
the first time in 1534. "In the year 7062 (1554) they were
again made to kiss the cross to the tsar and grand prince and
to his tsaritsa and Grand Princess Nasatasia [sic] and for
Tsarevich Ivan on the Feast of St. Peter."

In the second place, the text of the oath to Tsar Boris
contains a stated commitment not to seek Tsar Simeon
Bekbulatovich and his children for the throne of Muscovy.
"Do not think, conceive, speak, make friends with, refer to,
or quote Tsar Simeon either in speech or in writing." This
admonition is quite understandable. S. M. Soloviev spent
much time solving this riddle. The matter is explained in a
letter from Andrzej Sapieha to Christopher Radziwill dated
June 6 (16), 1598.

"Tsar — or, expressed more precisely, Khan — Sain-Bulet
Bekbulatovich of Kasimov (by baptism, Simeon) was rather
well known in the Moscow of the second half of the sixteenth
century. A great great-grandson of the last khan of the
Golden Horde, Akhmat, Simeon in his youth had become a

service "tsarevich" in Moscow. He had received the region of
Kasimov in appanage. He was baptized in 1573 and married
the daughter of the boyar Ivan Fedorovich Mstislavsky.
During the latter half of 1575 Ivan the Terrible placed
Simeon Bekbulatovich at the head of that part of Muscovy
which was known as the zemshchina. At the same time that
Ivan, as head of the oprichnina, carried the title "Prince of
Muscovy," Simeon was given the title "Grand Prince of All
Russia," and was treated as the bearer of supreme state
authority. We cannot define what this combination meant in
terms of governmental affairs. But it is completely clear that
Simeon had no real power; he was Ivan's puppet. "Simeon
Bekbulatovich had not been in the grand principality a full
year when his sovereign bestowed upon him a grand
principality in Tver, and reclaimed the whole of the tsardom
of Muscovy for himself."

The transfer of Simeon created a special order of
government in the district of Tver. The grand prince was the
sovereign there. He wrote letters patent, distributed pomestie
estates, collected taxes and quit-rent for himself, and
maintained a large court. The death of Ivan the Terrible put
an end to Simeon's comfortable position. When Boris came
to power Simeon "was no longer (sovereign) in Tver. He was
moved to the village of Kushalino (near Tver). His court
numbered very few people in those times, and they lived in
poverty." It was roughly during these years that Simeon went
blind. It was said that his blindness was due to the crafty
designs of Boris's regime, which "commanded the
ambassadors, who had been sent to Simeon, to blind him."
Apparently Simeon fell from favor together with his
father-in-law, Prince Mstislavsky who, as we know, tried
unsuccessfully to compete with Boris.

Andrzej Sapieha wrote concerning Simeon in the letter
to Radziwill dated June 6 (16), 1598. Godunov was just

starting out from Moscow on a campaign against the Tatars
(at the beginning of May) when "several princes and boyars,
first and foremost Belsky and Fedor Nikitich (Romanov) and
his brother Alexander, along with several others, began
plotting the election of Simeon to the throne instead of
Boris, whom they did not want." Sapieha did not know quite
what to call Simeon Bekbulatovich of Kasimov, and called
him "son of Shugal and Prince of Kazan." This does not
change matters since there was no one in Moscow with whom
to confuse "Tsarevich" Simeon. Boris, it seems, learned
of the boyar plot against him and managed to foil it. He
pointed out to the boyars that one cannot be occupied with
internal intrigues and discord while a Tatar attack threatened.
Having quashed his enemies Godunov, as yet uncrowned,
went out with his troops toward Serpukhov. Meanwhile the
people of Muscovy urged him to hasten his coronation.

So much for Sapieha's information. It completely
explains the episode of Simeon Bekbulatovich. Obviously
Boris's rivals did not lay down their arms after his election.
They had lost their game and could not reach for the throne.
But they did not wish to accept Boris's victory. Until Boris's
coronation they enjoyed a period of grace in which to find a
new rival and contender for the throne. This was Simeon —
"tsar" of Kasimov, at first "grand prince" of all Russia and
then "of Tver." He possessed titles and "pedigree," and he
had been persecuted by Boris; moreover, he was bound by
kinship to a most distinguished boyar family, that of Prince
Mstislavsky. Boris somehow managed to anticipate the *coup*.
Frightened by this new danger, he resolved to make his
subjects take a second oath. This oath contained the new
condition proscribing all contacts between his subjects and
Simeon. The first oath was taken at the end of February and
the beginning of March; the second, toward the end of May
and into June.

The final episode in the story of Boris's accession to the throne was his march toward Serpukhov. This campaign resulted from the incursion into Russia of the Crimean khan. Thanks to Boris it acquired unique characteristics. Apparently there was no real need either to gather a large military force or for the tsar to place himself at its head. At least contemporaries saw no military danger sufficient to justify Boris's call to arms. But Godunov attached a special significance to the campaign. So many troops gathered that eyewitnesses numbered them in the hundreds of thousands. The encampment along the river Oka (outside Moscow) appeared to occupy five square miles of meadowland. In the center of the camp "an entire city of tents" was erected for the tsar.

This city "was as white as snow" and its sheer size and intricate beauty enraptured all who gazed upon it. It seemed to them a city of white stone, with many gates and towers. This creation survived Boris. Its magnificent tents were restaked in Serpukhov for the false Dmitri when he came triumphantly to Moscow in 1605. Boris did not lie in wait of the Tatar host in this splendid camp. Probably he never intended to do so. He received an emissary of the Crimean khan outside Serpukhov and arranged for a series of reviews and parades. Meanwhile Boris lavished kindness on his troops, giving them of food and gifts. "They, learning his kindness, rejoiced and hoped to receive such favors from him in the future," recounted a chronicler. Such, in essence, was Boris's purpose: to seek popularity and support for his throne among Muscovy's military forces. After satisfying himself that most of the military people were well disposed toward him and recognized him as the new tsar, he returned to the capital. On New Year's Day 7107, that is, September 1, 1598, Boris was crowned tsar.

We have had occasion to mention how Boris behaved during the ceremony. Loudly he promised to all the people that he would care for the weak and the orphaned. "Taking hold of his blouse (that is, the collar of his long shirt), he said to the patriarch: 'Father Patriarch Job, as God is my witness, no one in my realm will be poor or a beggar! This last (his shirt) I am ready to share with all!' " Eyewitnesses recount that these words touched all those present. Later Muscovite recollections which allude to this story added another detail. For example, in 1651 a member of the Pushkin family said: "When Boris was elected to the throne of Muscovy, he swore before all the people that he would be 'neither friend nor enemy to anyone.'" Boris's contemporaries do not offer this kind of a picture. We may suppose that the story of his justice and impartiality as related by Pushkin grew out of his promises of charity.

It is difficult to believe Pushkin because the bulk of Muscovite tradition attests to exactly the opposite. Around 1730 the historian V.N. Tatishchev wrote the following words concerning Boris. "The boyars wanted Boris to take a written oath of allegiance to the state. This Boris did not wish to do, but he also did not want openly to refuse. He hoped that the common people would force his election without the consent of the boyars. Noting his stubbornness and refusals, the Shuiskys began saying that it was not right to entreat Boris, and recommended that another be chosen. Then the patriarch went to Boris in ceremonial procession, and Godunov accepted immediately."

Tatishchev was guided by the same uncertain tradition as was Pushkin. An historian cannot base an opinion on either statement. But he can believe that before and during the coronation Boris zealously sought to gain popular favor, both in Moscow and in the campaign to Serpukhov. He delayed the coronation ceremony itself until he could be certain of complete triumph over his rivals and enemies. Boris's customary discretion and caution did not desert him in this most decisive and triumphant moment of his political life.

VIII BORIS, THE ROMANOVS, AND BOGDAN BELSKY

We have presented a survey of all the events which accompanied Boris's election and accession to the throne. More precisely, we have shown the form of the election and accession. After consideration of the electoral struggle and of Boris's opponents in the contest for the tsarist crown, the difficulties and deadly complexities which created Boris's dilemma will stand in sharp relief. Boris was not challenged by a collateral branch of the dying dynasty or by representatives of other dynasties. It was, rather, private individuals who fought against Boris — his court friends and recent allies.

The closeness of Boris to the family of the "Nikitiches," the Romanovs, has been noted. That bond had been established during the time of old Nikita Romanovich. The "union of friendship" was sealed with vows of mutual aid and support. During Nikita Romanovich's illness and after his death Boris became father, guardian, and leader of the Romanovs. He "kept" them; that is, he guarded them until they passed from youth into positions of official responsibility. Boris had a long-standing friendship with Bogdan Belsky, an intimacy which had arisen when Boris came to the court of Ivan the Terrible as a boy and "was never out of reach of the tsar's sharp eyes." Together with

Belsky, Boris shared the protection and favor of the wrathful
tsar. When, after Ivan's death, Belsky provoked the
resentment of the people of Moscow and was exiled, Boris
befriended him and "provided" him with all that he needed,
and Bogdan "went from village to village in abundance and
peace, and passed his time most comfortably."

These people constituted the nucleus of the court
aristocracy as distinguished from the ancestral princely
aristocracy. They also opposed the old aristocracy. They had
to stand together were they to maintain supremacy at court
and in political life. As suggested earlier, those famous state
secretaries, the brothers Shchelkalov, placed their experience
and talents at Boris's disposal. So long as Tsar Fedor
Ivanovich reigned, the court aristocracy showed no sign of
internal disintegration. Only the elder Shchelkalov, Andrei,
was removed from his position, and that for some unknown
reason. If Andrei's dismissal owed to some disfavor, his guilt
was of a personal and incidental nature. His brother Vasili
not only did not suffer with Andrei, he even gained Andrei's
position and inherited his rank in the secretarial order.

But as soon as Tsar Fedor died, the disintegration of the
boyar circle immediately became evident. Friends quarrelled
over the question of succession. Bogdan Belsky came to
Moscow to try for the throne, to which, of course, he had
not the slightest claim. Fedor Romanov, not recognizing
Boris's seniority, also made known his ambition for the
throne, supported by his brother Alexander. Further, Vasili
Shchelkalov spoke with the people about swearing allegiance
to the Boyar Duma, an allegiance directed against Boris.

Godunov could be certain that it was the politics of Ivan
the Terrible, and not his own, that had weakened the
princely aristocracy. Not a single prince, be he Riurikovich or
Gediminovich, bid for the throne upon the death of Fedor.

All sat quietly under the heel of the Godunov administration. As candidates for the throne, no one mentioned the princes Shuisky or the princes of the Bulgakov clan (the Golitsyns and the Kurakins). Fedor Ivanovich Mstislavsky, the only designated candidate, declined nomination. Tacitly the princes yielded the road to the throne to the court aristocracy, and in particular to Boris. But Boris's own friends did not care to yield to him, and overlooked their debt to him for aid and comfort in times of trial. The struggle produced a savage display of hostility and hatred. Boris's friend Fedor Romanov even threatened him with a knife. Boris was charged with the murder of Dmitri. It was charged that Godunov intended to resurrect him — substitute an imposter — if Boris himself were not elected. Boris would then rule in Dmitri's name.

If the stories of the seventeenth century are accepted — that Boris sent his "zealous supporters" everywhere to frighten and cajole the people into electing him — it must be accepted also that the strongest methods available were set against him. These included personal violence and slander. Erstwhile friends became the cruelest enemies. Thanks to his own rise to power at the expense of the old court aristocracy, Boris could be certain that this faction would afford him no support. Nor could he count on the service princes, for heretofore they had been his opponents. Only those "who had sworn allegiance" to him, his friends, had rallied to him. But now that he was tsar these groups, and others as well, stood against him. Having created a dynasty, the Godunovs had also created their own isolation from the aristocracy. They must beware of everyone. Such was the chief difficulty of Boris's situation. It was compounded by the fact that his earlier friends, who had become his foremost enemies, were the most aggressive. They exhibited no inclination to ease their striving even after his election.

The story of Simeon Bekbulatovich underscores this fact. It defines, as it were, the psychology of the struggle. Given the situation, it is understandable that the contest produced support for an impostor. Boris's adversaries lost the scramble for election to a monarch chosen by the true will of the people. Thereafter it was impossible for anyone, whether boyar or prince, to overthrow Boris. His enemies had tried to bring forward a person honored before Boris with the title "tsar" through lineage from the khans, and "grand prince" by grant of Ivan the Terrible.

This proved to be a worthless attempt. Simeon, who was blind, was not strong enough to vie with Boris. He had neither the authority nor the resources for such a struggle. When the plot to use the blind and half-forgotten Tatar failed, it was natural to think of restoring the old dynasty and of abolishing the new one. "The name of Dmitri has risen again" announced the documents of 1598. But it is known from Andrzej Sapieha that Dmitri's name at first was not used as it was later. Initially, when Boris stood accused of the murder of the tsarevich, it was said that he planned to substitute a false Dmitri in his place were he not elected. Later the false Dmitri was set against Boris.

Confronted by such adversaries, Boris understood full well the extreme difficulty of his position — his political isolation and the aggressiveness of his enemies. Were only the princes hostile to him, he could have wielded an oprichnina terror to maintain state order. Had a political party opposed him, he could have resorted to open struggle. But against individuals and families so recently close to him each punitive measure would acquire a mean character injurious to his dignity. Still, Boris was not entirely unwilling to resort to such vengeance. While not yet in power he refrained from its use. He delayed until he could bring formal charges against Belsky and the Romanovs. Then he showed them no mercy. S. M. Soloviev castigates Boris for his pettiness and "evil envy of his old supporters." But later documents point to a different conclusion. Of course, Boris could have been generous and merciful — but his vengeance had been so long withheld! Those who hated him could have been rendered harmless only had they been punished much earlier. In the end Godunov's punitive measures did not arrest his ruin or the ruin of his house.

Apparently the Romanovs and Belsky were still sound in health and limb when Moscow heard the first word of the appearance of the pretender. During the first months of his reign Boris Godunov had even rewarded Alexander Nikitich Romanov with the rank of boyar, and Mikhail Nikitich was made an okolnichi. (The elder Romanov, Fedor Nikitich, became a boyar during the reign of Fedor Ivanovich.) But at the end of 1600, or the beginning of 1601, the storm of disfavor burst over Belsky and the Romanovs. Scholars vary in their chronology of events. A number of sources state that just at this moment a rumor spread "concerning Dmitri Ivanovich [the pretender]." Belsky was exiled, as were the Romanovs. Considering the time and the events, it is impossible to decide exactly what occurred. When the boyars were investigated they were not accused of creating a pretender. Consequently the information on Belsky and the Romanovs provides no grounds for connecting their misfortune with the pretender, though the affair of the pretender began at the moment of the destruction of the boyar families.

But other grounds, to be cited later, do allow for such a connection. In the words of a contemporary, Boris, having learned of the appearance of the pretender, "told the princes and boyars to their faces that it was their doing." ("In this I am not mistaken!" adds this source).

In the absence of relevant information about a connection between the pretender and the persecution of the boyars, it cannot be determined who suffered first at the hands of Boris, Belsky or the Romanovs. The precise time of the investigation of Belsky cannot be established. The "New Chronicle" puts the destruction of the Romanovs earlier than the persecution of Belsky. Bussow (who compiled a most curious "chronicle" of events in Moscow) places the news about the Romanovs later than the story of the punishment of Belsky.

The Belsky affair, which is always connected with the adventurer, Konrad Bussow, seems poorly understood. One chronicler recounts the affair as follows. Boris sent Belsky to the "Wild Field," to the Donets River at the mouth of the Oskol, to found the "New Town, Tsarev Borisov." Belsky received his orders during the summer of 1600.[16] The chronicler states that the distant South had been Belsky's place of honorable exile from Moscow. Belsky, "a rich man," went there "with great wealth" and "all sorts of supplies." He began the work "with his own court," that is, with his resources and people. He commanded the forces sent with him to build a fortress "according to plan," in other words, in line with his instructions from Moscow. In this way Belsky's "court," his servants and his slaves, captured the public eye in Tsarev Borisov as they had in Moscow in 1598 when Belsky "and the high aristrocracy" rushed there for the election of Boris.

The courtesies displayed by Belsky to the troops accompanying him to the new town could have aroused suspicion. He gave them food and drink, money, clothes, and supplies. Naturally they blessed and praised him in return. A

rumor had it that Belsky then distinguished himself by
holding that if Tsar Boris was tsar in Moscow, he was tsar in
Tsarev Borisov. This rumor reached Moscow and Belsky "was
widely praised for his good deeds by military men" (as the
chronicler has obliquely expressed it). "Great praise" of this
variety, in actuality an accusation, confused and embarrassed
Boris. According to Timofeev, Boris was already suspicious of
Belsky. Godunov suspected that Belsky lusted after the
throne. Belsky was summoned to Moscow, humiliated,
interrogated and, it is said, tortured. He was stripped of his
rank in the Duma and among the okolnichi. His estate was
confiscated and his "court" disbanded. He was even
subjected to corporal punishment and banished to the towns
in the Lower Reaches on the Volga where he was imprisoned.
There Belsky remained until the death of Boris and the
enthronement of the pretender, who showed him great
kindness and restored him to the rank of boyar.

The Belsky affair probably took place toward the end of
1600. It was about that time that the far-flung Romanov
affair began. Many families related to the Romanovs were
involved: the princes Cherkassky, the princes Sitsky, the
princes Repnin, Prince Shestunov, the Sheremetevs, the
Karpovs, and others. In the account of the chronicler, the
affair began with denunciations. By every conceivable means
the household slaves of the Romanovs were encouraged to
denounce and inform on their "sovereigns," over whom Boris
considered it essential to mount his own type of surveillance.
Nevertheless, the denunciations did not yield sufficient cause
for prosecution until word was received from Vtoroi
Bartenev, Alexander Nikitich Romanov's treasurer, that
Bartenev was ready to tell his sovereign all that he knew
[in Spring, 1601].

Then Semen Nikitich Godunov, who managed political

investigations during Boris's reign and who was "the chief
minion of the new tyranny" (according to Karamzin), placed
"various roots and herbs in bags" and instructed Bartenev to
put these bags "in the storehouse" of Alexander Nikitich.
Bartenev was then "to notify" the government of the
existence of these sacks of "herbs and roots." Bartenev did as
he was told. He informed on his lord. He said that his lord
engaged in "sorcery," or else fortune telling, and kept "herb
roots" in his storehouse.

A good deal had been said in the oath of allegiance
to Boris Godunov to the effect that no one was either to give
or receive "evil potions and roots," for they would be harmful [poisonous] to him and his family. No one was "to use
sorcerers and sorceresses for any evil whatsoever." When
investigation disclosed that Romanov had roots in his
possession, he and the entire "Nikitich" family were
suspected of witchcraft and brought before the patriarch.
"Many of the boyars who were present shoved and screeched
like animals." The trial of the Romanovs began amidst a
noisy scene of indignation directed at those "traitors" who
wished to gain the throne through witchcraft.

It would be a mistake to think that the possession of
herbs and roots used in sorcery was considered a minor
offense in those times. The charge of witchcraft was of the
gravest nature and the struggle against sorcery was of earnest
concern both to ecclesiastical and to secular authorities. According to Professor Novombergsky, "this crusade was no different from that in Western Europe. Muscovite Russia experienced a period of terrorizing investigations, torments, and
public burnings of those accused of magic." Except for burning
at the stake, the Romanovs endured all of these misfortunes.

When it was discovered that Alexander Nikitich had roots in
his possession, he was arrested together with all of his "kin," not

only the Romanovs but also their in-laws, the Cherkasskys, the Sitskys, and others. One of the princes Sitsky was even brought from Astrakhan for interrogation and investigation. Prince Ivan Borisovich Cherkassky, as well as Fedor Nikitich and his brothers, was seized under suspicion of a most grave offense. These persons "were brought to torture," that is, interrogated under ordeal. Their servants "underwent the worst of tortures" and "many died during their ordeals." The affair ended with the sentencing [in June] of those on trial. Fedor Nikitich was exiled to the Monastery of St. Anthony Siisky on the Northern Dvina. When he took monastic vows [and the name Filaret], he swore to give up forever his claim to the throne and his dreams of the crown. His brothers and their families were also banished. His wife, Ksenia Ivanovna, and his mother-in-law, Maria Shestova, took the veil. The guards assigned to the convicted persons considered them to be villains and traitors who wished to seize the throne through witchcraft and sorcery.

Thus ended the trial of the Romanovs. From the "official files concerning the exile of the Romanovs" their ultimate fate is learned. Fedor Nikitich, now the monk Filaret, languished in the Siisky Monastery until the accession of the pretender to the throne. His wife was incarcerated in the Zaonezhsky settlement (between lakes Ladoga and Onega). His children, Mikhail and Tatiana, together with the family of Alexander Nikitich and his aunt, Princess Cherkasskaia, were banished to Lake Beloozero. From there they were taken to the village of Kliny near Yuriev-Polsky. Alexander Nikitich was banished to the region of Perm and imprisoned in the village of Nyroba. Vasili Nikitich was held in Yaransk, and Ivan Nikitich, in Pelym. Of all the Romanov brothers only Filaret and Ivan survived. The remainder died

in exile, perhaps as victims of the "simple-minded" cruelty of
their jailers.

The surviving documents concerning the exile of the
Romanovs make clear that the Godunov government
frequently restrained the zeal of its police. It treated the
prisoners well by giving them "adequate food" and clothing.
The exiled were even allowed to have their own servants. In
May, 1602, the youngest of the Romanovs, Ivan Nikitich,
was released from exile and entered "into service" in Nizhni
Novgorod. In September of the same year he and Prince
Cherkassky were returned to Moscow. At the same time the
fate of the others still living was eased, except for Filaret and
his wife. Hence Boris did not wish to exterminate the
Romanovs. By resort to the monk's cowl he rendered his
enemy Filaret harmless, and kept him imprisoned in a monastery.
The fate of the remainder of the surviving Romanov's was
not so terrible.

IX   THE POLITICAL ISOLATION OF THE
GODUNOVS

There was another factor that frightened Boris. Earlier it was
suggested that when the Godunovs became a dynasty, they
isolated themselves from the Muscovite aristocracy. In
contesting for the throne they lost their friends and acquired
new enemies. They had to beware of everyone and to suspect
and spy on all those around them. Police security and the
conduct of investigations were given to Boris's kinsman,
Simeon Nikitich Godunov. He executed his duty in such
frightful manner that he earned widespread hatred, spite,
and fear. He converted security measures and investigation
into   terror.   Openly   he   encouraged   and   rewarded

denunciations. It is said that denunciations became quite common after an informer, the slave of Prince Shestunov, was rewarded publicly even though his information was false. Prince Shestunov was left in peace, but the informer was told that "he would receive the grace and favor of the sovereign bestowed upon him in public." For his service and zeal he was given a pomestie and commanded thenceforth "to serve as a service gentleman." For his information the slave was rewarded with "land and freedom."

After this event slaves were wont to inform on their lords, and priests and monks on their brothers. Sextons and the women who baked the communion bread, as well as every sort and variety of plain folk, fell to informing on others. "Wives informed on their husbands, and children on their fathers." "Much innocent blood" was shed because of these denunciations, and everywhere there were rumblings of dissatisfaction and insurrection.

The Godunov family was not generally popular. This was because, apart from Boris, the family included no other bright and talented persons. Only one uncle, Dmitri Ivanovich Godunov, was considered to be an outstanding official. But he was already elderly at the time of Boris's reign. (He had been made a boyar in 1578). Although he was still active in governmental affairs, he gave outsiders the impression that he was an extremely aged man. Danes, who were in Moscow with Duke Hans, said he was "a decrepit old man," "a little old man of around ninety or more." He appeared at the ambassadorial court to pay the duke compliments, and nothing more. During the last years of his life he prayed more than he worked, and diligently cared for and watched over the monasteries, providing them with sumptuously "illuminated and decorated" copies of the Psalter. This fact is well-known among paleographers.

Besides Dmitri Ivanovich, there was another noted courtier, Stepan Vasilievich Godunov, "a very handsome, attractive patriarch" (as the Danes described him). There was also Ivan Ivanovich Godunov, Boris's great grand-nephew. The reputation of this member of the younger Godunov generation derived from his marriage to Irina Nikitichna Romanova. After the fall of the Godunovs in 1605, Ivan Ivanovich joined the Romanovs. They supported him, and through their friendship he gained recognition, and after his death during the Time of Troubles, a complete pardon. But these members of the Godunov family mentioned here were not statesmen and could not form their own ruling circle.

Boris's misfortune lies in the fact that he was unable to form such a circle. According to the custom of his time, he organized "a group [duma] close to him," consisting of his relatives. But he derived no aid or support from this group. Only rarely did Boris reach out among the boyars. Evidently, he had no favorites at court, with the possible exception of the Basmanovs.

Two little Basmanov boys, Peter and Ivan Fedorovich, had been orphaned during the reign of Ivan the Terrible. Their father, Fedor Alexeevich, died early in life in exile at Lake Beloozero, a victim of Ivan's disfavor. His young widow and his children were sent to her brother, Prince Andrei Vasilievich Sitsky in Novgorod the Great. Then, by the tsar's favor, the widow married Prince Ivan Konstantinovich Kurliatev, and Ivan the Terrible "took her children, Peter and Ivan, to himself." He gave them patrimonies, and reared them as earlier he had reared Boris and Irina Godunova. Boris inherited Ivan the Terrible's disposition toward the Basmanovs. He took tender care of Peter Fedorovich (Ivan Fedorovich previously had died in battle). "The Tsar and Grand Prince Boris Fedorovich rewarded me for my service!"

cried Peter Basmanov on the eve of his desertion to the
pretender.

Close members of his own family and other
undistinguished persons such as the Basmanovs did not lessen
Boris's isolation. From the height of the throne he observed
only resistence, not friendship. All of the difficulties of rule,
all of the dangers of the struggle against both open and
clandestine enemies fell directly upon Boris's shoulders. No
one can be blamed for this but Boris himself, the product of
a narrow world where power was prince. Political isolation
was the natural result of his success and in the course of time
became the setting for the downfall of his dynasty.

X   FAMINE AND BRIGANDAGE: 1601 – 1603

Muscovites found that God did not bless the reign of Tsar
Boris. His rule was without peace from the very beginning.
During and following his election in 1598 plots and intrigues
placed Boris in difficult straits. Then there followed still new
problems and complications. According to a remarkable
account by the Frenchman [Jacques] Margeret, [17] who was
in Moscow, a rumor circulated in 1600 saying that the
tsarevich was still alive. At the same time exploded the affair
of Bogdan Belsky and the Romanovs. The boyar investigation
began at this point as well, and according to Margeret, very
few aristocratic families escaped Boris's suspicion. He was
searching for the thread of a plot against him. Life in Moscow
was now anxious and uneasy. To cap these troubles, a famine
began in 1601. A chronicler has described the beginning of
the famine.

The summer of 1601 was exceptionally rainy. By the
middle of August, when the grain should have been ripe, it

was still "green as grass." Then on the Feast of the Dormition
there was a frost which killed the rye and oats. Out of
necessity the people ate old grain and planted the winter
and spring crops with the frozen grain from the bad harvest.
In 1602 "nothing grew; the whole crop perished in the
earth." Then began a terrible famine; grain could not be
purchased at any price. Men died as they had not died even
"during Plague." Special officers collected the bodies of the
dead from houses and from the streets and buried them in
mass graves. People of that time numbered the dead in the
tens, even hundreds, of thousands. They described horrible
scenes of human suffering — starving people driven to
cannibalism.

        The famine lasted into the year 1603 and rent the entire
social fabric. Those among the starving who were still able
took to plundering and pillage. There was no other way for
them to get bread. Slaves and peasants, driven away by their
lords for lack of food to feed them, wandered off into robber
gangs and committed violence on the roads. "One could not
travel at all; everywhere around Moscow there were large
gangs of bandits." It became necessary to dispatch entire
troop detachments against these brigands. Near Moscow itself
took place a battle between a robber band headed by a leader
named Khlopko, and the okolnichi Ivan Fedorovich
Basmanov. Basmanov was killed; Khlopko was captured,
covered with wounds, and was executed. His band dispersed
and fled to the "Borderland"[18] where most unfortunates
fled to escape Muscovy.

        Boris's administration labored to feed the starving
masses in Moscow and to give them money but, of course, it
could not satisfy everyone. The government provided work
"for food." "It ordered much stone construction to be
undertaken in order to feed the people." A large stone

palace on the place where Tsar Ivan is buried was built in
the Kremlin.

Understandably, construction projects could not aid
many people. The need was far too great and the area caught
in the grip of famine far too large for success in fighting the
elements. The complexity of the situation was augmented by
the fact that abuses by the people accompanied the disasters
inflicted by nature. They cheated and stole during the
distribution of alms, food, and work. They speculated in
grain. Farmers — clergy as well as peasants — and people living
on minimum subsistance, "hoarded their grain and demanded
inflated prices for it in order to make profit." Grain buyers
appeared on the scene. These individuals controlled the
distribution of grain on the market through clever deals, and
thereby managed to raise its cost.

A most interesting decree by Boris has been preserved.
This decree enumerated steps to be taken to halt the evil:
prohibition of grain purchases; establishment of tariffs;
obligatory sale of grain at low retail prices, "little by little,
but not stingily;" survey of grain reserves and their market
distribution; punishment of speculators; prohibition of grain
distilling and brewing of beer, and so on. Persons who have
survived a time of great crisis can easily imagine the horrors
of the famine which overtook a backward country at the
beginning of the seventeenth century. The troubles brought
on by the famine and its accompanying social disintegration
created very favorable conditions for the success of the
pretender, the false Dmitri.

XI   THE PRETENDER AND HIS PROBABLE
        BACKGROUND

In 1603 it became known that a person terming himself
Tsarevich Dmitri Ivanovich had turned up in the
Polish-Lithuanian Commonwealth. He called himself the son
of Ivan the Terrible and claimed that he had been saved from
an attempt on his life made by Boris Godunov. This person
was recognized by the Polish government as the authentic
tsarevich, despite the fact that in Moscow he was called an
imposter and officially identified as the monk Grigori
Otrepiev. In March, 1604, the pretender reached agreement
with the Jesuits, and on April 24 embraced Catholicism. He
notified Pope Clement VIII of this fact in a formal letter
written in the Polish language. From this moment on, so to
speak, there was an official pretender to the throne of
Muscovy. Boris must expect an armed invasion of his
realm. 19
    Of all extant opinions concerning the origin of the
pretender, the most probable is that he was a Russian,
prepared for his role by boyar enemies of Boris, and sent by
them to Poland. At least his letter to the Pope clearly shows
that it was not written by a Pole (although it was in excellent
Polish), but by a Muscovite who poorly understood the
manuscript of which he had to make a clean copy from a
preliminary draft obligingly prepared for him by the Jesuits.
It is vain to search in Poland or Lithuania for a cabal with the
initiative to contrive and to train the Muscovite tsarevich.
Boris himself, according to contemporaries, as soon as he
learned of the appearance of the pretender, told the "princes
and boyars to their faces" that it was their doing. Evidently
an inquiry undertaken by Boris convinced him that the role
of the pretender was being played by the monk Grigori

Otrepiev, and he did not hesitate to explain this to the Polish authorities. It would have been easy, of course, to accuse the Polish government of supporting a pretender as well as of putting forward a person calling himself Dmitri. But Boris did not throw that charge at the Poles. This allowed him grounds to search in Moscow for the guilty schemers. It is doubtful that he detected them, though obviously he suspected that the intrigue had its roots among the Romanovs.

There are several circumstances that support Boris's suspicion of Romanov involvement. In 1605, during the declaration to the people of war with the pretender, Godunov's officials called him Grishka Otrepiev and stated that he had "lived in the household of the Romanovs." Not long afterward, when the pretender was overthrown, the Muscovite embassy in Poland announced that the fallen Grishka "had been a slave of the Nikitiches (Romanovs) and of Prince Boris Cherkassky, and that he had been a thief before taking vows and becoming a monk." This declaration reiterated the essence of an announcement made at the end of 1604 while Boris still reigned. The earlier statement was sent to Emperor Rudolph II in Vienna. It stated that Grishka had been in the service of Mikhail (Nikitich) Romanov. Private accounts also attest that Otrepiev was connected with the household of the Romanovs and Cherkasskys. One of these accounts about Grishka related that he was "spirited off" to a monastery by Boris because Grishka "was often honored by Ivan Borisovich Cherkassky in the wealthy home of Boris Cherkassky, and this aroused the indignation of Tsar Boris." Indeed, Prince Ivan Borisovich Cherkassky, a close relative of the Romanovs, was one of the chief suspects in the Romanov affair. He later became a person of great importance close to the pretender.

This cozy story about the "honor" offered Otrepiev in

the home of the Cherkasskys lends weight to a passing, but important reference made by Margeret (who believed in the authenticity of the false Dmitri). Margeret wrote that the Romanovs were instrumental in saving the young Dmitri from perishing in Uglich. Thus several hints cause the historian to suspect, just as did Boris, that the root of the plot lay hidden somewhere in the heart of the court aristocracy hostile to Boris, most probably among the Romanovs and their relatives or in-laws.

When the troops of the pretender appeared on the borders of Muscovy and the Muscovite forces had taken the field against them, Boris did not hesitate to entrust them to the high-born "princes" Trubetskoi, Mstislavsky, Shuisky, and Golitsyn. He did not fear that they would betray him, for he knew that these high-born princes were far from being supporters of the pretender. He was not mistaken. The princes drove the pretender to Putivl. Only by chance did they fail to kill him. On the other hand, Boris did not include in his forces persons of the Romanov circle who had survived disgrace and exile unharmed. It was clear to Boris that they were unreliable and "unsteady." No one bearing names connected with the Romanov affair can be found among the commanders of the forces sent against the pretender. There were sure to be persons who did not wish Boris well among those connected with the Romanovs. They would have welcomed the pretender's success. One contemporary said that such persons "rejoiced in his (the pretender's) arrival in Muscovy and would be glad when they heard of his victory over Boris's forces. When they learned that Dmitri had been driven back, they walked stooped and in sorrow, hanging their heads."

The behavior of the monk Filaret Romanov at the time of the pretender's appearance on the borders of Muscovy can serve as an indice of the mood of those who opposed Boris. It is interesting to compare two reports about Filaret given by his guards. One dates from November, 1602; the other from February, 1605.

In the first report Filaret's utter spiritual collapse is described. He wished that he, his wife, and his children might die. "My dear little children (he lamented) are left small and poor. . . evil for me are a wife and children. When I remember them, something pierces my heart like a boarspear!. . . Grant, O Lord, that God shall take them soon!" The Siisky Monastery where Filaret was held prisoner was visited by outsiders both in winter and in summer. "Trading people of those towns came by road to pray." Other people came "from other towns to live" in the monastery. From these visitors the brothers as well as the prisoner Filaret learned news of the outside world. They learned of the resurrected Dmitri and of civil war in Muscovy. The prisoner revived at the beginning of 1605. "The monk Filaret does not live according to the monastic rule," reported his guard to Moscow. "He is always laughing and talks of life in the world, of falcons and hounds, and about how he lived in secular life. He is cruel to the monks." Filaret threatened the monks. They constantly complained that "he barks at them and wants to beat them." He even "ran at one of them with a crozier." "Filaret the monk tells the other monks how it will be with him in the future."

Hope for freedom and a chance to live again in the world had seized Filaret. The monastic authorities yielded to his mood. They lessened their surveillance of him and abandoned their previous "solicitude." Such was the situation in February, 1605. In the summer of that year Filaret gained his freedom, granted by that very pretender whose first appearance had filled him with such bright hopes.

In their struggle with the pretender the Godunovs behaved as the Muscovite government generally did when confronted with contending factions in Muscovite society. One element of the Moscow aristocracy had inspired a pretender to opposition to Boris. These aristocrats had entered a "sworn union of friendship." The other part of the aristocracy, namely the princes, awaited an opportune moment to attempt the overthrow of Boris's successors with the aid of the pretender. The approaches were different but the goals were the same — to destroy the hated dynasty of the Godunovs. When the people of the Borderland came to the support of the "true Tsar Dmitri Ivanovich," they attacked the Godunovs as defenders of serfdom and of the hated order whose symbols were stately, palatial dwellings and rich, arable lands. Should the "evil boyars" who opposed the Godunovs seek power for themselves, the people of the Borderland would resist them no less. The people wanted their freedom. They hoped that the "true tsarevich" would be generous to them and bring about the social changes for which they longed.

XII   THE PRETENDER'S CAMPAIGN. THE UP-
      RISING IN THE "WILD FIELD" AND THE
      BORDERLAND

The pretender established himself in the castle of the Mniszechs[20] in Sambor. He recruited a small force of local Poles who were ready to support the venture of the [so-called] Muscovite tsarevich. At the time this force was regarded with some scorn for it comprised but a small handful of people, and possessed no notable strength. The force numbered not more than 3,500 or 4,000 men when (in

October, 1604) the pretender launched his campaign against Boris. He crossed the Dnieper River to the Muscovite side near Kiev, "at the Seversk border."

But this small force did not constitute the whole of the pretender's strength. During the summer of 1604 he had cultivated the population of the Borderland and incited insurrection there in his behalf. The whole summer he spent recruiting people from Muscovy and distributing his "seductive letters" (as the proclamations were then called) throughout the lands of Muscovy. The pretender sent "free" Cossacks to the Don to spread news about himself. Sources suggest that people coming from the Don were with the pretender in Sambor. They also joined his march enroute. On the banks of the Dnieper and the Desna thousands of Cossacks joined him. At Chernigov his troops numbered close to 10,000. Moreover, to the east of the pretender and his troops, a separate force of Cossacks and peasants gathered under his banners and for his support on the roads south of Moscow. Thus it was that the pretender and his agents and supporters began their struggle against Boris with the help of forces organized from among the insurrectionary regions in the South who also opposed Moscow's authority.

The causes of this insurrection are familiar. The movement southward of dissatisfied Russians had populated the Borderland with "belligerent people" who opposed the encroachment of the central government. The famine of 1601-1603 joined new groups of people to these masses in the South. The new "arrivals" sought to escape the long arm of the state. Those recently arrived in the South could not long enjoy the spacious lands there. This was because the rapid extension of government administration to the "Wild Field" had brought the free population of the "Field" into subservience to the government. The recent arrivals became peasants or were enserfed on pomestie lands. Even the Cossacks were drawn into state service. These latter were unable to put down roots or to provide for themsleves in the "Field" or on the "rivers." They found service in frontier towns and in sentry posts along the border. So it was that the Moscow authorities overtook and again enslaved a population which had sought freedom in flight. These developments explain the discontent and dissatisfaction of those who had "gone to the Field," away from service to the sovereign. When they worked, it was without zeal.

Popular discontent was surely aggravated by the imposition of indiscriminate taxation, and that without warrant. The people of the border towns and regions had been drawn into obligatory labor on crown lands in addition to service in the fields or in the settlements. Crown *desiatinnaia* lands had been established in the southern portions of the "Field." In Elets, Oskol, Belgorod and Kursk the expanse of these lands under Tsar Boris had become so great that subsequent rulers, even when stable conditions returned, did not venture to reinstate the practices established during Boris's reign. Tsar Mikhail Fedorovich re-established desiatinnaia lands only one-half as great as those which existed. In the towns mentioned only 300 *desiatiny* were ordered plowed in 1620 instead of the former 600. In Belgorod it was planned originally to put 900 desiatiny into cultivation. Yet only 600 desiatiny were plowed during Boris's time, the remainder being distributed to the peasants.

It is not difficult to imagine the tremendous burden placed upon the peasant populace forced to cultivate such a vast expanse of land. The people had not yet built their own economic order. Yet they must spend their time and energy working lands owned by someone else, the fruits of which they would never see. Grain harvested from the crown lands either lay rotting in the granaries or was shipped further south to areas where farming did not exist. Grain was transported from Elets and Oskol to Tsarev Borisov, while all of the grain of Voronezh was sent to the Don Cossacks.

Both the permanent and transient residents of a given town could not be sure of receiving compensation for their labor. Often people had to be content with "daily provisions," and sometimes they were forced to find their own food. Boris's agents in Voronezh took 300 desiatiny for inclusion among the sovereign's lands. Later practice shows that the authorities considered it fair to borrow seed grain from peasants, returning it without the slightest payment of interest.

The people of the South who served the government in the new towns also could not have been satisfied with their lot. They were gathered from the local population and placed in the work force. Many of the town people had arrived from the North in recent times. The town population consisted of streltsy and Cossacks, couriers and guides, cannoneers, and stockade guards originally engaged for service on a contract basis. They carried with them the memory of life in the central provinces of Great Russia where they or their fathers had been reduced to serfdom. They had traded one evil for another. Instead of working manorial lands they now labored on crown lands — and were equally enslaved. Formerly their enemy had been the landowners. Now their enemy was the state, with its agents who drove the people into servitude and forced them to plow crown lands. During the famine surely the mood of these people grew more and more sullen.

The "seductive letters" of the pretender fell on fertile ground. The Borderland rose up and moved against the heart of Muscovy. Thirsting for vengeance, the people of the South thought to join other oppressed people with the aid of the "oppressed tsarevich." Townspeople and "free Cossacks" supporting the pretender formed a large "Cossack" crowd. This sizable mass consisted of military men from the towns and wandering bands of Cossacks. It included also people from Don Cossack settlements and military camps. Creeping northward, this multitude awaited the moment when it, according to his instructions, might join the pretender.

So it was that the pretender's campaign began on two fronts at once. The pretender himself invaded Muscovy from Kiev, following the Desna upstream. He kept to the river's right bank, hoping to gain the upper reaches of the Oka. From that point the trade roads led to Moscow. At the same time, the Cossack masses followed the "Crimean roads" towards the north. The Cossacks planned to join the pretender somewhere near Orel or Kromy and from there to advance with him on Moscow via Kaluga or Tula.

Meanwhile the army of Godunov delayed its march against the pretender. Briansk was the mustering point designated by Boris for his main force. Briansk was a town lying halfway between Smolensk and the Seversk border. No matter whence the enemy might strike, from Orsha or from Kiev, at Briansk the army could meet them head-on. When it was clear that the pretender approached "from Seversk," the voevody marched there, arriving in time, though not at the border itself.

They met the pretender at the town of Novgorod Seversky. Dmitri had succeeded in taking the towns along the Desna, even the town of Chernigov. But he lingered too long at Novgorod Seversky. The direct road northward to Moscow was tightly closed against him. Then he learned that to the east, in the "Field," town after town was recognizing his authority. In the course of two weeks Putivl, Rylsk, Sevsk, the Komaritsky district, Kursk, and Kromy went over to him.

Then Belgorod and Tsarev Borisov recognized him and joined his cause. So rapid was the submission of the "Field" and the "Borderland" that the pretender was enticed onward. He broke off the siege of Novgorod Seversky and moved eastward toward Sevsk where he might join the Cossacks. But Boris's troops overtook him along the way and smashed his Polish-Lithuanian and Russian followers. The pretender fled southward, unable to join the Cossacks. In Putivl he withdrew into seclusion. His strength was spent and he had scant hope of being spared himself. It seemed that his song had been sung.

But another Cossack uprising in the Borderland spared him. Though the pretender met defeat, the Cossacks continued to capture towns in his name. In Putivl he learned that Oskol, Valuiki, Voronezh, Elets, and Livny had recognized his banner. The whole "Field" was swept up by the movement against the Muscovite regime. By spring the boyars heading Boris's army had to abandon the pursuit of the pretender and move their troops northward lest they be cut off from Moscow. The army was led by the boyars to the fortifications of Kromy, an important road junction. At Kromy roads converged from the entire region caught in the grip of the revolt. Cossacks were already at Kromy. The Moscow army surrounded the town, preventing the Cossacks from escaping northward toward Moscow. Kromy long remained the focal point of military operations. Though the Cossacks could not move forward, Boris's troops could not drive them southward from Kromy. In this way passed the winter of 1604-1605.

In early spring a decisive turn occurred. Tsar Boris died on April 13, 1605.

XIII   GODUNOV'S DEATH AND THE FALL OF
         HIS FAMILY

Boris had been ill since 1602, although he was far from being old. It is difficult to establish the precise nature of his illness. It is thought that he was "hidropic," that he suffered from dropsy. It was said that he suffered a stroke in 1604 and that "he dragged one leg behind him." He was often quite ill and did not venture out for long periods. His death at fifty-three seemed quite sudden and unexpected all the same, so much so that it was thought he had committed suicide. Rumor related that Boris suffered a dizzy spell in the middle of the day, either during an ambassadorial reception or after dinner. He was barely able to receive the Eucharist. According to ancient custom, he took the vows of a monk (with the name Bogolep), and that day departed to eternity.

Just three weeks after his death the Moscow troops at Kromy turned against the Godunovs and went over to the side of the pretender, "the true Tsar Dmitri Ivanovich." Within three more weeks Boris's family was taken from the palace to Boris's old residence. There, on June 10, 1605, his widow and son were murdered and his daughter desecrated and made a prisoner.

The tragedy of Boris culminated with the death of his family and the complete "impoverishment" of all the Godunov kin. The Godunovs suffered chiefly because they had themselves become a dynasty and one which was politically isolated. More than once it has been shown that the friendly ties which had strengthened the court nobility during the reign of Tsar Fedor Ivanovich had been broken by the quarrel of the Romanovs and Godunovs in 1598, during the struggle for the throne. This strife opened the way to intrigue, which took the form of the scheme involving the pretender. The name of Dmitri became a weapon in the conflict. The Romanovs would not have suffered defeat had they abstained from this intrigue, had they upheld the "sworn union of friendship" with Boris. Godunov and his family stood alone against the princely aristocracy which he had demeaned and weakened. This princely caste never reconciled itself to its new situation and never forgot its past primacy. When the pretender appeared, this aristocracy recognized Boris's authority and talent, and served him. But when Boris died it declined to support his dynasty and to serve his family. Among this titled group all the old pretensions revived: past injuries were again relived, and the hunger for vengeance and the thirst for power sharpened. The princes knew that the dynasty founded by Boris possessed neither a leader capable of ruling nor adherents and admirers. It was weak, it would be easy to destroy, and in fact it was destroyed.

Young Tsar Fedor Borisovich recalled the princes Mstislavsky and Shuisky to Moscow from Kromy. In their place he sent Prince Mikhail Petrovich Katyrev-Rostovsky and Peter Fedorovich Basmanov. The two Golitsyn brothers, Vasili Vasilievich and Ivan Vasilievich, remained in Kromy. This change in command was probably done out of caution, but it served to harm the Godunovs. The troops remaining in Kromy came under the influence of the Golitsyns, who were the most important and influential of all the voevody, and of Peter Basmanov, who was extremely popular and successful. Moscow naturally had to court Vasili Ivanovich Shuisky who was thought to have been an eyewitness to the events in Uglich in 1591. If he was not an eyewitness to the death of the tsarevich, he witnessed his rescue, it was thought.

The boyar-princes became the masters of the situation, both in the army and in the capital. Immediately they

declared themselves against the Godunovs and for "Tsar
Dmitri Ivanovich." The Golitsyns and Basmanov persuaded
the army to go over to the side of the pretender. Not only
did Prince Vasili Ivanovich Shuisky not resist the overthrow
of the Godunovs and the triumph of the pretender but,
according to some accounts, he also testified, when
questioned, that the true tsarevich had been rescued. Then he
and a large number of other boyars went directly to the new
tsar, Dmitri, and swore allegiance to him. This boyar
camarilla then returned to Moscow and assembled the people
to take the oath to the new monarch. So it was that the
princely aristocracy behaved at a decisive moment in the
Moscow drama. Their actions dealt the deathblow to the
Godunovs. Vasili Vasilievich Golitsyn did not deny himself
the pleasure of witnessing the final moments of Boris's wife
and son, Tsar Fedor Borisovich.

The Godunovs were not spared even after their death.
Their remains did not immediately find a final resting place.
Boris's body was removed from the Cathedral of the
Archangel and taken to the Varsonofiev Monastery (in
Moscow itself). His body was finally removed to the
Trinity-St. Sergius Monastery where the other members of his
family also were eventually buried.

* * * *

The tragedy of Boris ended with the death of a hero, so
Pushkin's marvelous work, *Boris Godunov*, leads us to believe.
For Pushkin, in his notes and letters, could not accept the
portrait of Boris that he had created under the influence of
Karamzin — the portrait of a victim of the criminal lust for
power. "You will ask me," he wrote, "whether my tragedy is

one of character or of manners." His correspondent received
no clear answer to this question. "I have tried," he said, "to
unite both." But this was an important historical error. In
reality Pushkin's *Boris* is a tragedy not of character, but of
fate. Boris died exhausted by the grave imponderables of his
reign. He did not die exhausted by a struggle with his own
sin-filled conscience. By the standards of his time he was
guilty neither of sin nor of crime.

Boris was placed at the head of the Russian government
during a period of complex crises. He was forced to attempt
to reconcile the irreconcilable and to bring together that
which could not be joined. He carried peace to a society
uprooted by the horrors of Ivan the Terrible, and at the same
time he strengthened that society while adding to the
authority of the state. To some he gave privileges; others he
suppressed. Some were exalted, some humbled, but all for
the good of the state. He labored for the Russian land while
at the same time building his road to the throne. Boris
refused the robes of the monarch when in fact he was
monarch. His complex and multifaceted activities displayed
in full brilliance his administrative talents and his fine
personal qualities — gentleness and kindness.

But these qualities earned him not wonder, delight, and
praise alone, but also envy, hatred, and slander. Fate willed
that slander and malice grew common among crude minds
and gullible hearts, and became weapons for political struggle
and intrigue. While Boris lived and enjoyed health, intrigue
failed to undermine his rule. But when his terrestrial life
closed amid the heat of struggle and the weariness of labor,
intrigue and malice marched triumphant over his family and
sundered it. The memory of Boris was clouded by grave
accusations. Yet these accusations were never proven. Their

merit rested only upon their official affirmation by state and church, which together passed to posterity his blighted image. We hold that it is the duty of historical scholarship to restore the true character of Boris Godunov.

NOTES TO THE INTRODUCTION

1. "Neskol'ko vospominanii o studencheskikh godakh," *Dela i dni*, bk. 2 (1921), 104-133; "Avtobiografiia akademika S.F. Platonova," *Ogonek*, 28 August 1927, pp. 10-11; "Iz vospominanii," *Izvestiia Tavricheskogo obshchestva istorii, arkheologii i etnografii*, fasc. 1 (1927), 1-6; and O. Hoetzsch, ed., "Aus Platonovs Selbstbiographie," *Zeitschrift für osteuropäische Geschichte, VII*, no. 4 (1933), 465-486.
2. "Aus Platonovs Selbstbiographie," pp. 465-466.
3. "Neskol'ko vospominanii," p. 104.
4. Ibid., p. 105.
5. G.H. Lewes (1817-1878) was an English journalist and popularizer of Comtean positivism whose translated works on philosophy and psychology enjoyed considerable popularity in Russia from the 1860s onward, as did the writings of John Stuart Mill.
6. "Neskol'ko vospominanii," p. 106.
7. Ibid., p. 112.
8. Ibid., p. 113.
9. Ibid., p. 113.
10. Ibid., p. 114.
11. Ibid., p. 118.
12. Ibid., p. 119.
13. Ibid., p. 120.
14. Ibid., p. 121.
15. On the Tetraxite (or Trapezite) Goths, see A.A. Vasiliev, *The Goths in the Crimea* (Cambridge, Mass., 1936), pp. 57-69.
16. "Neskol'ko vospominanii," p. 122.

17. Platonov, "Iz vospominanii," p. 2. On Vasilievsky see G.L. Kurbatov, "V.G. Vasil'evskii i nachalo vizantinovedeniia v Peterburgskom universitete," *Problemy otechestvennoi i vseobshchei istorii: Sbornik statei k 150-letiiu Leningradskogo universiteta*, ed. V.G. Revunenkov (Leningrad, 1969), pp. 133-152.

18. "Neskol'ko vospominanii," pp. 122-123.

19. Ibid., p. 125; E.M. Zhurkov et al., eds., *Sovetskaia istoricheskaia entisiklopediia* (Moscow, 1968), IX, 204.

20. "Neskol'ko vospominanii," pp. 125-126. Zhelyabov and Vera Figner were among those present at these disturbances. See Franco Venturi, *Roots of Revolution*, trans. F. Haskell (New York, 1960), p. 695.

21. "Neskol'ko vospominanii," pp. 123-124.

22. Lenin's brother, Alexander Ul'ianov, served as secretary of the society's scientific section until he resigned in January, 1887, six weeks before his arrest for complicity in a plot to kill Alexander III. The authorities used his membership in the society as a pretext for its dissolution. On the formation and activities of the society, see Platonov, "Neskol'ko vospominanii," pp. 126-127; I.M. Grevs, "V gody iunosti," *Byloe*, XII, bk. 6 (June 1918), 42-88; and V. V. Mavrodin, ed., *Leningradskii universitet v vospominaniiakh sovremennikov* (Leningrad, 1963), I, 202, 205-207, 223-224.

23. Platonov, "Neskol'ko vospominanii," pp. 131-132. On Lappo-Danilevsky's special position among these groups, see A.E. Presniakov, *Aleksandr Sergeevich Lappo-Danilevsky* (Petersburg, 1922), pp. 26-28.

24. "Neskol'ko vospominanii," pp. 127-128.

25. Ibid., pp. 128-129.

26. Ibid., p. 130. See Kliuchevsky's letters to him in M.V. Nechkina, ed., *V.O. Kliuchevskii: pis'ma, dnevniki, aforizmy i mysli ob istorii* (Moscow, 1968), pp. 165, 196, 200—especially the last, written in 1904, wherein Kliuchevsky coldly responded to Platonov's criticism of one of his works.

27. Platonov, "Avtobiografiia," pp. 10-11; E.P. Trifil'ev, "Tridtsatiletie nauchno-pedagogicheskoi deiatel'nosti professora Sergeia Feodorovicha Platonova," *Letopis' Istoriko-filologicheskogo obshchestva pri Novorossiiskom universitete*, XXII (Odessa, 1913), p. 1-2; "K portretu

Sergeia Fedorovicha Platonova," *Russkaia starina,* No. 8 (1911), pp. 193-195.

28. S.N. Valk et al., eds., *Sankt-Peterburgskie vysshie zhenskie (Bestuzhevskie) kursy (1878-1918 gg.): sbornik statei* (Leningrad, 1965), pp. 7-10, 14, 17; Nicholas Hans, *History of Russian Educational Policy (1701-1917)* (1931; reprint ed., New York, 1964), pp. 128-131, 147, 175-176, 241; E. P. Mikheeva, "Iz istorii vysshego zhenskogo obrazovaniia v Rossii," *Istoriia SSSR,* No. 2 (1969), pp. 174-179.

29. Valk et al., pp. 18, 78, 81, 84.

30. Ibid., p. 220.

31. Ibid., p. 220. Platonov's university lectures were likewise very crowded. Viktor Shklovsky, who attended St. Petersburg University in 1911-1914, was impressed by the "calm voice of a person who is not surprised by anything, who had attained a liberal, talented omniscience." *(Zhili-byli: vospominaniia, memuarnye zapiski, povesti o vremeni: s kontsa XIX v. po 1962 g.* [Moscow, 1964], p. 87).

32. Platonov, "Avtobiografiia," pp. 10-11.

33. *The Life of a Chemist: Memoirs of Vladimir N. Ipatieff,* ed. X.J. Eudin et al., trans. V. Haensel and Mrs. Ralph H. Lusher (Stanford, 1946), pp. 177-178. If N.O. Lossky is to be believed, however, Platonov possessed a temper and did not appreciate unexpected obstacles, as when Lossky was reluctant to accept a position at the Pedagogical Institute. N.O. Lossky, *Vospominaniia* (Munich, 1968), p. 132. I am indebted to Professor Emeritus George Vernadsky for this reference; in a note to me of 28 June 1969, he comments: "I never witnessed and never heard of any of such."

34. "Tri stila russkoi istoricheskoi nauki i S.F. Platonov," reprinted in P.B. Struve, *Sotsial'naia i ekonomicheskaia istoriia Rossii* (Paris, 1952), p. 342.

35. D. I. Ilovaisky, *Kratkie ocherki Russkoi istorii: kurs starshago vozrasta,* 24th ed. (Moscow, 1887). An outspoken nationalist and bitter critic of the Normanist interpretation of early Slavic history, Ilovaisky (1832-1920) was on bad terms with Vasilievsky and his associates of the *Journal of the Ministry of Public Education.* The conservative liberal V. A. Maklakov maintained that the pre-1905 school authorities had sought to convert history into simple chronology. "An example of

the history permitted was Ilovaisky. This became a negative name. When his textbooks were attacked in print, he would complacently declare that he answered such reproaches in a few words: 'write a better one.' He knew that for the purpose which the Ministry [of Public Education] had set, i.e., to kill interest in history, a more appropriate textbook than his could not have been invented." (V.A. Maklakov, *Iz vospominanii* [New York, 1954], p. 4). In 1891 Platonov had sharply criticized Ilovaisky's study of Muscovite Russia (" 'Istoriograficheskoe sochinenie nashego vremeni," reprinted in his *Sochineniia,* 2d ed. (St. Petersburg, 1912; reprinted, The Hague, 1966), I, 103-126, while he later recalled Ilovaisky's extreme vanity ("Iz vospominanii," pp. 4-5).

36. Quoted by S.N. Valk, "Istoricheskaia nauka v Leningradskom universitete za 125 let," *Trudy iubileinoi nauchnoi sessii: sektsiia istoricheskikh nauk* (Leningrad, 1947), p. 45, no. 1.

37. See Kliuchevsky's positive estimate of the work for the prize committee, reprinted in his *Sochineniia* (Moscow, 1959), VII, 439-453.

38. Quoted by Valk, "Istoricheskaia nauka," p. 51.

39. Ibid., p. 52; Platonov, "Avtobiografiia," pp. 10-11. For a list of works edited, see "Spisok trudov S.F. Platonova," *Sbornik statei po russkoi istorii, posviashchennykh S.F. Platonovu* (Petersburg, 1922), pp. vii-xii.

40. M.V. Nechkina et al., eds., *Ocherki istorii istoricheskoi nauki v SSSR* (Moscow, 1963), III, 575-576, 581; N.E. Nosov in *Vsesoiuznoe soveshchanie o merakh uluchsheniia podgotovki nauchno-pedagogiches-kikh kadrov po istoricheskim naukam* (Moscow, 1964), pp. 342-344.

41. George Vernadsky, "Some of My Reminiscences about S.F. Platonov," unpub. MS [New Haven, 1969], p. 3. I am deeply grateful to Professor Vernadsky for this five-page essay. See also the recent, somewhat different Russian version of this memoir: G. Vernadsky, "Iz vospominanii (Gody ucheniia S.F. Platonov)," *Novy zhurnal,* No. 100 (New York, 1920), pp. 196-221.

42. Ibid., p. 4

43. *Imperatorskoe russkoe istoricheskoe obshchestvo, 1866-1916* (Petrograd, 1916), pp. 153-154; "Aus Platonovs Selbstbiographie," p. 482.

44. "Spisok trudov S.F. Platonova," pp. vii-xii; Platonov, "Avtobiografiia," pp. 10-11.
45. "Spisok trudov," p. xii (no. 88); A. Presniakov, "Historical Research in Russia during the Revolutionary Crisis," *American Historical Review, XXVIII,* no. 2 (January 1923), 250; A.E. Presniakov, "Reforma arkhivnago dela," *Russkii istoricheskii zhurnal,* bk. 5 (1918), 205-222; and "Khronika," ibid., bk. 7 (1921), 219-220.
46. Konstantin F. Shteppa, *Russian Historians and the Soviet State* (New Brunswick, 1962), p. 27. *Letopis' zaniatii arkheograficheskoi komissii za 1917 god,* fasc. 30 (Petrograd, 1920); for 1918, fasc. 31 (Petrograd, 1923), pp. 7-18; for 1919-1922, fasc. 32 (Petrograd, 1923). Of the 54 sessions recorded in these two volumes (January-December 1917 and January 1919 to December 1922), Platonov was present at fifty. He attended the six sessions held in 1918 for which attendance was enumerated (one other session was recorded, but no attendance given).

For a recent, positive appraisal of the Archaeographic Commission's post-1917 activities (which, however, ignores Platonov's role therein and repeats without comment the orthodox version of his "resignation"), see L.V. Ivanova, "Arkheograficheskaia komissiia, 1917-1931 gg.," in M.A. Alpatov et al., eds., G.M. Ameshina, comp., *Problemy istorii obshchestvennogo dvizheniia i istoriografii [k 70-letiiu akademika Militsy Vasil'evny Nechkinoi]* (Moscow, 1971), pp. 401-418.

On the formation of PIAK, see Platonov, "Istoriia," in *Akademiia nauk SSSR za desiat' let, 1917-1927* (Leningrad, 1927), pp. 83-95; and *Otchet o deiatel'nosti Akademii nauk SSSR v 1927 g.* (Leningrad, 1928), pp. 394-400.
47. "Khronika," *Russkii istoricheskii zhurnal,* bk. 8 (1922), 304-307, 309-311.
48. Presniakov, "Historical Research," p. 225; Pokrovsky's review is reprinted in M.N. Pokrovsky, *Istoricheskaia nauka i bor'ba klassov* (Moscow and Leningrad, 1933), II, 87-93; Barskov's review in *Russkii istoricheskii zhurnal,* bk. 8 (1922), 280-290.
49. Z.M. Androsenkova, "Organizatsiia izucheniia istorii rabochego dvizheniia v Rossii v pervyi period razvitiia istoricheskoi nauki (do

serediny 30-kh godov)," *Vestnik Leningradskogo universiteta*, no. 14, fasc. 3 (1966), p. 17.

50. Michael T. Florinsky, ed., *McGraw-Hill Encyclopedia of Russia and the Soviet Union* (New York, 1961), p. 437.

51. Presniakov, "Historical Research," pp. 254-255; "Aus Platonovs Selbstbiographie," pp. 484-485.

52. Platonov, "Avtobiografiia," pp. 10-11.

53. *Sovetskaia istoricheskaia entsiklopediia*, Vol. IX (Moscow, 1968), 204.

54. For example, P. Miliukov, "Dva russkikh istorika (S.F. Platonov i A.A. Kizevetter)," *Sovremennyia zapiski*, LI (1933), 312; and A.M. Petrunkevich, "S.F. Platonov–istorik 'Smutnago vremeni'," *Vozrozhdenie*, no. 189 (September 1967), p. 75.

55. Bernard W. Eissenstat, "M.N. Pokrovsky and Soviet Historiography: Some Reconsiderations," *Slavic Review*, XXVII, no. 4 (December 1969), 605-606, 612-613.

56. Loren R. Graham, *The Soviet Academy of Sciences and the Communist Party*, 1927-1932 (Princeton, 1967), p. 31.

57. Ibid., pp. 96-129, 174-176. See also Vladimir V. Tchernavin, *I Speak for the Silent Prisoners of the Soviets*, trans. N.M. Oushakoff (Boston and New York, 1935), pp. 359-368.

58. Miliukov, *"Dva russkikh istorika,"* p. 313.

59. Tchernavin, *I Speak for the Silent*, pp. 367-368, says two daughters accompanied Platonov, whereas Otto Hoetzsch, "S.F. Platonov," *Zeitschrift für osteuropäische Geschichte*, no. 7 (1933), p. 468, says only one went.

60. L.V. Danilova, "Stanovlenie Marksistskogo napravleniia v sovetskoi istoriografii epokhi feodalizma," *Istoricheskie zapiski*, LXXVI (1965), 114-115, cautiously implies that the charges against Platonov were unfounded.

61. On National Bolshevism, see S.V. Utechin, *Russian Political Thought: A Concise History*, paper ed. (New York, 1964), pp. 253-256.

62. L.V. Ivanova, *U istokov sovetskoi istoricheskoi nauki (Podgotovka kadrov istorikov-marksistov v 1917-1929 gg.)* (Moscow, 1968), pp. 177-190; O.D. Sokolov, "Bor'ba M.N. Pokrovskogo protiv dvoriansko-burzhuaznoi istoriografii," *Istoriia SSSR*, no. 5 (1969), pp. 33-47.

63. Valk, "Istorischeskaia nauka," p. 64.

64. V.P. Volgin et al., eds., *Dvadtsat'piat' let istoricheskoi nauki v SSSR* (Moscow and Leningrad, 1942), pp. 92-93.

65. *Sochineniia*, VII, 446.

66. *Smutnoe vremia* (Prague, 1924), p. 14.

67. N.L. Rubinshtein, *Russkaia istoriografiia* (Moscow, 1941), pp. 504-505; V.I. Picheta, *Vvedenie v russkuiu istoriiu* (Moscow, 1923), pp. 158-159; and J.-J. Gapanovitch, *Historiographie Russe*, trans. B.P. Nikitin (Paris, 1946), pp. 43-45, wherein Platonov is termed "un des meilleurs maitres de l'historie russe."

68. The latest authoritative Soviet works on the subject, R.G. Skrynnikov's *Nachalo oprichniny* and *Oprichnyi terror* (Leningrad, 1966, 1969), confirm the accuracy of part of Platonov's thesis; namely that the oprichnina began as a specifically anti-princely policy.

69. G.E. Orchard, "The Historiography of the 'Time of Troubles' in Muscovy," unpub. paper presented at the Annual Meeting of the Canadian Association of Slavists, York University, 12 June 1969. Professor Orchard kindly provided me with a copy of his paper.

70. "Pamiati S.F. Platonova," reprinted in Struve, *Sotsial'naia i ekonomicheskaia istoriia Rossii*, p. 337.

71. V.V. Mavrodin, ed., *Istoriia Leningradskogo universiteta: ocherki (1819-1969)* (Leningrad, 1969), p. 302, which also prints a picture of Platonov and others meeting with Lunacharsky (p. 187).

72. V.E. Illeritsky and I.A. Kudriavtsev, eds., *Istoriografiia istorii SSSR* (Moscow, 1961), pp. 365, 438-441. For a much more favorable view, see A. L. Shapiro, *Russkaia istoriografiia v period imperializma* (Leningrad, 1962), pp. 45-47.

NOTES TO THE TEXT

CHAPTER ONE

1. The Trinity-St. Sergius Monastery, founded in the mid-fourteenth century, has been active from its founding to the present time. It is located in Zagorsk, northeast of Moscow, and is now called officially the Zagorsk State Art Museum and Ancient Monument.

2. Tsarevich Dmitri was the third son of Ivan the Terrible, born to his seventh wife, Maria Nagaia.

3. The Zemsky Sobor, or Assembly of the Land, was a kind of primitive estates-general in Muscovy which appeared in the mid-sixteenth century and disappeared toward the end of the seventeenth century.

4. Dmitri the Pretender, or the false Dmitri, was crowned tsar on July 21, 1605. He claimed to be, and may have believed he actually was, the son of Ivan the Terrible, whom Boris was accused of having assassinated in Uglich on May 15, 1591 (see Chapter Three, Part I). Who he really was is open to question. The Moscow authorities declared that he was a fugitive monk named Grigori Otrepiev from the Chudov Monastery in Moscow.

5. Professor A. Ya. Shpakov, *Uchrezhdenie patriarchestva v Rossii* (Odessa, 1912) pp. 56-60. (Platonov's note).

6. The Boyar Duma, or Council of Nobles, was a strong element in the Muscovite government until the second half of the sixteenth century, when it lost strength. There was no written law outlining its functions and rights. The Duma was abolished by Peter the Great early in the eighteenth century.

7. *Boris Godunov,* scene I.

8. "That the Godunovs were a very noble family," notes the historian A. I. Markevich, "is very easy to see. The family gave four boyars before the enthronement of Boris. His relatives the Veliaminovs, the Saburovs and others were also considered great boyars." From *O Mestnichestve,* p. 643. (Platonov's note).

9. Maliuta Skuratov was among the most notorious henchmen in Ivan the Terrible's oprichnina.

10. Ivan the Terrible was married seven times.

11. The year 7089 is counted from the mythological date of the creation of the world.

12. Ivan the Terrible had four sons. The first, Dmitri, born during the campaign against Kazan, drowned in June, 1553. Two more sons, Ivan and Fedor, were born to Ivan the Terrible's first wife, Anastasia Romanova. His fourth son, Tsarevich Dmitri, was born to his seventh wife, Maria Nagaia. In 1582 Ivan the Terrible accidentally killed his eldest son, Ivan Ivanovich, in a burst of violent anger. Thus Fedor Ivanovich stood in succession to the throne upon the death of his father in 1584.

13. The Russians first applied the title tsar to the Byzantine emperor, or *basileus autocrator.* Later Tatar khans were also called tsar.

14. Moscow considered itself the "third Rome" after the fall of the "second Rome" (Constantinople) to the Turks in 1453.

15. Baron Sigismund Herberstein (1486-1566), a diplomat and traveler, was ambassador to Moscow from Maximilian I in 1517-1518 and 1526 — 1527. In 1549 he published *Rerum Moscoviticarum Commentarii,* based on his observations as ambassador from the Hapsburg court.

16. In Muscovy, kniazhata was a collective term for the service princes.

17. Ivan III (1462-1505) was the son of Vasili II (the Blind).

18. Literally "boyar's son." The deti boyarskie (plural) were a lower rank of the nobility who comprised the majority of the tsar's military servitors in the sixteenth and seventeenth centuries.

19. From the thirteenth to the sixteenth century, appanage (or *udel*) was a term used for inherited land, sometimes relatively small in area. The lord of an appanage often functioned both as political ruler and private landlord.

20. In the early sixteenth century a dispute raged within the church concerning whether or not the church should possess land

and other forms of wealth, and whether or not there should be close relations between church and state. The question was settled in the general church council of 1503. The prevailing party, which took the affirmative position in the debate, was led by the learned and capable abbot, Joseph Volotsky (or Joseph of Volokolamsk). The party taking the opposing view was led by another distinguished abbot, Nil Sorsky. Those who sided with Sorsky came to be called the "Trans-Volga Elders." Later the materialist clergy, basing their position upon Volotsky's writings, organized into a school of monastic administrators known as "Josephites."

21.   The okolnichie (plural) formed a service rank immediately below that of the boyars.

22.   Pomestie estates were lands granted in return for military service. The master of a pomestie, the pomeshchik, held his position by rendering military service to the sovereign.

23.   Riurik the Varangian (d. 879 A.D.) is the traditional founder of the Principality of Novgorod and originator of the main Great Russian dynasty.

24.   Prince Gedimin came to power in 1316 in Vilna after a period of intermittent civil war which followed the assassination of Prince Mindovg in 1263. Mindovg had united the Russians and Lithuanians and led them both in wars against the Germans. Gedimin further united the two disparate peoples. He considered himself king of Lithuania and of the Russians.

25.   Ivan the Terrible did not choose Muscovite princesses for his own or his sons' wives. He usually took to wife women from untitled families, who brought with them to court members of the simple boyar or gentry class. This practice formed a new court aristocracy dominated by the Godunovs and the Yurievs. The Yurievs previously had been called the Zakharins; later they were known as the Romanovs. A given generation of this family usually took the name of the grandfather as its surname. The key phrase in the text is *Bog byl v kike* (God was in, or wore, a headdress). The *kika* was a horned headdress worn by women in old Russia. Platonov parenthetically compares the *kika* to the *povoinik,* worn by Russian married women of the time, and the *kokoshnik,* another type of woman's headdress. The intent of the joke appears to demean men whose positions at court depended upon women.

26.   Somewhat later Sapieha asserted this fact, writing in July of the same year: "Whether indeed he has little reasoning power or

whether it is as others say, I have paid close attention to this matter and know that he has nothing more" [that is, he was not possessed of full mental powers] . (Platonov's note).

27.   The streltsy, or musketeers, were professional infantry armed with harquebuses. Established in the 1550's, they were recruited from various strata of society. In their spare time from service duties they engaged in petty trade and crafts.

28.   The zemsky boyars were from that part of the country (the zemshchina) which had not been under the oprichnina and which had retained the traditional administration.

29.   There is a tradition written under the year 7093 (1585) by one chronicler (in the so-called Latukhinsky Book) that, according to the boyars, Mstislavsky "had in mind to have a feast at his home and, having called Boris there, to kill him," but that "Boris was informed of this, became cautious and was immune from them." (Platonov's note).

30.   Muzhik is the diminutive of *muzh* (man). The term was applied to men of the lower classes.

31.   The adjective ploshchadnye (from *ploshchad* - "square" or "plaza") was used to refer to the crowd which milled around and occupied the squares close to the Kremlin. This mob is sometimes called simply "the square."

32.   Konrad Bussow lived in Moscow from 1601 to 1611 and compiled an account entitled *A Muscovite Chronicle,* treating the years 1584-1613.

33.   Peter Petrei-de-Erlezund (Petreus) was envoy to Muscovy from Karl IX of Sweden. In 1615 he wrote *Regni Muscovitiici Sciographia* in which he described Muscovy between 1608 and 1611.

34.   A voevoda was originally a military governor. In sixteenth-century Muscovy the title was also used to mean governor in a non-military sense.

35.   The terms "tsar" and "tsarevich" here refer to Tatar khans and their sons.

36.   This quote from Horsey is from Hakluyt's *Principal Navigations, Voyages, etc., of the English Nation,* Vol. I (London, 1809-1812).

37.   Isaac Massa, a Calvinist, was born in 1587 into a wealthy and aristocratic Italian merchant family which had emigrated to Holland during the Reformation. In 1609, he went on a trading mission to Moscow where he lived eight years, leaving a description of the reigns of

Tsar Boris, Dmitri the Pretender, and Vasili Shuisky. His writings were first published in Russian translation in 1874 by the Archeographical Commission. They were republished in Moscow, in 1937, under the title *Kratkoe izvestie o Moskovii v nachale XVII v.*

38.   Facsimilies of these may be seen in *Chteniia Moskovskogo obshchestva istorii i drevnostei rossiskikh* (1897), Book I. (Platonov's note).

39.   Avraami (or Avraamy) Palitsyn was a monk and chronicler of the period.

CHAPTER TWO

1.   Stefan Batory was king of the Commonwealth of Poland-Lithuania (1576 - 1587).

2.   The translation of this quotation is based upon J. L. I. Fennell's *The Correspondence Between Prince A. M. Kurbsky and Tsar Ivan IV of Russia, 1564-1579* (Cambridge, 1963), p. 237.

3.   "Eternal peace'. was not achieved. The war ended with a ten-year truce concluded with Batory in January, 1582. A three-year truce was made with the Swedes in August, 1583. To accomplish an "absolute end" or eternal peace was difficult in light of the mutually unacceptable views and aspirations of the belligerents. (Platonov's note).

4.   "German" was a general term for foreigners from Northwestern Europe.

5.   Literally "land along the sea," the term Pomorie designated the northern region adjoining the White Sea and Barents Sea, and extending several hundred miles inland. (See map).

6.   This city is now called Volgograd; previously it was Stalingrad.

7.   The unsettled plains lying to the northeast of the Dnieper River and extending in a southerly direction from the town of Orel. (See map).

8.   The Nogais were a splinter of the Golden Horde which, after the Muscovite conquest of the Khanate of Kazan in 1552, itself split apart, some fragments remaining under Muscovite suzerainty and roaming along the lower Yaik (Ural) River. Other fragments went south and submitted, fitfully, to the overlordship of the Crimean khan.

9.   Kakhetia was one of the Georgian principalities in the Caucasus.

10.   The apostasy of the patriarch of Rome refers to the Great Schism of 1054, during which the patriarchs of Rome and Constantinople excommunicated each other.

11.   The pomeshchiki were owners of pomestie estates (see note 22 of Chapter One).

12.   The so-called "black lands" were directly under the prince. On these lands peasant self-government was organized and supervised by the prince's agents.

13.   The Divine Liturgy of the Russian Orthodox Church is always sung. Thus this expression indicates that the churches stood empty.

14.   The posad was an urban settlement in Muscovy located around a town's fortress which included the government offices and main churches.

15.   The word desiatinnaia is an adjectival form of *desiatina,* a unit of measurement equal to about 2.7 acres.

16.   In Muscovy, the gosti were the richest and highest ranking merchants. They received their honorary title *(gost)* from the tsar and functioned also as tax collectors and overseers of trading operations.

17.   By the second decade of the seventeenth century, the city of Moscow was divided into four walled areas. The first and oldest of these was the Kremlin, consisting of over sixty acres. It is situated on the northern bank of the Moscow River and is surrounded on four sides by a wall. To the east of the Kremlin was the "Walled City" (Kitaigorod), about one-fourth mile in width and one-half mile in length. Surrounding these two areas on the east, north and west was a rather large area (for the time) known as the "White City." Beyond these sections and spreading out in all directions was what was known as the "Earthen City," which was also walled. The whole of these areas comprised no more than what is today's central Moscow.

18.   One verst, or *versta,* equals 1.067 kilometers, or 0.663 miles.

19.   The Kitaigorod was named for a certain type of basket, known as *kit,* which was filled with earth and used to reinforce the wall that surrounded this section. Foreign markets and the business of the city were located there.

CHAPTER THREE

1. All material concerning the question of the death of the tsarevich, up until the last decade, is examined in an article by A. I. Tiumenev, "Peresmotr izvestii o smerti tsarevicha Dmitriia," in *Zhurnal Ministerstva Narodnogo Prosveshcheniia*, (May and June, 1908). (Platonov's note.)

2. Vladimir Klein, *Uglichskoe sledstvennoe delo o smerti tsarevicha Dmitriia 15 maia 1591 goda*. Part I: *Diplomaticheskoe issledovanie podlinnika*. Part II: *Fototipicheskoe vosproizvedenie podlinnika i ego transkriptsiia* (Moscow, 1913). (Platonov's note).

3. The game the children were playing was *tychka,* in which the player throws the knife so that it turns in the air before striking its target.

4. The reproduction of this sketch is taken directly from Platonov's work. The labeling of the Church of the Transfiguration is based on textual information.

5. The sloboda was a settlement or group of settlements exempt from ordinary taxation.

6. The word in question here is *sud* meaning both "court" and "vessel." "Vessels" or "boats" makes the best sense in the context.

7. The exile of the Uglich townsmen contributed to the colonization of Siberia.

8. *Ocherki po istorii Smuty v Moskovskom gosudarstve XVI-XVII vv.* Chapter 3, Section 2. (Platonov's note).

9. The end of this long quote from Platonov's *Ocherki* is not indicated in the original.

10. Mikhail Fedorovich Romanov, born about 1596, was elected tsar by the Zemsky Sobor in 1613. This ended the Time of Troubles which began in 1598.

11. Uglichsky, "of Uglich," was spelled variously "Uglitsky" and "Ugletsky."

12. According to testimony, the fire was the work of arsonists hired by agents of Afanasi Alexandrovich Nagoi.

13. The child lived only about a year.

14. Sapieha states that Dmitri was the son of the sixth wife of Ivan the Terrible.

15. The Mnogoletie is a prayer beseeching God to grant long life and health to the sovereign.

16.   Professor Bagalei dates the orders to 1600. At the beginning of his document it is stated that the tsar commanded Belsky to go "to the Donets at the mouth of the Oskol in the year 7108 (1600) on the fifth day of July." Later in the text of the document Belsky is ordered "to remain until the feast of St. Ilya in the present year of 107 (1599)." We follow the date accepted by Bagalei, that is, 1600, not 1599. (Platonov's note).

17.   Jacques Margeret, a soldier of fortune, commanded a squadron of foreign cavalry in Muscovy during the reign of Boris. He had entered Russian service in 1601. He later served the pretender, escaping death in the massacre of 1606. In 1611 he returned to Muscovy in the service of the Poles. His memoirs are an important historical source: *Etat de L'empire Russie, et Grand Duché de Moscovie avec ce qui s'y est passé de plus memorable et tragique, depuis l'an 1590 jusques en l'an 1606* (Paris, 1607, second edition, 1669).

18.   The Borderland refers to the area along Muscovy's southern border.

19.   There is no necessity in presenting here the well-known details concerning the appearance of the pretender in Poland and his personal adventures before his march on Moscow. Those who desire can read about this in the works of Paul Pierling, most of all in his book *La Russie et le Saint-Siège,* Volume III, (Paris, 1901). It appeared in *Sphinx* (1912) in Russian translation under the title *Dmitri Samozvanets. Polnyi perevod s frantsuzskogo V. P. Potemkina.* (Platonov's note).

20.   Yuri Mniszech, an extremely wealthy man, was voevoda of Sandomir and prefect of Lvov. Mniszech used his youngest daughter, the beautiful Marina, to gain control of the pretender. An excellent account of the affair of Dmitri and Marina is to be found in George Vernadsky, *A History of Russia,* Volume V, *The Tsardom of Moscow, 1547-1682, Part I* (New Haven, 1969), pp. 225-234.

TRANSLATOR'S REFERENCES

Barbour, Philip L. *Dmitri Called the Pretender. Tsar and Great Prince of All Russia, 1605-1606.* Boston, 1966.

Dal', Vladimir. *Tol'kovyi slovar' zhivogo Velikorusskogo iazyka.* 2nd. ed., Moscow, 1956.

Entsiklopedicheskii slovar'. I.E. Andreevskii, et. al., eds. 43 vols. St. Petersburg, 1890-1907.

Fennell, J.L.I. *The Correspondence Between Prince A.M. Kurbsky and Tsar Ivan IV of Russia.* Cambridge, 1963.

Fennell, J.L.I. *Kurbsky's History of Ivan IV.* Cambridge, 1965.

Fletcher, Giles. *Of the Russe Common Wealth* in *Russia at the Close of the Sixteenth Century.* Ed. E. A. Bond. London, 1856.

Horsey, Sir Jerome. *Sir Jerome Horsey His Travells* in *Russia at the Close of the Sixteenth Century.* Ed. E.A. Bond. London, 1856.

Kliuchevskii, Vasili O. *Kurs russkoi istorii* in *V.O. Kliuchevskii. Sochineniia.* 8 vols. Moscow, 1956-1959.

Kliuchevskii, Vasili O. *A Course in Russian History. The Seventeenth Century.* Trans. Natalie Duddington. Chicago, 1968.

Platonov, Sergei F. *Ivan Groznyi.* Leningrad, 1926.

Platonov, Sergei F. *The Time of Troubles.* Trans. John T. Alexander. Lawrence, Kansas, 1970.

Pushkarev, Sergei G., comp. *Dictionary of Russian Historical Terms From the Eleventh Century to 1917.* Eds. George Vernadsky and Ralph T. Fisher, Jr.. New Haven, 1970.

Smirnitsky, A.I. *Russian-English Dictionary.* New York, 1959.

Soloviev, Sergei M. *Istoriia Rossii s drevneishikh vremen.* 15 Vols. Moscow, 1962-1966..

The Testaments of the Grand Princes of Moscow. Trans. and ed. Robert C. Howes. Ithaca, New York, 1967.

PLATONOV'S SOURCES

Karamzin, N.M. *Istoriia Gosudarstva Rossiiskogo.* Volumes IX-XI.

Soloviev, S.M. *Istoriia Rossii s drevneishikh vremen.* Volumes VII-VIII.

Bestuzhev-Riumin, K.N. "Obzor sobytii (1584-1613)" in *Zhurnal Ministerstva Narodnogo Prosveshcheniia.* July, August, 1887 (Pt.252).

Kliuchevskii, V.O. *Kurs russkoi istorii.* Parts 2,3.

Platonov, S.F. *Ocherki po istorii Smutnogo vremeni v Moskovskom gosudarstve.*

Le P. Pierling S.J. *La Russie et le Saint-Siège.* Volume III (Russian translation: *Dmitri Samozvanets.* Trans. V.P. Potemkin. Moscow, 1912).

Waliszewski, K. *La crise revolutionnaire 1584-1614. (Smoutnoie vremia).* Paris, 1906. (Russian translation: *Smutnoe vremia.* Ed. E.N. Shchenkinaia. St. Petersburg, 1911).

Kraevskii, A.A. *Tsar Boris Fedorovich Godunov.* St. Petersburg, 1836.

Pavlov, P.V. *Ob istoricheskom znachenii tsartvovaniia Borisa Godunova.* St. Petersburg, 1863.

Suvorin, A.S. *O Dimitrii samozvantse.* St. Petersburg, 1906.

Klein, Vladimir. *Uglichskoe sledstvennoe delo o smerti tsarevicha Dimitriia 15 maia 1591 goda.* Moscow, 1913.

Russkaia Istoricheskaia Biblioteka, izdavaemaia Arkheograficheskoi Komissiei. Volume XIII *(Pamiatniki drevnei russkoi pis'mennosti, otnosiashchiesia k Smutnomu vremeni).* 2nd enl. ed., St. Petersburg, 1909.

Polnoe Sobranie Russkikh Letospisei. Volume XIV. First Half. (I. *Povest' o chestnem zhitii tsaria i velikogo kniazia Fedora Ivanovicha.* II. *Novyi Letopisets).*

INDEX

Platonov, Sergei Fedorovich, 1860 - 1933.
    Boris Godunov, tsar of Russia [by] S.F. Platonov. Translated
from the Russian by L. Rex Pyles. With an introductory essay,
"S.F.Platonov: eminence and obscurity," by John T. Alexander.
[Gulf Breeze, Florida] Academic International Press, 1973.

    xlii, 230 p. maps, port. 22 cm. (The Russian series, vol. 10)

    Includes bibliographical references.

    1. Boris Godunov, czar of Russia, 1551? - 1605. 2. Russia-
Hist.-Boris Godunov, 1598-1605. I.Pyles, Lewis Rex, 1937 - tr.

DK109.P713   947.04   73-176467
ISBN 0-87569-024-6